Garfield
SPILLS THE BEANS

BY JIM DAVIS

Ballantine Books • New York

A Ballantine Books Trade Paperback Original

Copyright © 2008 by PAWS, Inc. All rights reserved.
"GARFIELD" and the GARFIELD characters are trademarks of PAWS, Inc.

Published in the United States by Ballantine Books, an imprint of The Random House Publishing Group,
a division of Random House, Inc., New York.

BALLANTINE and colophon are registered trademarks of Random House, Inc.

ISBN 978-0-345-49177-0

Printed in the United States of America

www.ballantinebooks.com

9 8 7 6 5 4

MYTH MADNESS

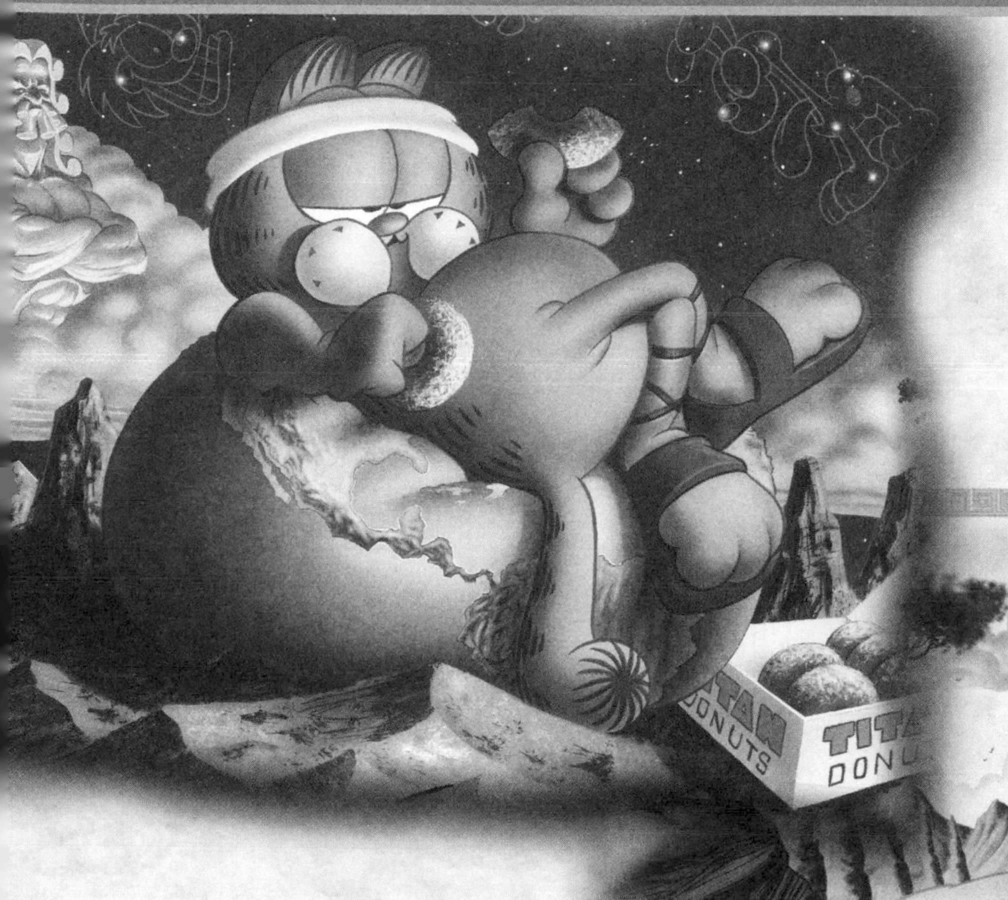
DONUTS

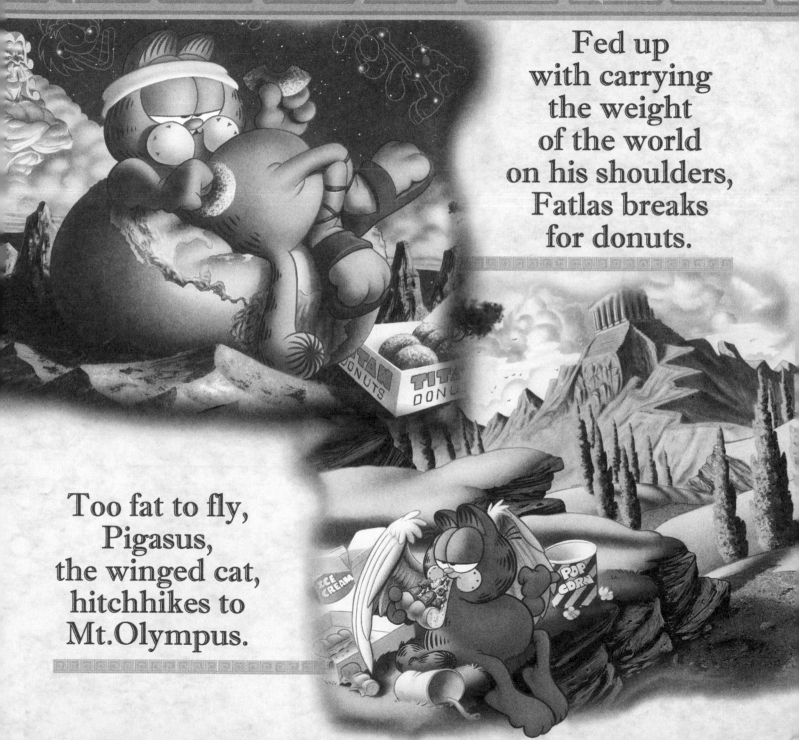

Fed up
with carrying
the weight
of the world
on his shoulders,
Fatlas breaks
for donuts.

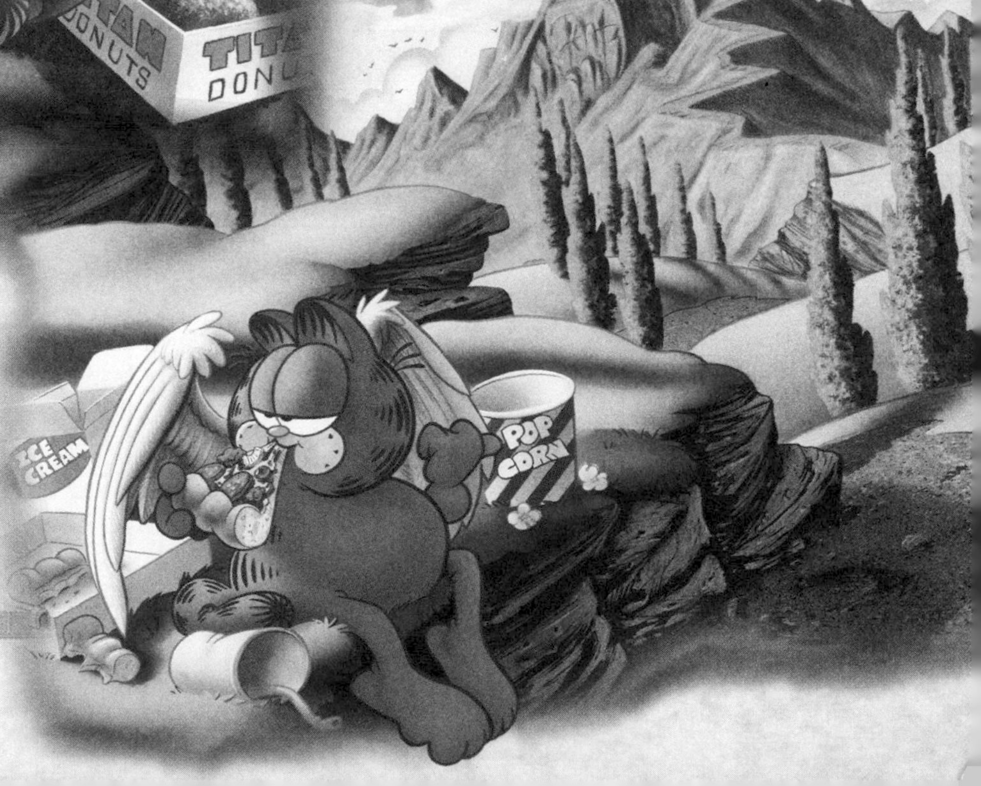
ICE CREAM
POP CORN

Too fat to fly,
Pigasus,
the winged cat,
hitchhikes to
Mt.Olympus.

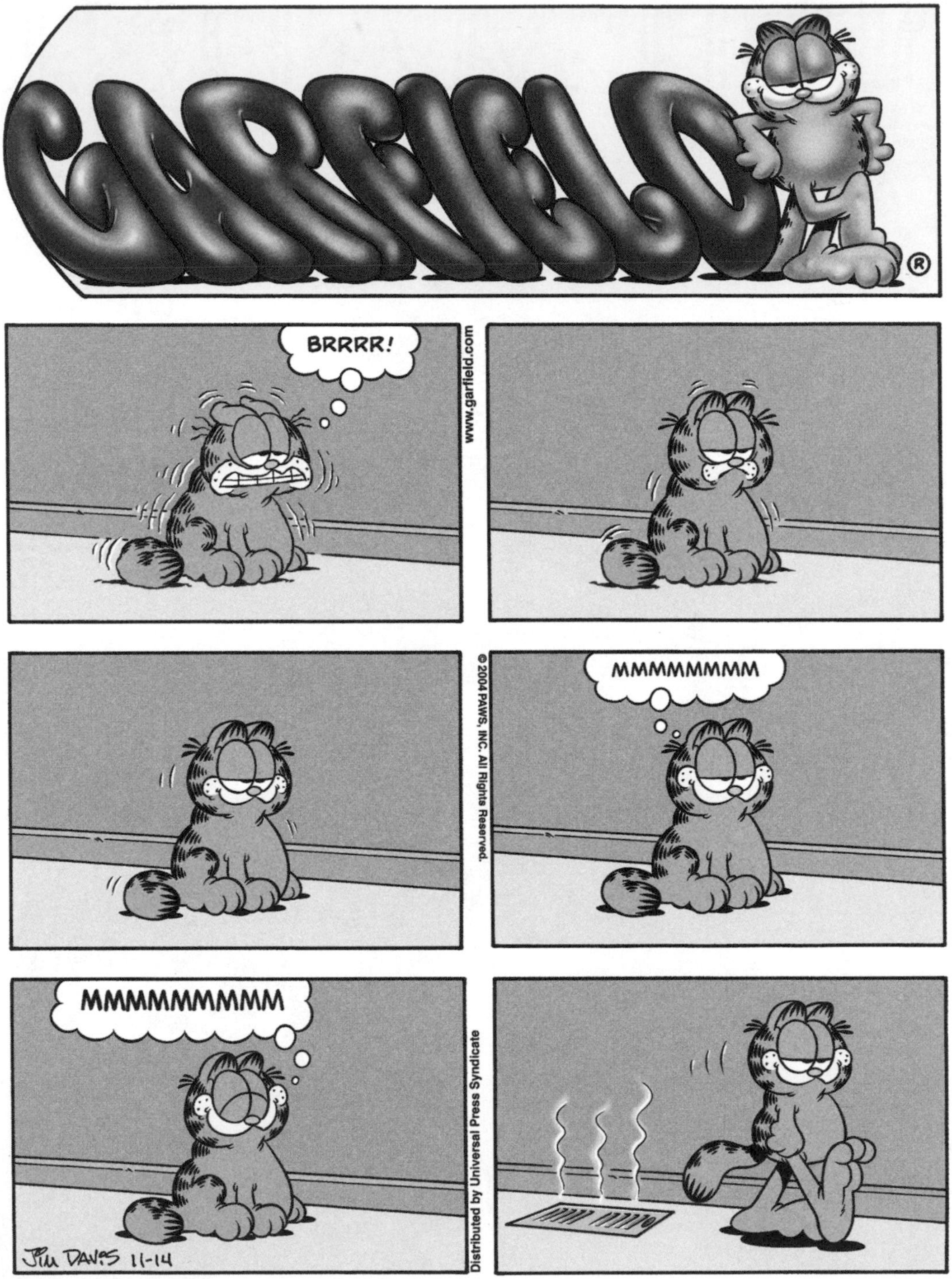
GARFIELD
BRRRR!
MMMMMMMMM
MMMMMMMMMM
JIM DAVIS 11-14
www.garfield.com
© 2004 PAWS, INC. All Rights Reserved.
Distributed by Universal Press Syndicate

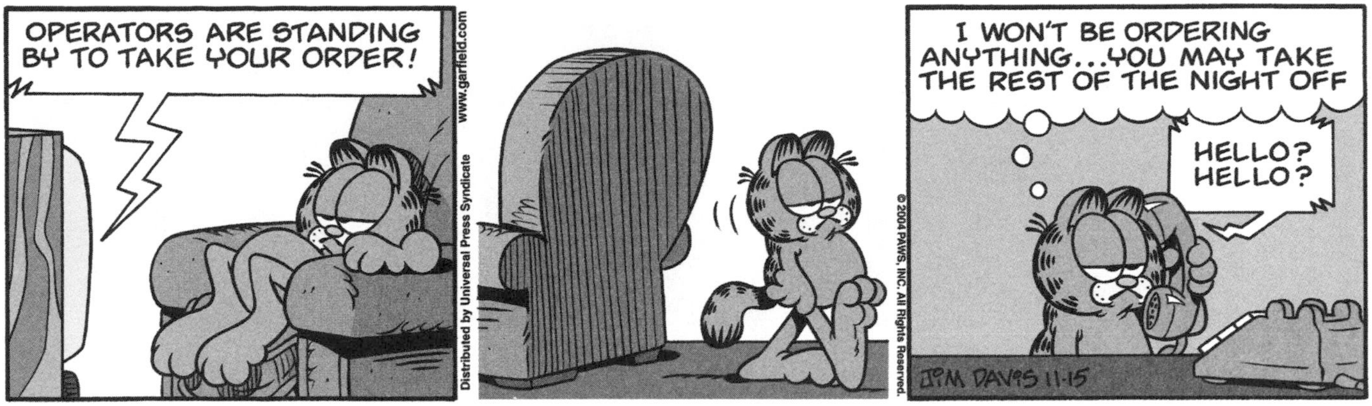
OPERATORS ARE STANDING BY TO TAKE YOUR ORDER!
www.garfield.com
Distributed by Universal Press Syndicate
© 2004 PAWS, INC. All Rights Reserved.
I WON'T BE ORDERING ANYTHING...YOU MAY TAKE THE REST OF THE NIGHT OFF
HELLO? HELLO?
JIM DAVIS 11-15

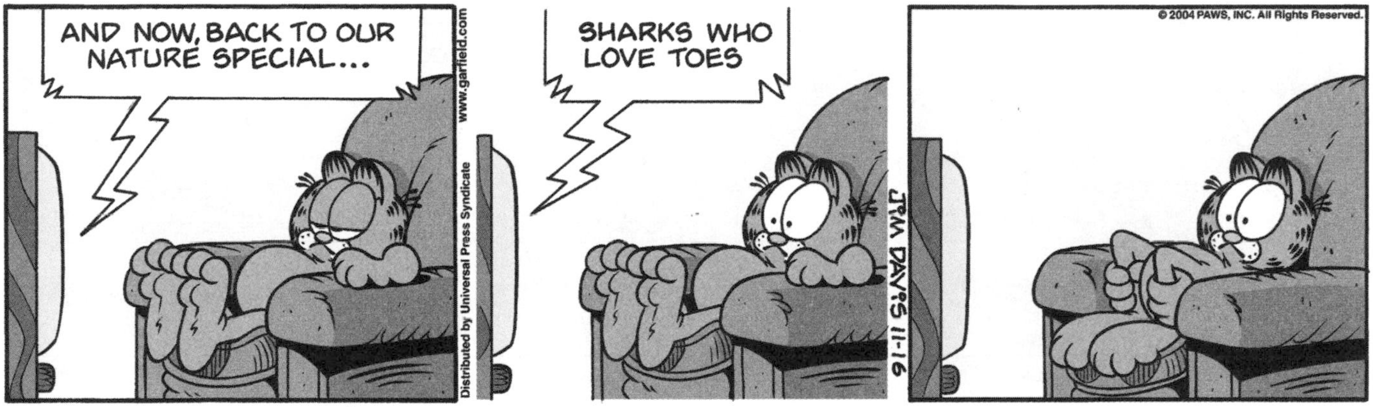
AND NOW, BACK TO OUR NATURE SPECIAL...
www.garfield.com
Distributed by Universal Press Syndicate
SHARKS WHO LOVE TOES
JIM DAVIS 11-16
© 2004 PAWS, INC. All Rights Reserved.

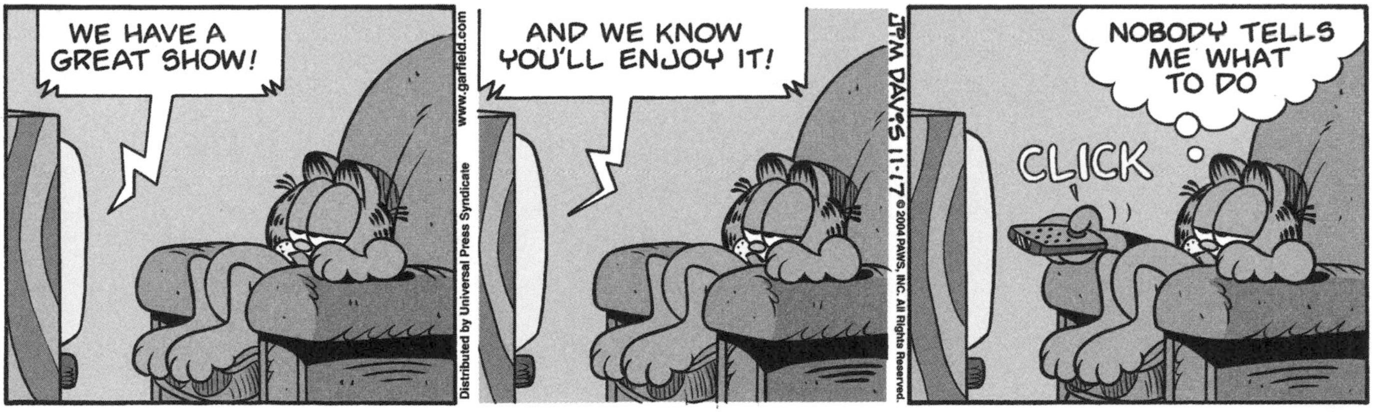
WE HAVE A GREAT SHOW!
www.garfield.com
Distributed by Universal Press Syndicate
AND WE KNOW YOU'LL ENJOY IT!
JIM DAVIS 11-17
© 2004 PAWS, INC. All Rights Reserved.
NOBODY TELLS ME WHAT TO DO
CLICK

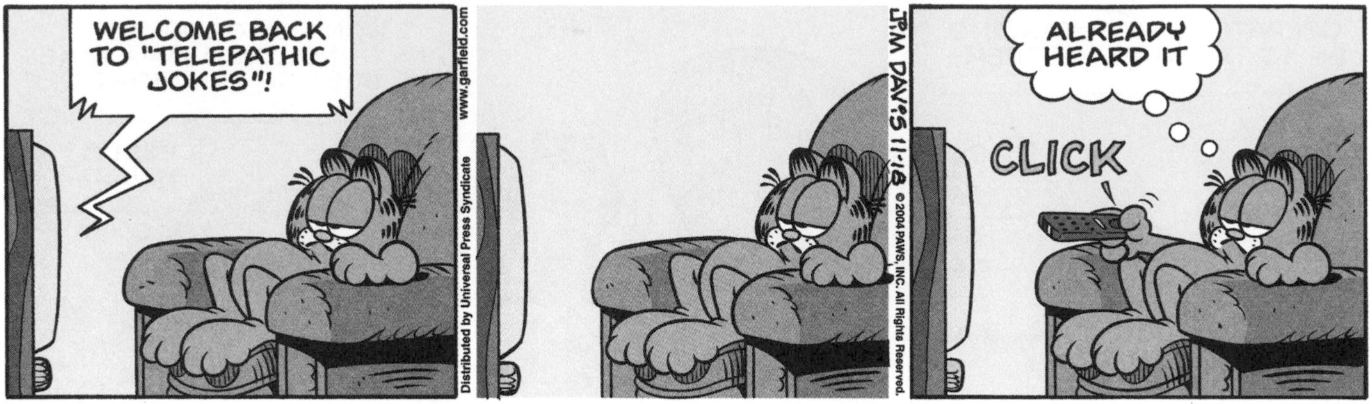
WELCOME BACK TO "TELEPATHIC JOKES"!
www.garfield.com
Distributed by Universal Press Syndicate
JIM DAVIS 11-18
© 2004 PAWS, INC. All Rights Reserved.
ALREADY HEARD IT
CLICK

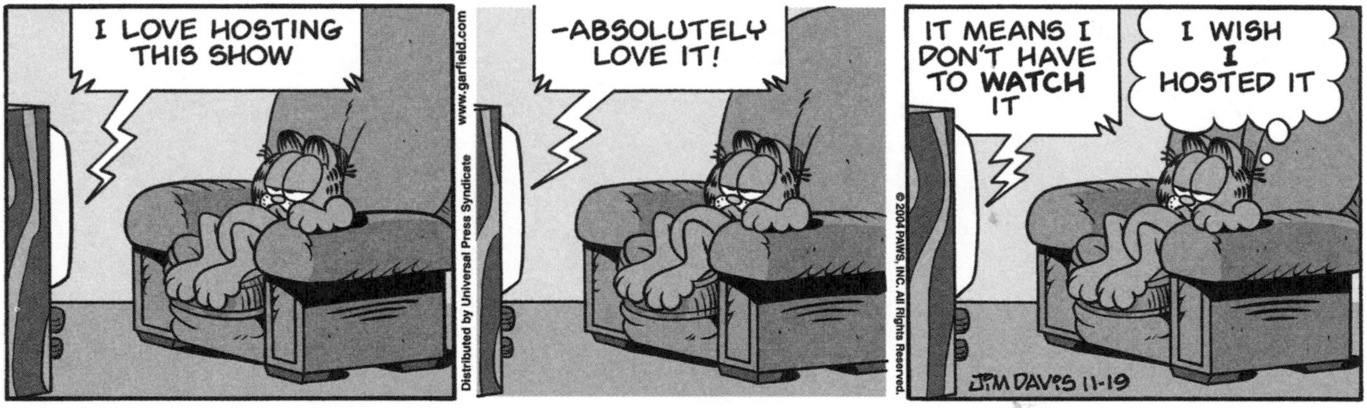
I LOVE HOSTING THIS SHOW
www.garfield.com
Distributed by Universal Press Syndicate
-ABSOLUTELY LOVE IT!
© 2004 PAWS, INC. All Rights Reserved.
IT MEANS I DON'T HAVE TO WATCH IT
I WISH I HOSTED IT
JIM DAVIS 11-19

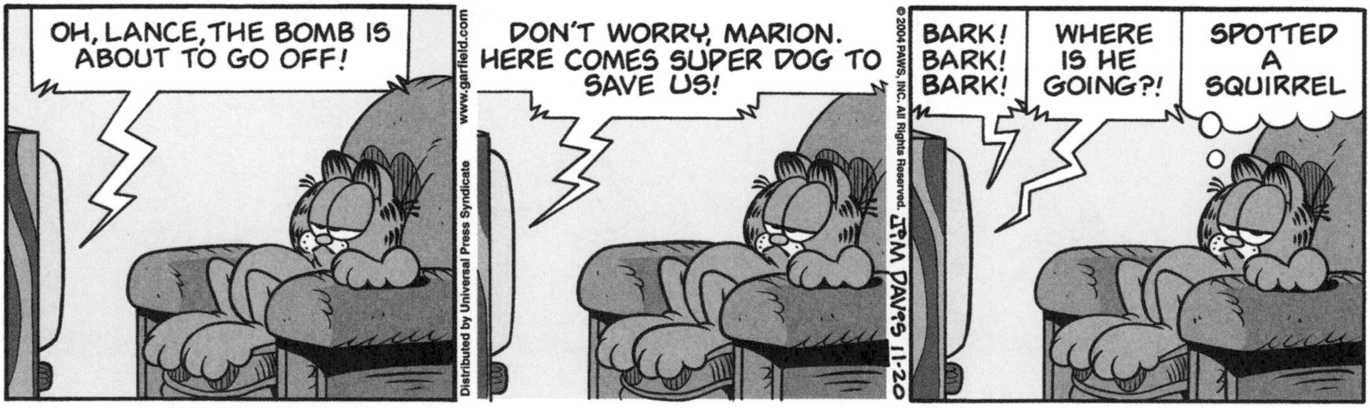
OH, LANCE, THE BOMB IS ABOUT TO GO OFF!
www.garfield.com
Distributed by Universal Press Syndicate
DON'T WORRY, MARION. HERE COMES SUPER DOG TO SAVE US!
JIM DAVIS 11-20
© 2004 PAWS, INC. All Rights Reserved.
BARK! BARK! BARK!
WHERE IS HE GOING?!
SPOTTED A SQUIRREL

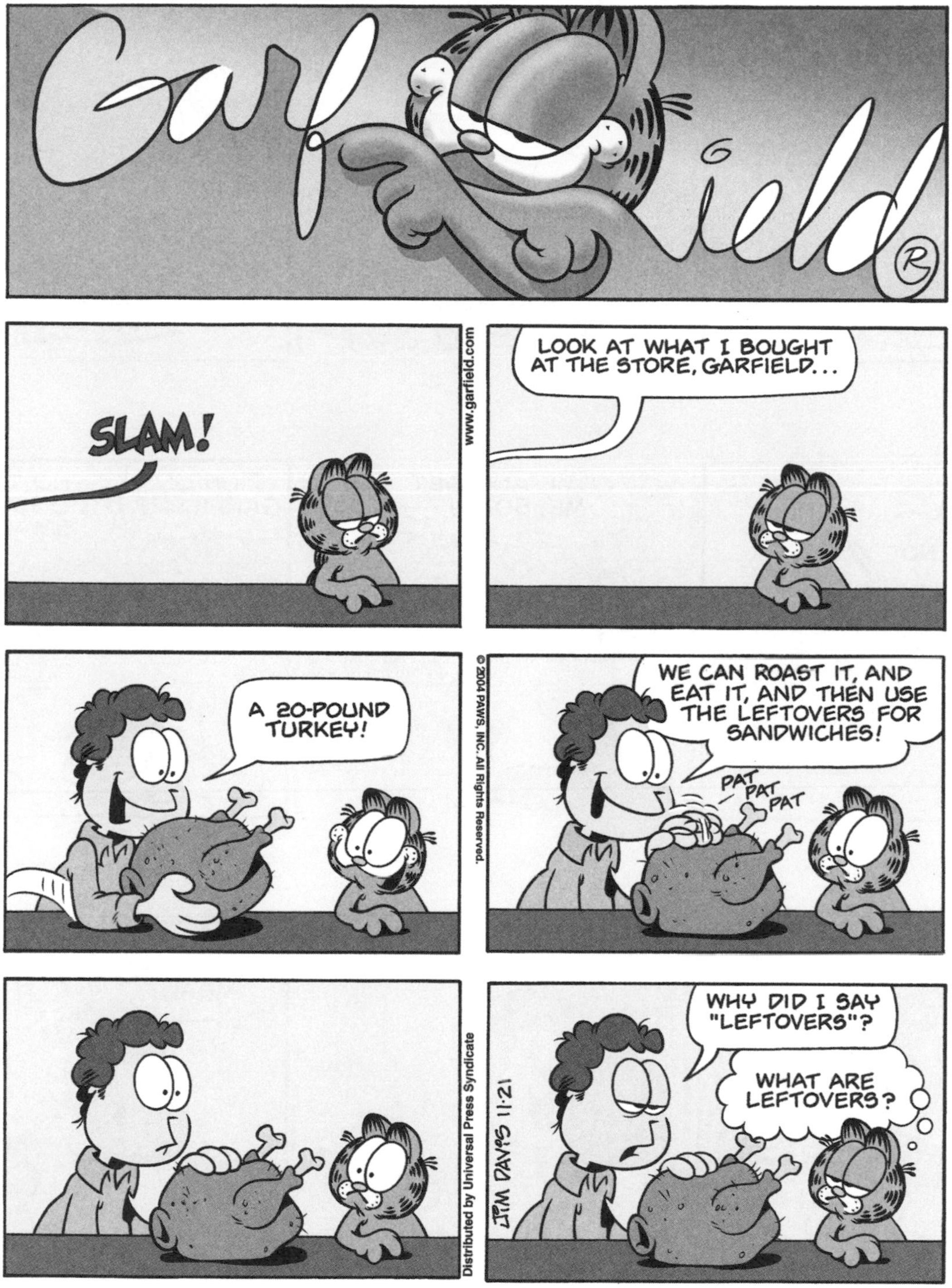
Garfield®
SLAM!
www.garfield.com
LOOK AT WHAT I BOUGHT AT THE STORE, GARFIELD...
A 20-POUND TURKEY!
© 2004 PAWS, INC. All Rights Reserved.
WE CAN ROAST IT, AND EAT IT, AND THEN USE THE LEFTOVERS FOR SANDWICHES!
PAT PAT PAT
Distributed by Universal Press Syndicate
JIM DAVIS 11-21
WHY DID I SAY "LEFTOVERS"?
WHAT ARE LEFTOVERS?

GARFIELD, ARE YOU HAPPY?
GARFIELD
Distributed by Universal Press Syndicate
www.garfield.com
GARFIELD
© 2004 PAWS, INC. All Rights Reserved.
NO FOOD, NO HAPPY
JPM DAVIS 11-22
GARFIELD

COME ON OUT!
NO!
JPM DAVIS 11-23
Distributed by Universal Press Syndicate
www.garfield.com
COME AND GET ME, BOZO!
© 2004 PAWS, INC. All Rights Reserved.
DINNER, GARFIELD?
NO THANKS. I JUST ATE A SMALL HOUSE

Distributed by Universal Press Syndicate
www.garfield.com
© 2004 PAWS, INC. All Rights Reserved.
THAT WAS A NUTRITIOUS MEAL!
YEAH, I DIDN'T LIKE IT EITHER
JPM DAVIS 11-24

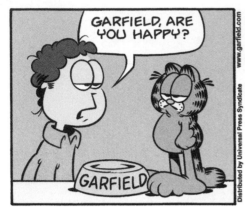

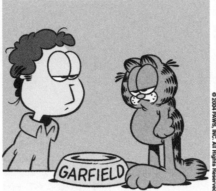

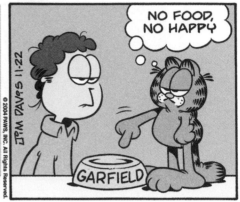

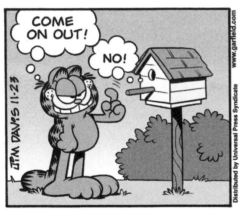

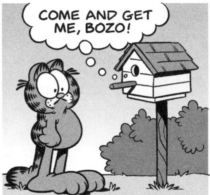

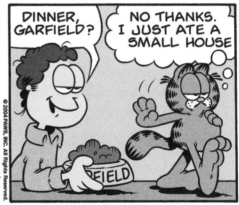

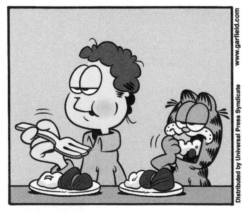

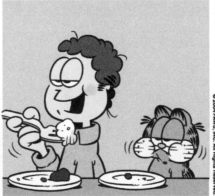

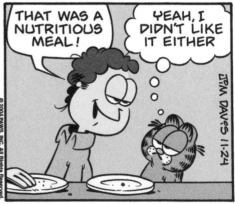

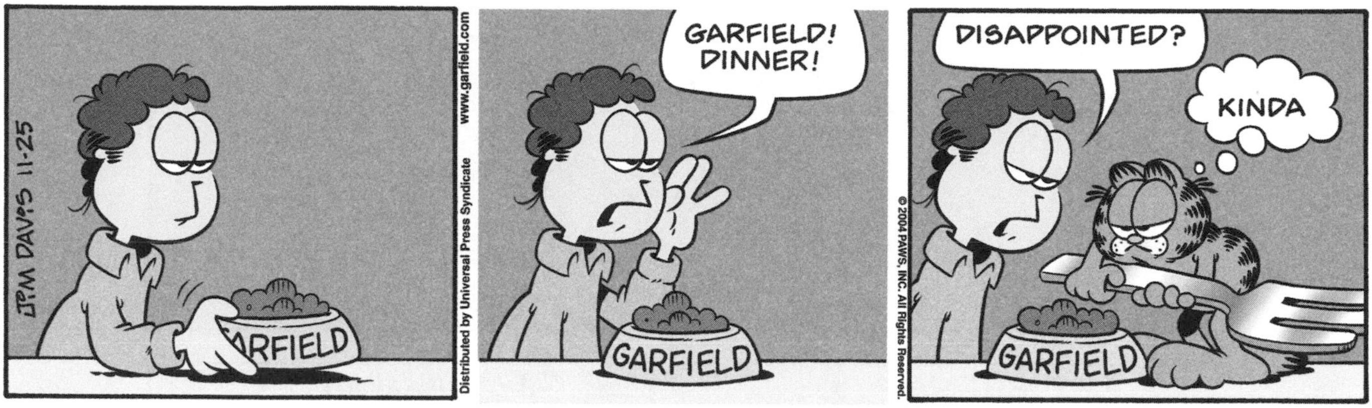
JIM DAVIS 11-25
GARFIELD
Distributed by Universal Press Syndicate www.garfield.com
GARFIELD! DINNER!
GARFIELD
DISAPPOINTED?
KINDA
© 2004 PAWS, INC. All Rights Reserved.
GARFIELD

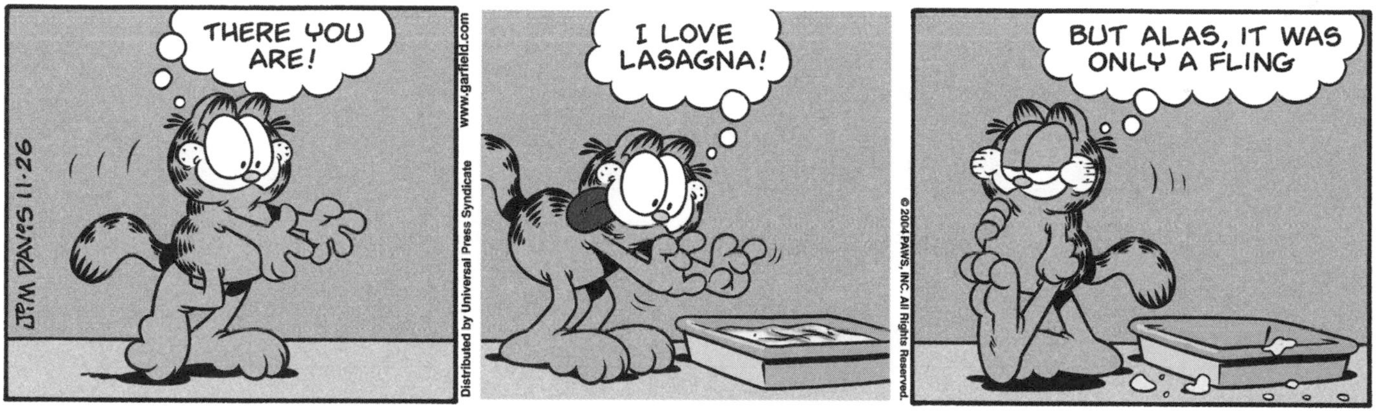
JIM DAVIS 11-26
THERE YOU ARE!
Distributed by Universal Press Syndicate www.garfield.com
I LOVE LASAGNA!
© 2004 PAWS, INC. All Rights Reserved.
BUT ALAS, IT WAS ONLY A FLING

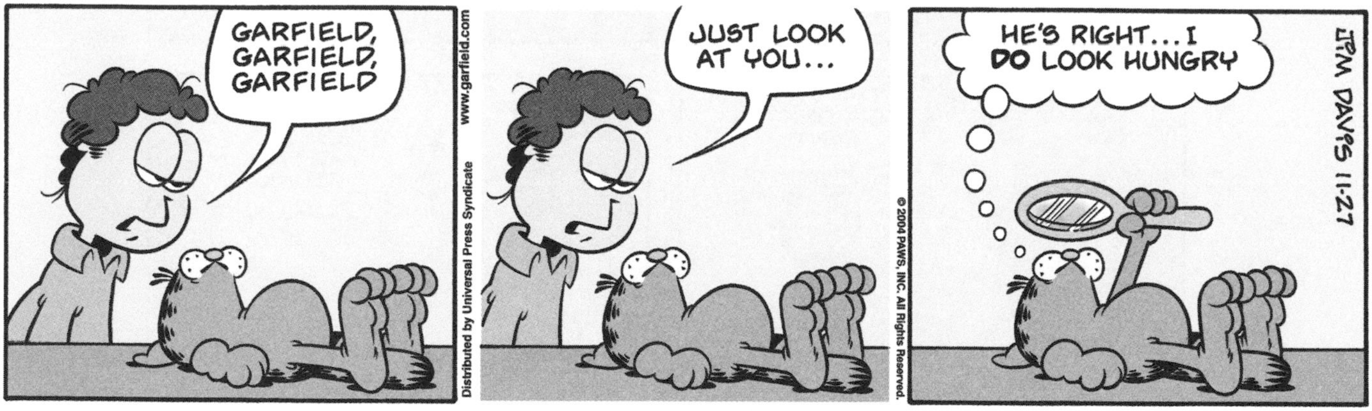
GARFIELD, GARFIELD, GARFIELD
Distributed by Universal Press Syndicate www.garfield.com
JUST LOOK AT YOU...
© 2004 PAWS, INC. All Rights Reserved.
HE'S RIGHT... I **DO** LOOK HUNGRY
JIM DAVIS 11-27

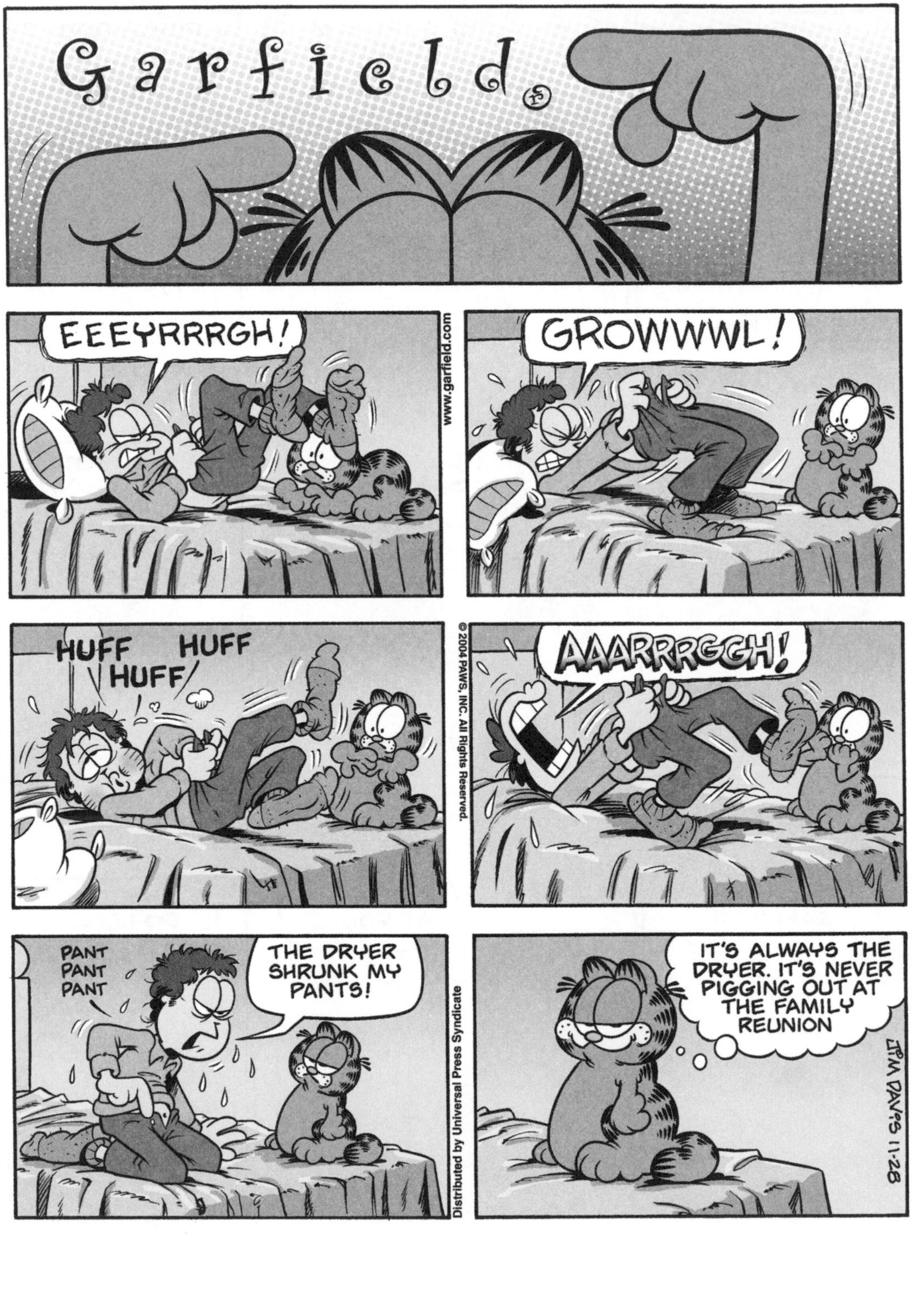
Garfield
EEEYRRRGH!
GROWWWL!
HUFF HUFF HUFF
AAARRRGGH!
PANT PANT PANT
THE DRYER SHRUNK MY PANTS!
IT'S ALWAYS THE DRYER. IT'S NEVER PIGGING OUT AT THE FAMILY REUNION
JIM DAVIS 11-28
www.garfield.com
© 2004 PAWS, INC. All Rights Reserved.
Distributed by Universal Press Syndicate

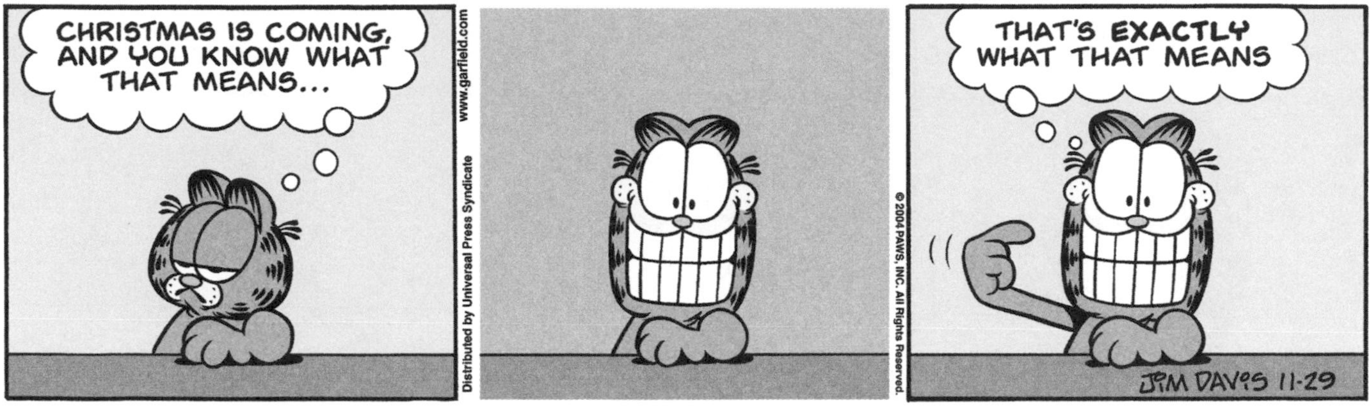
CHRISTMAS IS COMING, AND YOU KNOW WHAT THAT MEANS...
THAT'S EXACTLY WHAT THAT MEANS
JIM DAVIS 11-29
www.garfield.com
Distributed by Universal Press Syndicate
© 2004 PAWS, INC. All Rights Reserved.

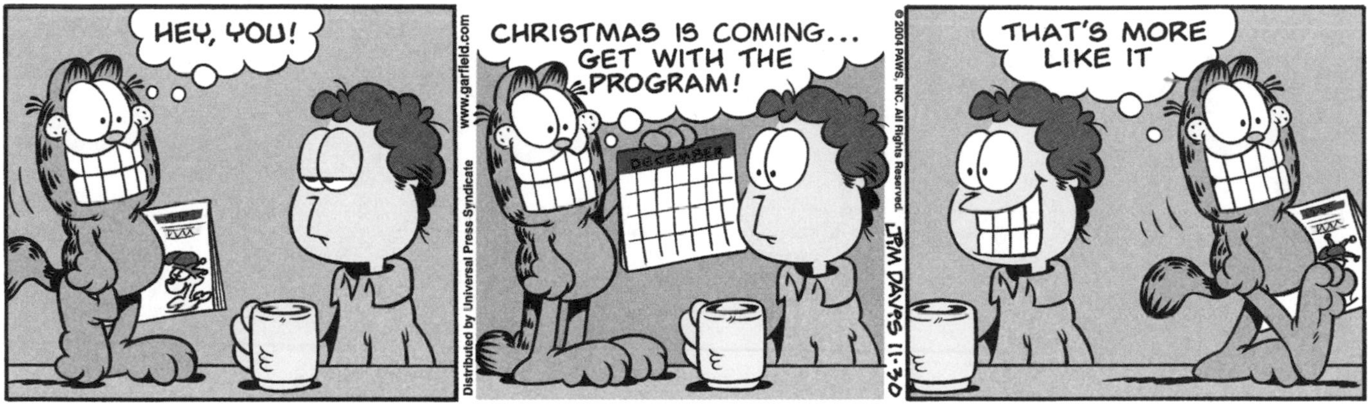
HEY, YOU!
CHRISTMAS IS COMING... GET WITH THE PROGRAM!
DECEMBER
THAT'S MORE LIKE IT
JIM DAVIS 11-30
www.garfield.com
Distributed by Universal Press Syndicate
© 2004 PAWS, INC. All Rights Reserved.

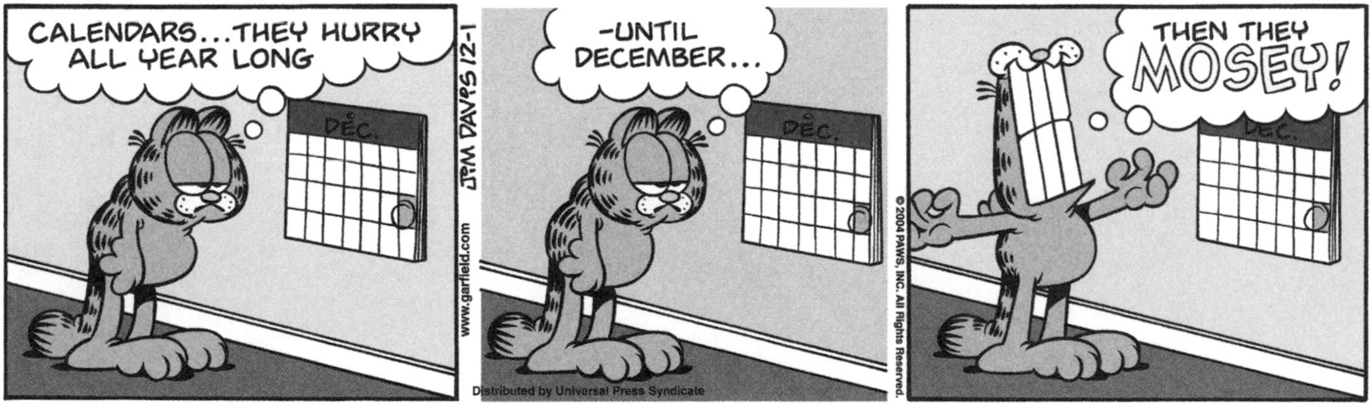
CALENDARS...THEY HURRY ALL YEAR LONG
DEC.
-UNTIL DECEMBER...
THEN THEY MOSEY!
JIM DAVIS 12-1
www.garfield.com
Distributed by Universal Press Syndicate
© 2004 PAWS, INC. All Rights Reserved.

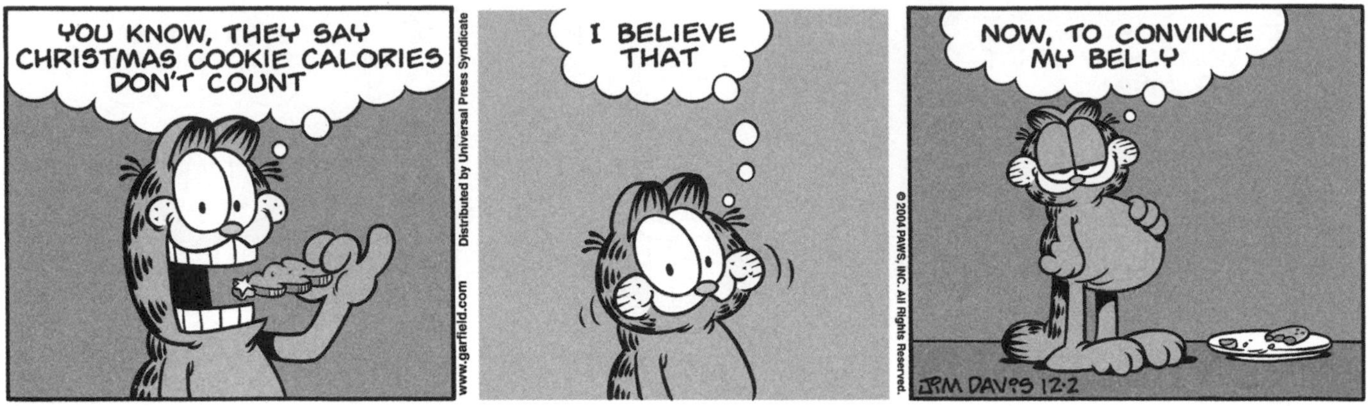
YOU KNOW, THEY SAY CHRISTMAS COOKIE CALORIES DON'T COUNT
www.garfield.com Distributed by Universal Press Syndicate
I BELIEVE THAT
© 2004 PAWS, INC. All Rights Reserved.
NOW, TO CONVINCE MY BELLY
JIM DAVIS 12·2

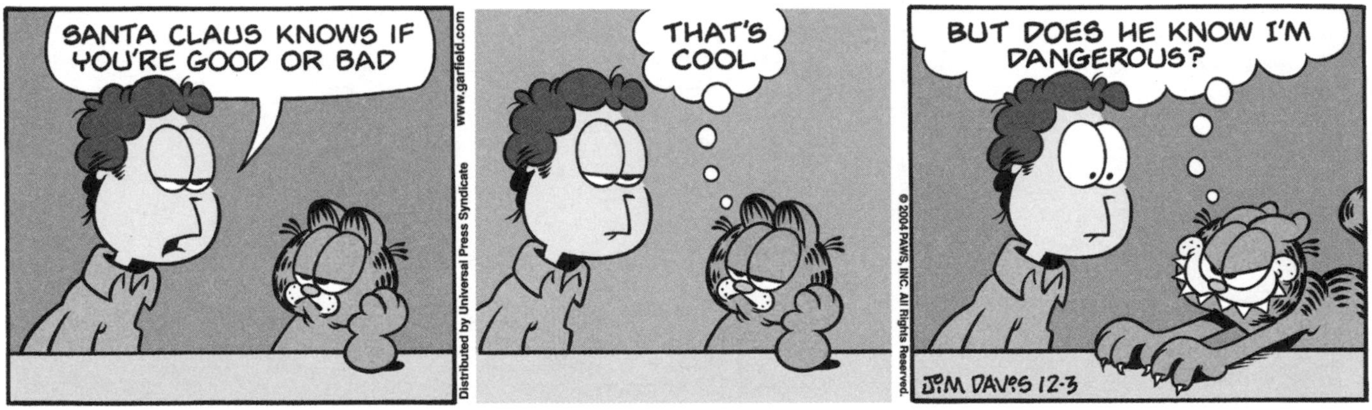
SANTA CLAUS KNOWS IF YOU'RE GOOD OR BAD
Distributed by Universal Press Syndicate www.garfield.com
THAT'S COOL
© 2004 PAWS, INC. All Rights Reserved.
BUT DOES HE KNOW I'M DANGEROUS?
JIM DAVIS 12-3

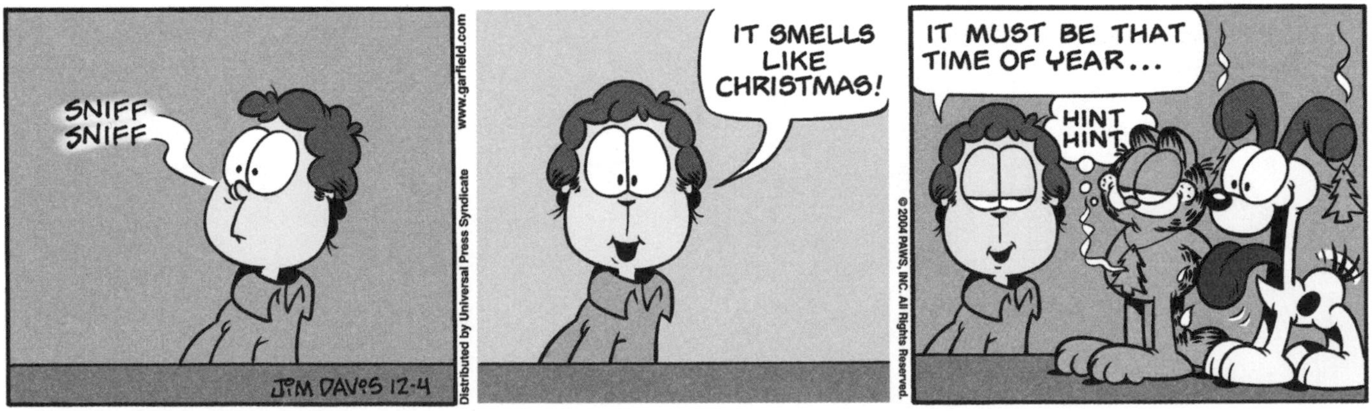
SNIFF SNIFF
JIM DAVIS 12-4
Distributed by Universal Press Syndicate www.garfield.com
IT SMELLS LIKE CHRISTMAS!
© 2004 PAWS, INC. All Rights Reserved.
IT MUST BE THAT TIME OF YEAR...
HINT HINT

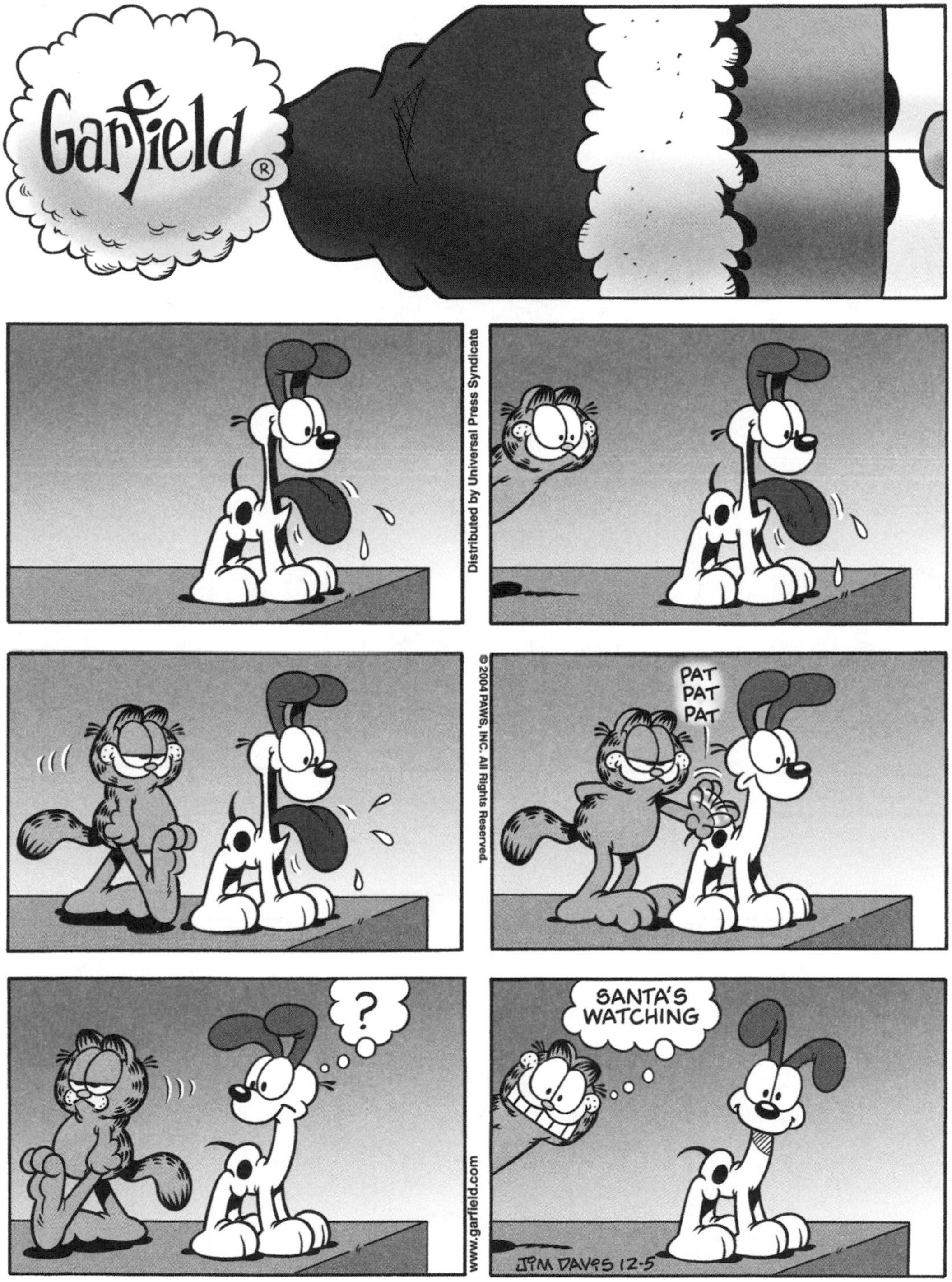

Garfield®
Distributed by Universal Press Syndicate
© 2004 PAWS, INC. All Rights Reserved.
PAT
PAT
PAT
?
www.garfield.com
SANTA'S WATCHING
JIM DAVIS 12-5

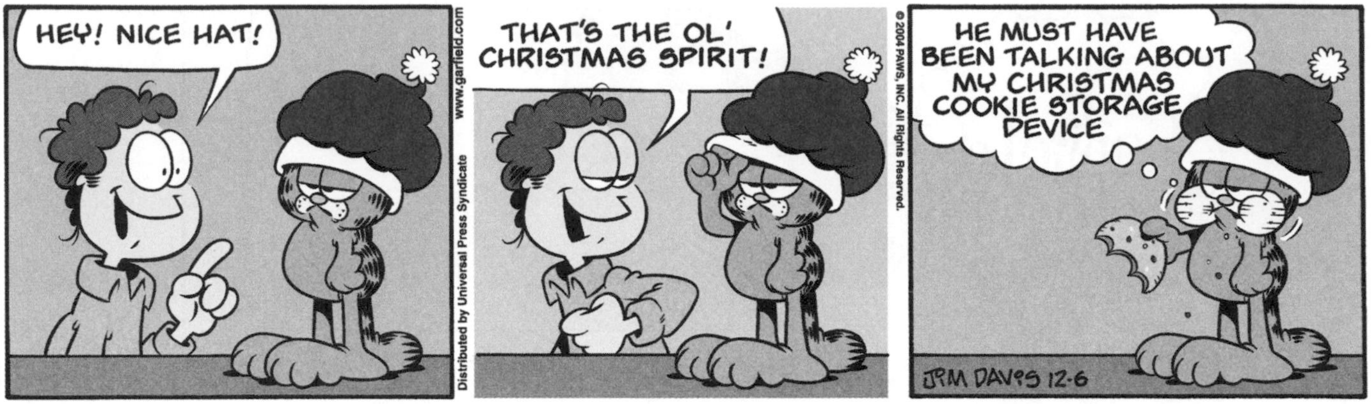
HEY! NICE HAT!
THAT'S THE OL' CHRISTMAS SPIRIT!
HE MUST HAVE BEEN TALKING ABOUT MY CHRISTMAS COOKIE STORAGE DEVICE

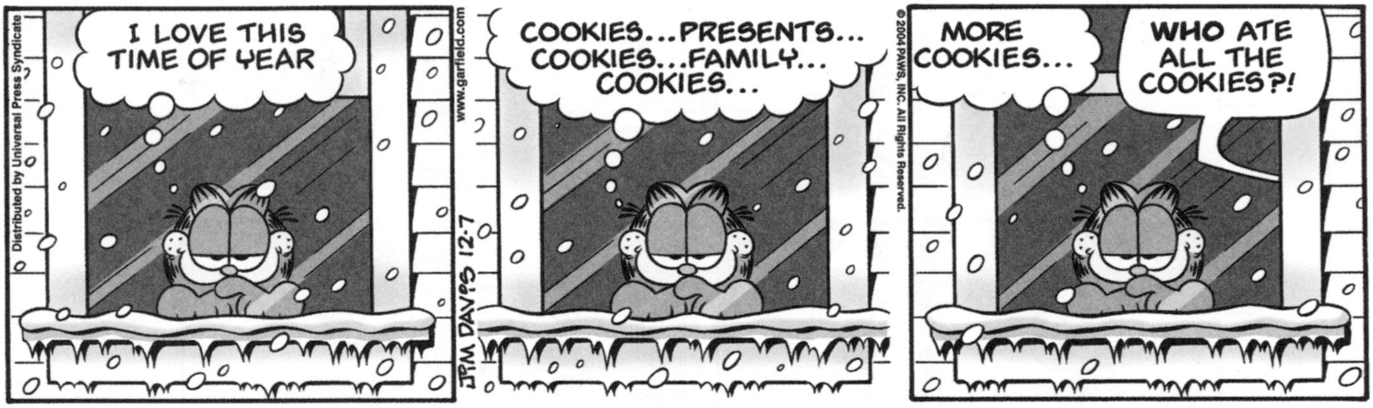
I LOVE THIS TIME OF YEAR
COOKIES...PRESENTS... COOKIES...FAMILY... COOKIES...
MORE COOKIES...
WHO ATE ALL THE COOKIES?!

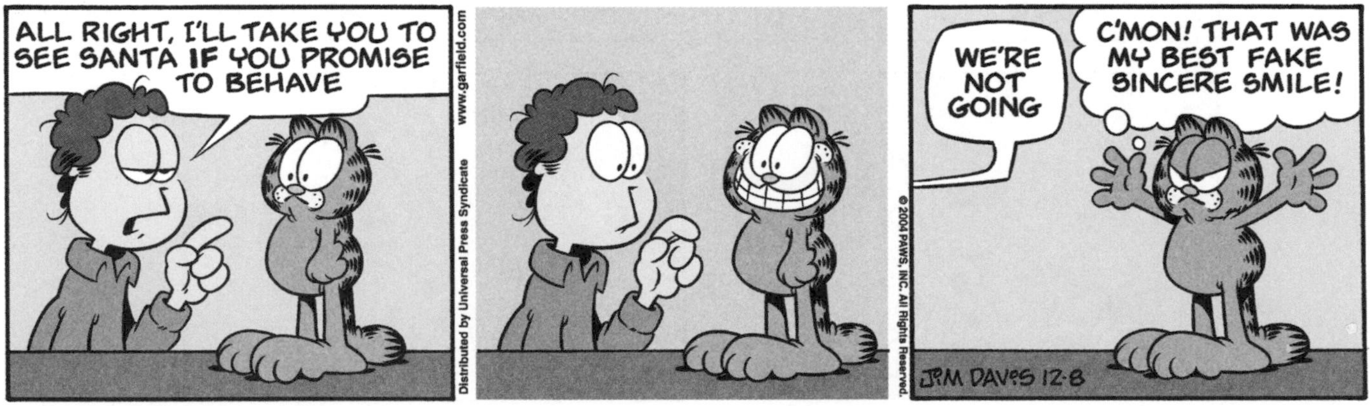
ALL RIGHT, I'LL TAKE YOU TO SEE SANTA IF YOU PROMISE TO BEHAVE
WE'RE NOT GOING
C'MON! THAT WAS MY BEST FAKE SINCERE SMILE!

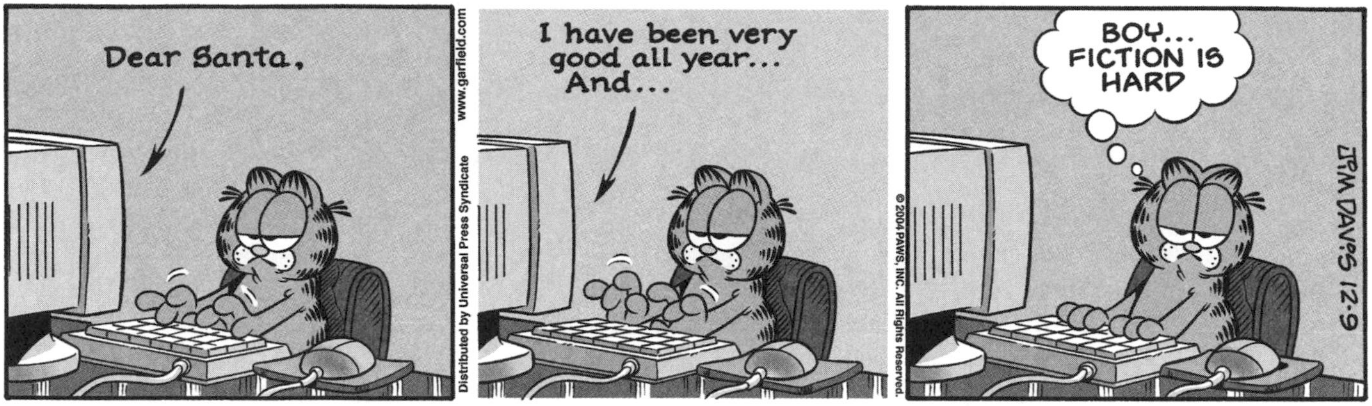
Dear Santa,
I have been very good all year... And...
BOY... FICTION IS HARD
JIM DAVIS 12-9
www.garfield.com
Distributed by Universal Press Syndicate
© 2004 PAWS, INC. All Rights Reserved.

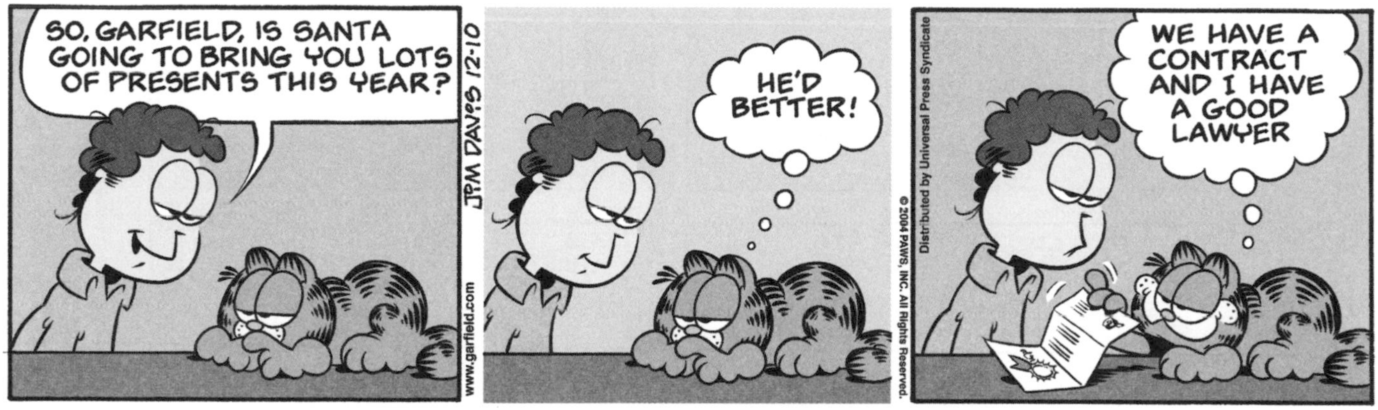
SO, GARFIELD, IS SANTA GOING TO BRING YOU LOTS OF PRESENTS THIS YEAR?
HE'D BETTER!
WE HAVE A CONTRACT AND I HAVE A GOOD LAWYER
JIM DAVIS 12-10
www.garfield.com
Distributed by Universal Press Syndicate
© 2004 PAWS, INC. All Rights Reserved.

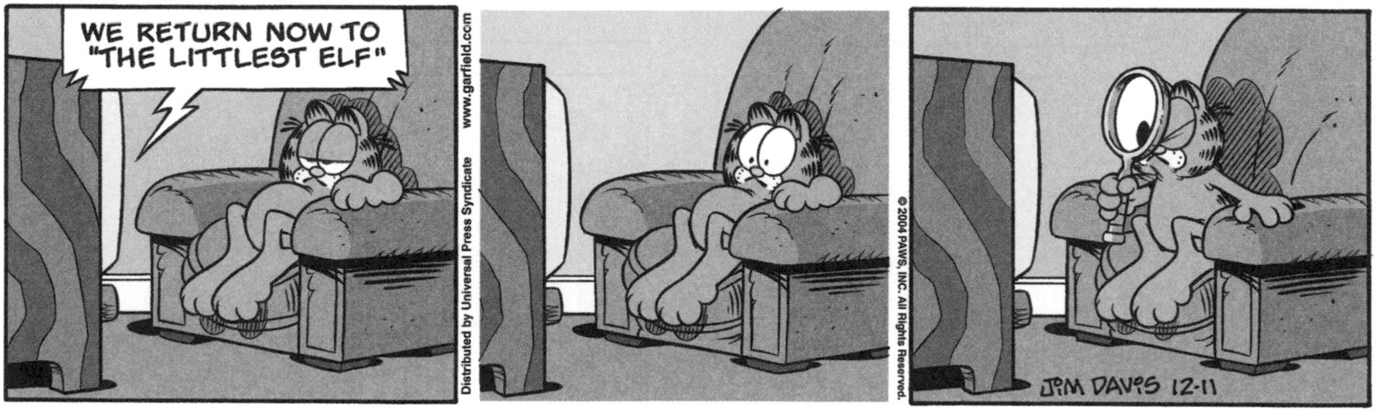
WE RETURN NOW TO "THE LITTLEST ELF"
JIM DAVIS 12-11
www.garfield.com
Distributed by Universal Press Syndicate
© 2004 PAWS, INC. All Rights Reserved.

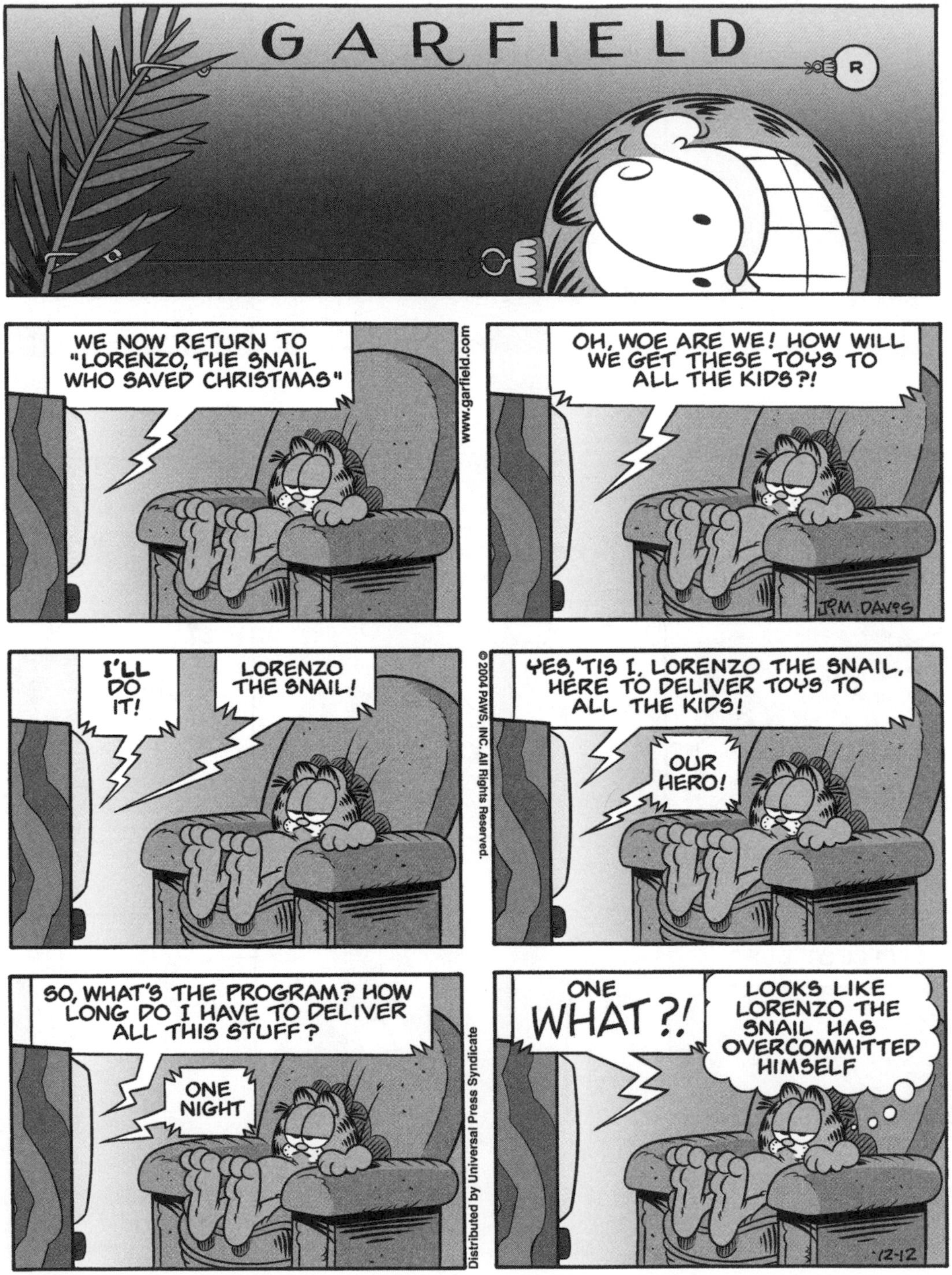
GARFIELD
WE NOW RETURN TO "LORENZO, THE SNAIL WHO SAVED CHRISTMAS"
OH, WOE ARE WE! HOW WILL WE GET THESE TOYS TO ALL THE KIDS?!
JPM DAVPS
I'LL DO IT!
LORENZO THE SNAIL!
YES, 'TIS I, LORENZO THE SNAIL, HERE TO DELIVER TOYS TO ALL THE KIDS!
OUR HERO!
SO, WHAT'S THE PROGRAM? HOW LONG DO I HAVE TO DELIVER ALL THIS STUFF?
ONE NIGHT
ONE WHAT?!
LOOKS LIKE LORENZO THE SNAIL HAS OVERCOMMITTED HIMSELF
12-12
www.garfield.com
© 2004 PAWS, INC. All Rights Reserved.
Distributed by Universal Press Syndicate

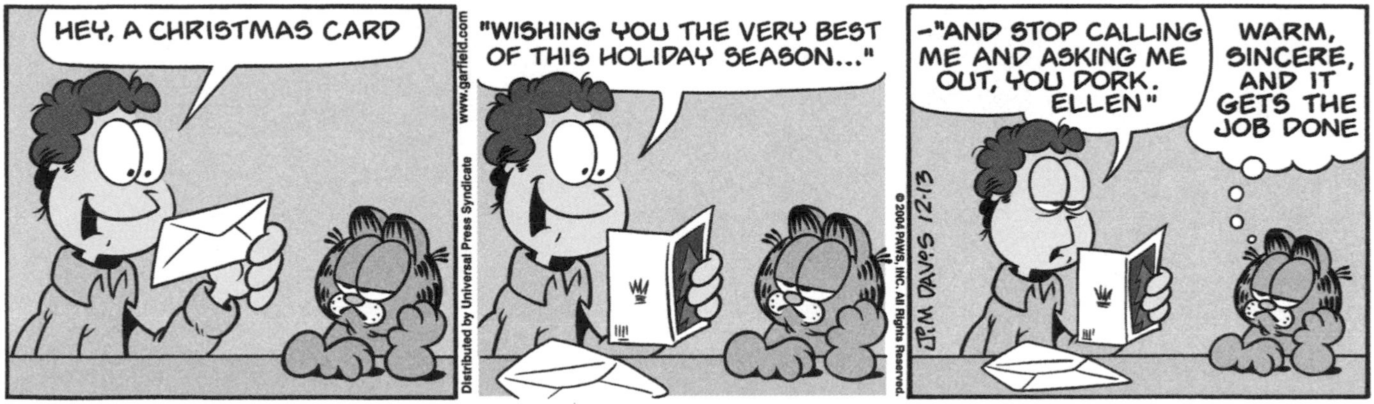
HEY, A CHRISTMAS CARD
www.garfield.com
Distributed by Universal Press Syndicate
"WISHING YOU THE VERY BEST OF THIS HOLIDAY SEASON..."
© 2004 PAWS, INC. All Rights Reserved.
-"AND STOP CALLING ME AND ASKING ME OUT, YOU DORK. ELLEN"
WARM, SINCERE, AND IT GETS THE JOB DONE
JIM DAVIS 12-13

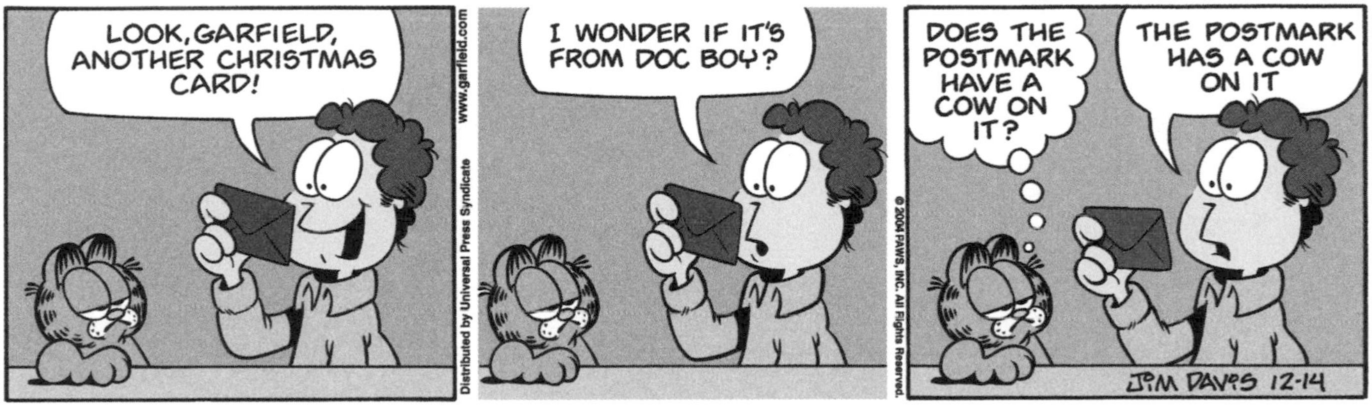
LOOK, GARFIELD, ANOTHER CHRISTMAS CARD!
www.garfield.com
Distributed by Universal Press Syndicate
I WONDER IF IT'S FROM DOC BOY?
© 2004 PAWS, INC. All Rights Reserved.
DOES THE POSTMARK HAVE A COW ON IT?
THE POSTMARK HAS A COW ON IT
JIM DAVIS 12-14

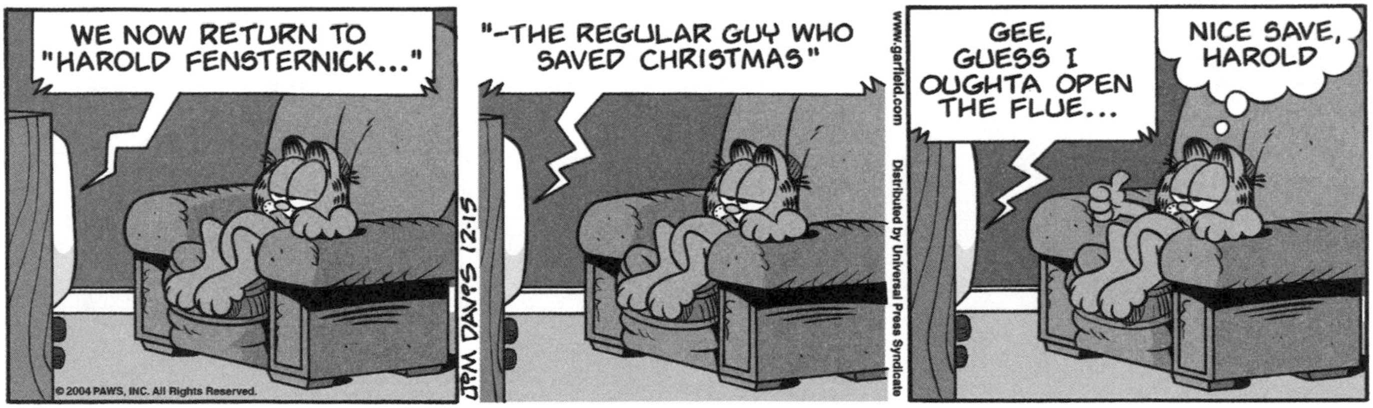
WE NOW RETURN TO "HAROLD FENSTERNICK..."
© 2004 PAWS, INC. All Rights Reserved.
JIM DAVIS 12-15
"-THE REGULAR GUY WHO SAVED CHRISTMAS"
www.garfield.com
Distributed by Universal Press Syndicate
GEE, GUESS I OUGHTA OPEN THE FLUE...
NICE SAVE, HAROLD

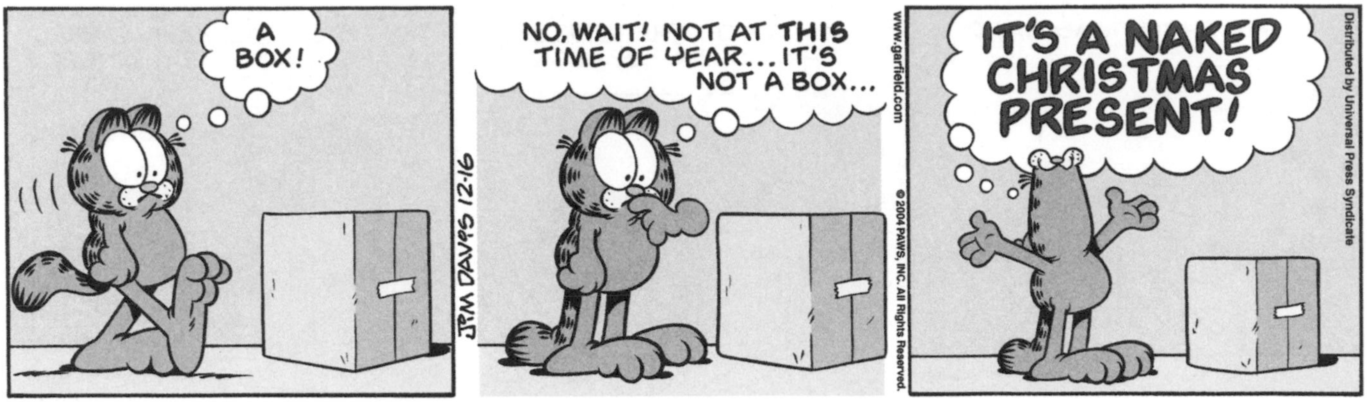
A BOX!
NO, WAIT! NOT AT THIS TIME OF YEAR... IT'S NOT A BOX...
IT'S A NAKED CHRISTMAS PRESENT!
JIM DAVIS 12-16
www.garfield.com
© 2004 PAWS, INC. All Rights Reserved.
Distributed by Universal Press Syndicate

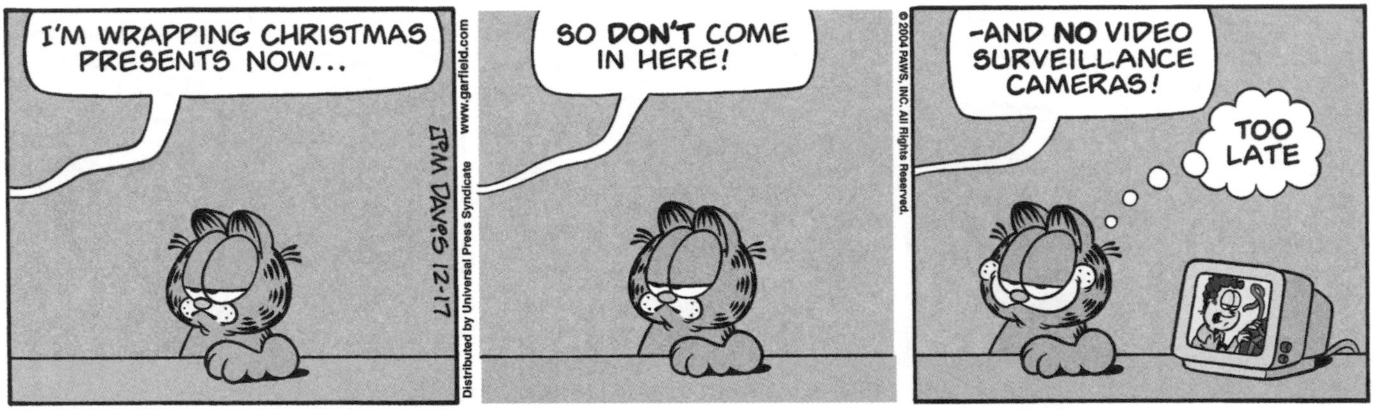
I'M WRAPPING CHRISTMAS PRESENTS NOW...
SO DON'T COME IN HERE!
-AND NO VIDEO SURVEILLANCE CAMERAS!
TOO LATE
JIM DAVIS 12-17
www.garfield.com
Distributed by Universal Press Syndicate
© 2004 PAWS, INC. All Rights Reserved.

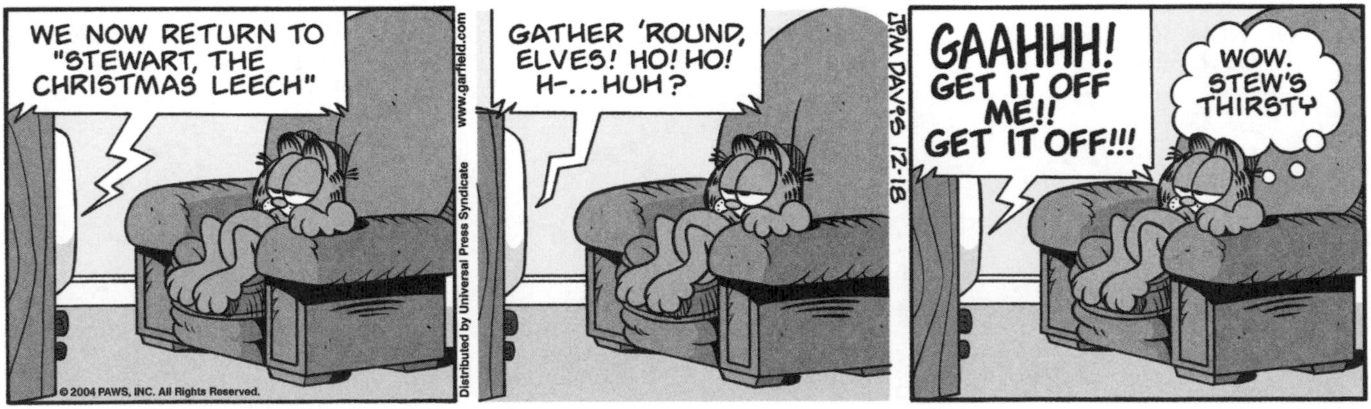
WE NOW RETURN TO "STEWART, THE CHRISTMAS LEECH"
GATHER 'ROUND, ELVES! HO! HO! H-...HUH?
GAAHHH! GET IT OFF ME!! GET IT OFF!!!
WOW. STEW'S THIRSTY
JIM DAVIS 12-18
www.garfield.com
Distributed by Universal Press Syndicate
© 2004 PAWS, INC. All Rights Reserved.

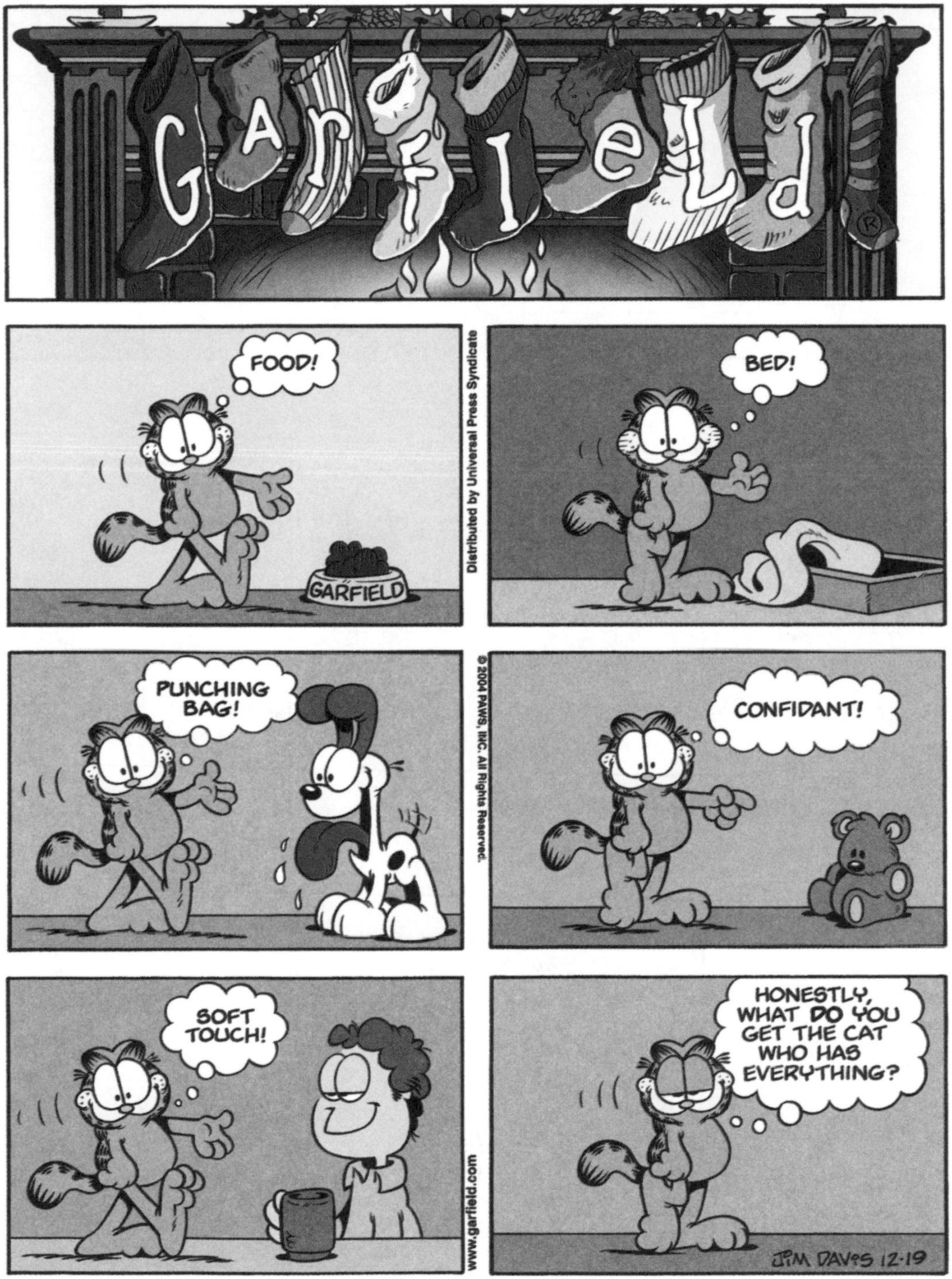

Garfield
FOOD!
GARFIELD
Distributed by Universal Press Syndicate
BED!
PUNCHING BAG!
© 2004 PAWS, INC. All Rights Reserved.
CONFIDANT!
SOFT TOUCH!
www.garfield.com
HONESTLY, WHAT DO YOU GET THE CAT WHO HAS EVERYTHING?
JIM DAVIS 12-19

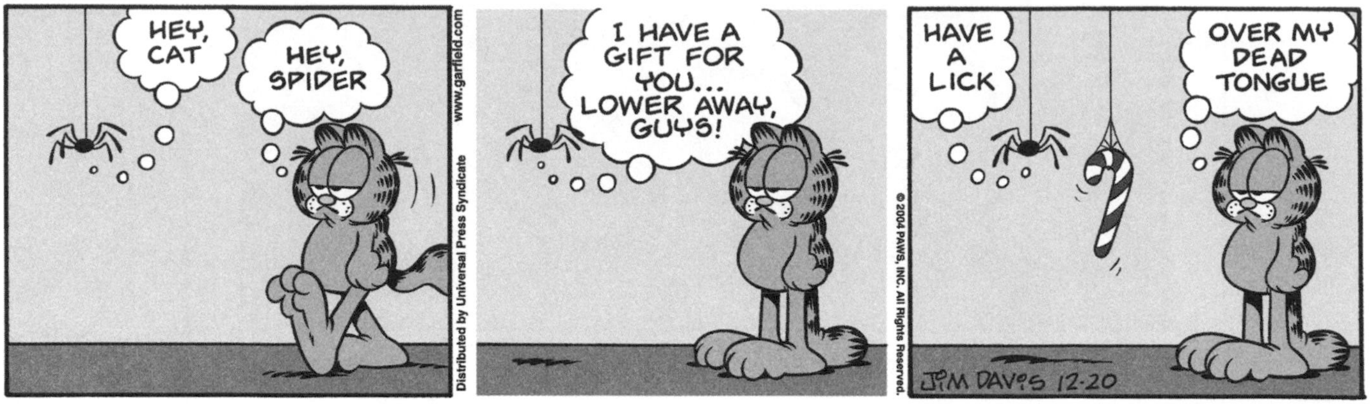
HEY, CAT
HEY, SPIDER
www.garfield.com
Distributed by Universal Press Syndicate
I HAVE A GIFT FOR YOU... LOWER AWAY, GUYS!
© 2004 PAWS, INC. All Rights Reserved.
HAVE A LICK
OVER MY DEAD TONGUE
JIM DAVIS 12-20

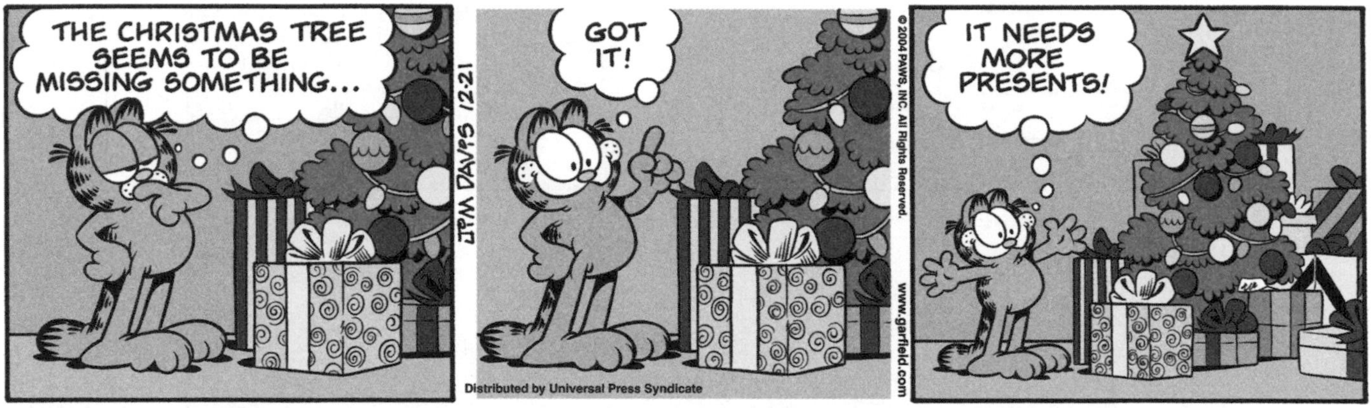
THE CHRISTMAS TREE SEEMS TO BE MISSING SOMETHING...
JIM DAVIS 12-21
GOT IT!
Distributed by Universal Press Syndicate
© 2004 PAWS, INC. All Rights Reserved.
www.garfield.com
IT NEEDS MORE PRESENTS!

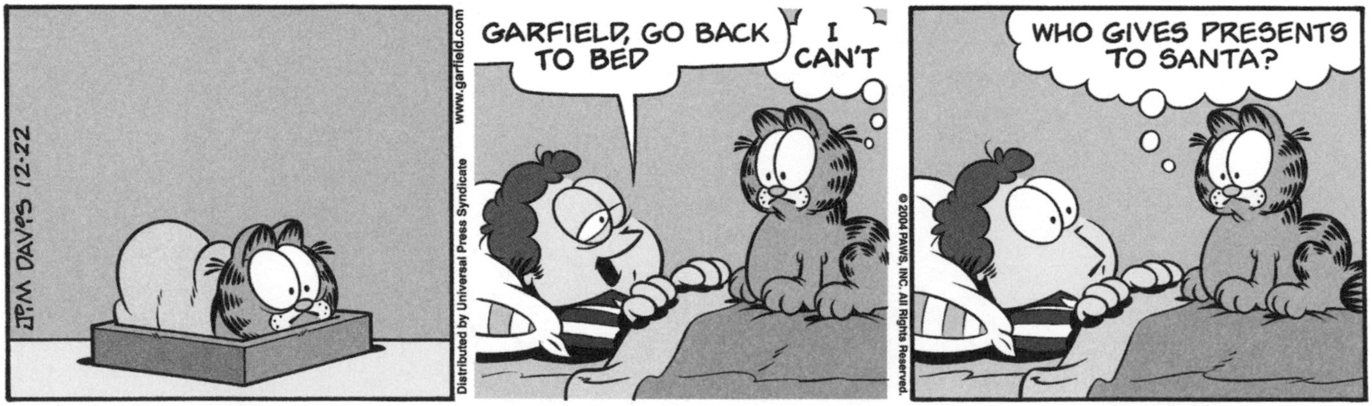
JIM DAVIS 12-22
www.garfield.com
Distributed by Universal Press Syndicate
GARFIELD, GO BACK TO BED
I CAN'T
© 2004 PAWS, INC. All Rights Reserved.
WHO GIVES PRESENTS TO SANTA?

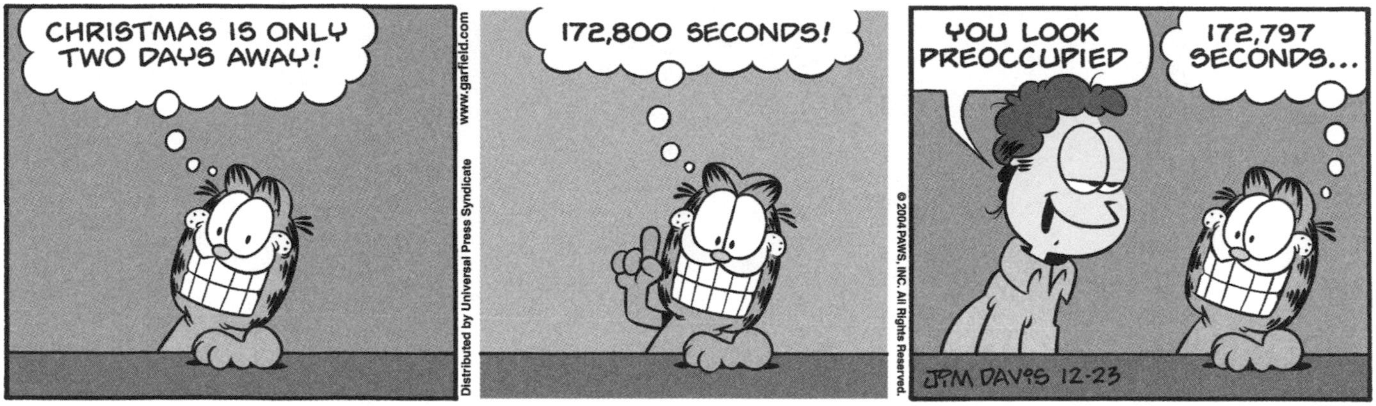
CHRISTMAS IS ONLY TWO DAYS AWAY!
www.garfield.com
Distributed by Universal Press Syndicate
172,800 SECONDS!
© 2004 PAWS, INC. All Rights Reserved.
YOU LOOK PREOCCUPIED
172,797 SECONDS...
JIM DAVIS 12-23

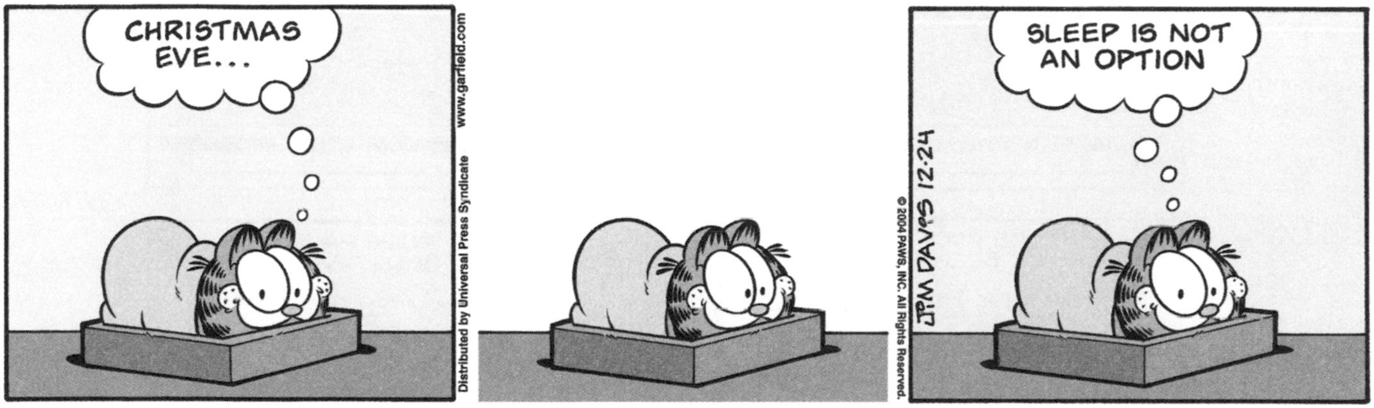
CHRISTMAS EVE...
www.garfield.com
Distributed by Universal Press Syndicate
© 2004 PAWS, INC. All Rights Reserved.
JIM DAVIS 12-24
SLEEP IS NOT AN OPTION

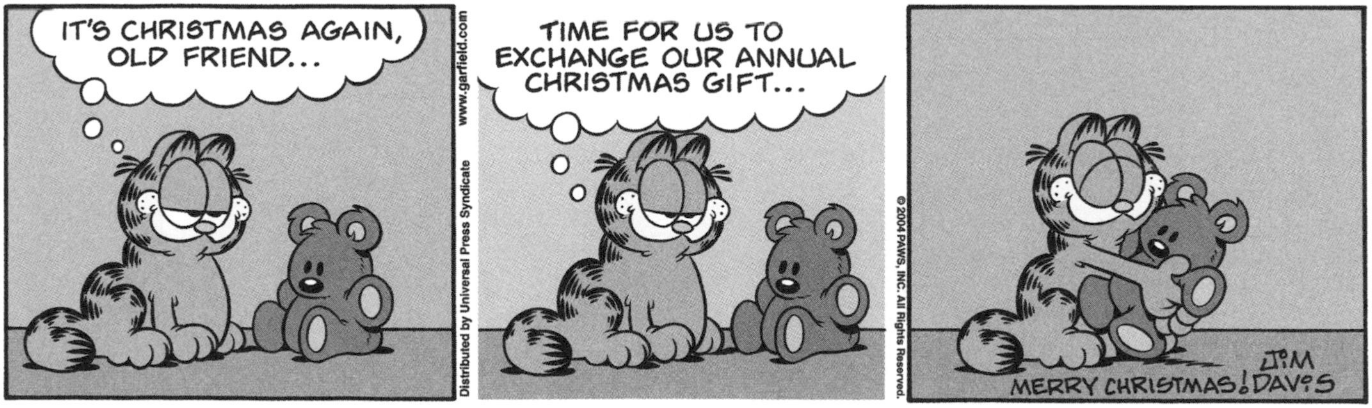
IT'S CHRISTMAS AGAIN, OLD FRIEND...
www.garfield.com
Distributed by Universal Press Syndicate
TIME FOR US TO EXCHANGE OUR ANNUAL CHRISTMAS GIFT...
© 2004 PAWS, INC. All Rights Reserved.
MERRY CHRISTMAS!
JIM DAVIS

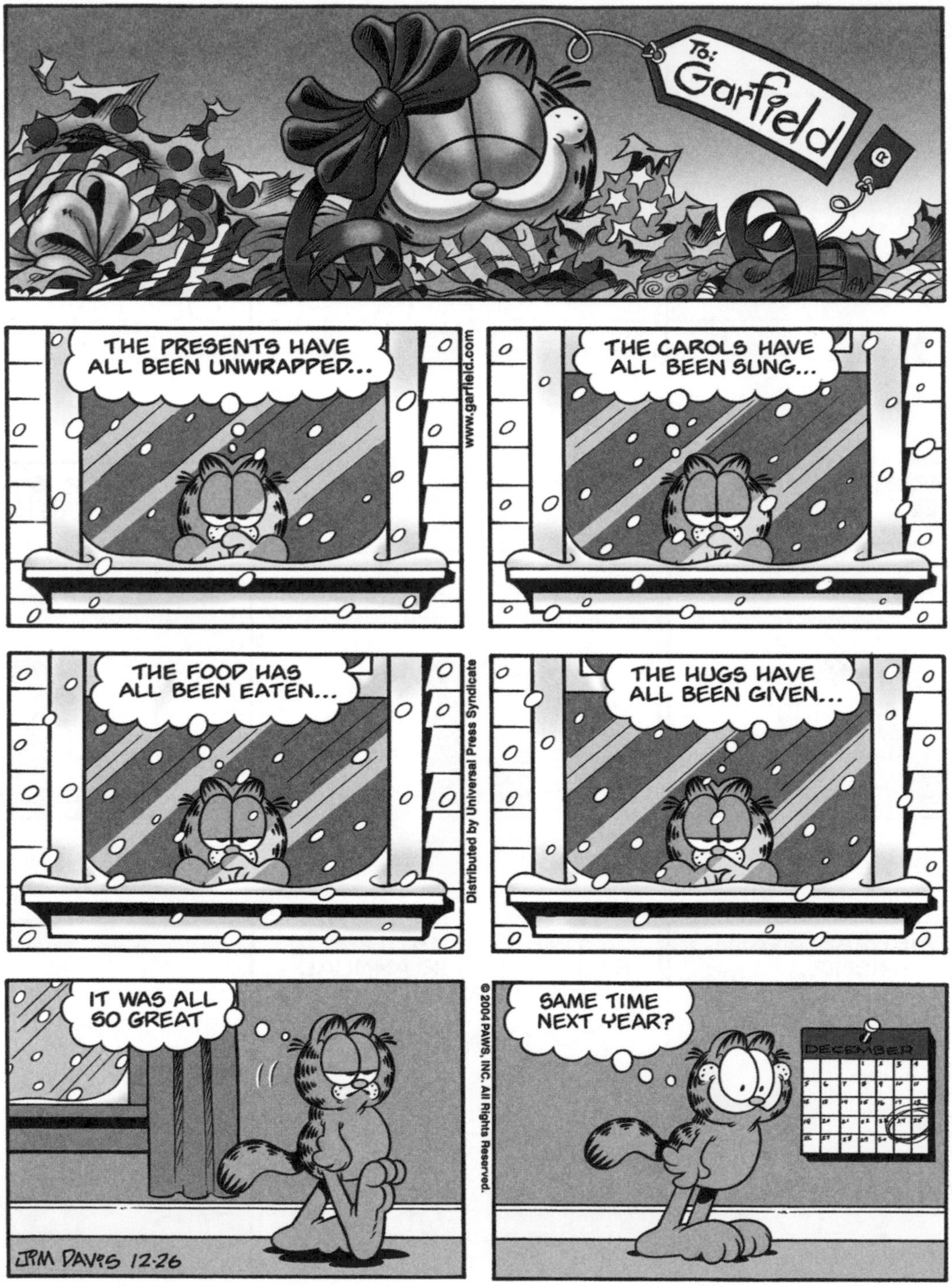

To: Garfield
THE PRESENTS HAVE ALL BEEN UNWRAPPED...
THE CAROLS HAVE ALL BEEN SUNG...
THE FOOD HAS ALL BEEN EATEN...
THE HUGS HAVE ALL BEEN GIVEN...
IT WAS ALL SO GREAT
SAME TIME NEXT YEAR?
DECEMBER
JIM DAVIS 12·26
www.garfield.com
Distributed by Universal Press Syndicate
© 2004 PAWS, INC. All Rights Reserved.

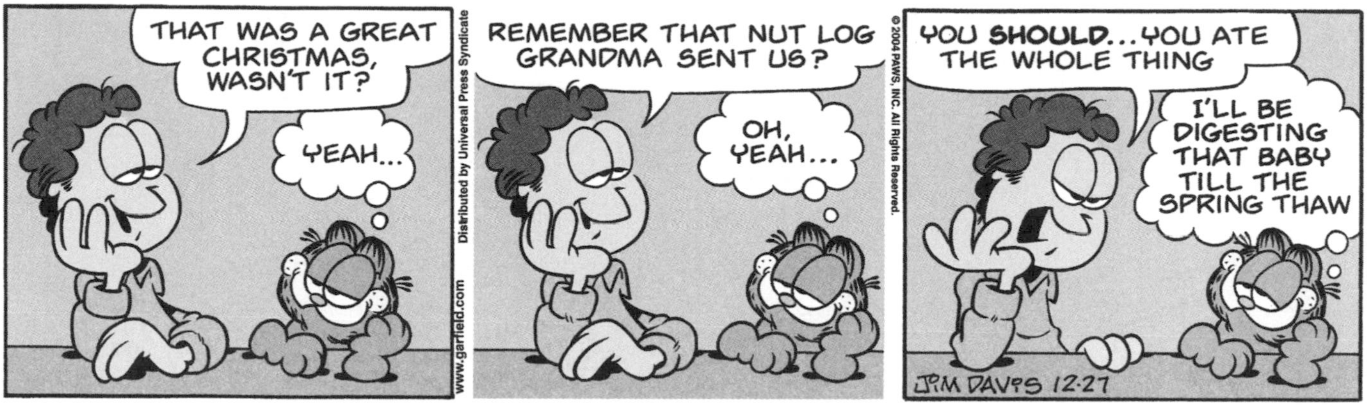
THAT WAS A GREAT CHRISTMAS, WASN'T IT?
YEAH...
www.garfield.com
Distributed by Universal Press Syndicate
REMEMBER THAT NUT LOG GRANDMA SENT US?
OH, YEAH...
© 2004 PAWS, INC. All Rights Reserved.
YOU SHOULD...YOU ATE THE WHOLE THING
I'LL BE DIGESTING THAT BABY TILL THE SPRING THAW
JIM DAVIS 12·27

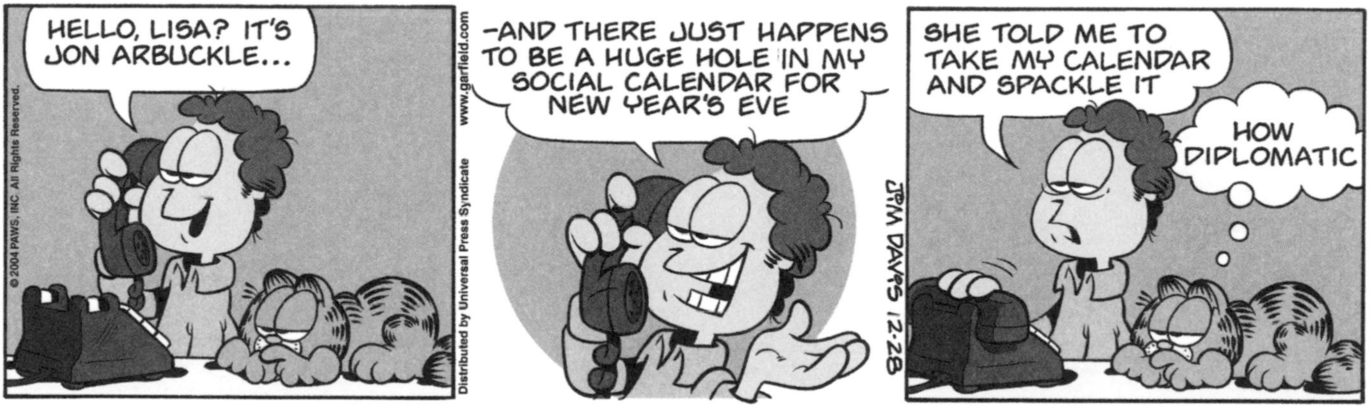
HELLO, LISA? IT'S JON ARBUCKLE...
© 2004 PAWS, INC. All Rights Reserved.
www.garfield.com
Distributed by Universal Press Syndicate
-AND THERE JUST HAPPENS TO BE A HUGE HOLE IN MY SOCIAL CALENDAR FOR NEW YEAR'S EVE
JIM DAVIS 12·28
SHE TOLD ME TO TAKE MY CALENDAR AND SPACKLE IT
HOW DIPLOMATIC

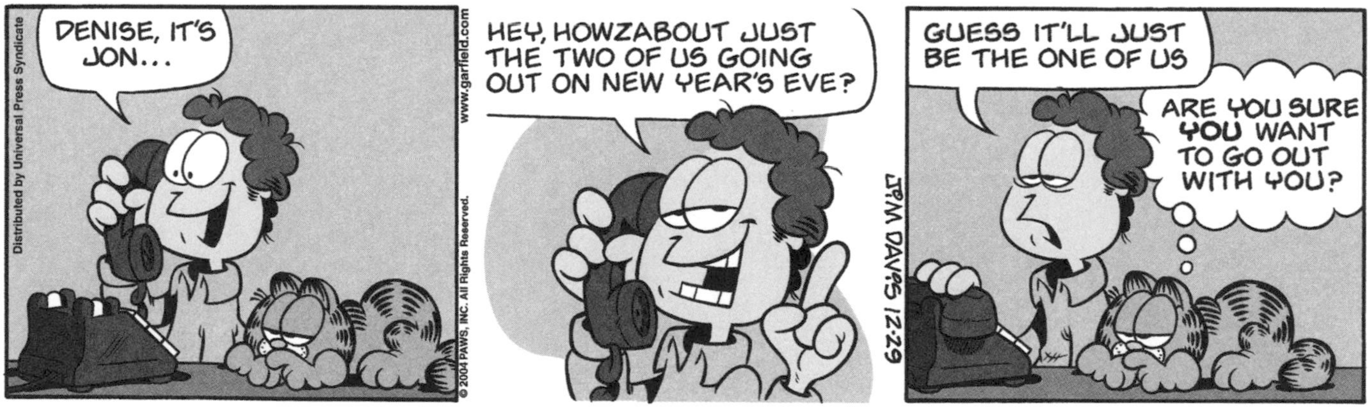
DENISE, IT'S JON...
Distributed by Universal Press Syndicate
www.garfield.com
© 2004 PAWS, INC. All Rights Reserved.
HEY, HOWZABOUT JUST THE TWO OF US GOING OUT ON NEW YEAR'S EVE?
JIM DAVIS 12·29
GUESS IT'LL JUST BE THE ONE OF US
ARE YOU SURE YOU WANT TO GO OUT WITH YOU?

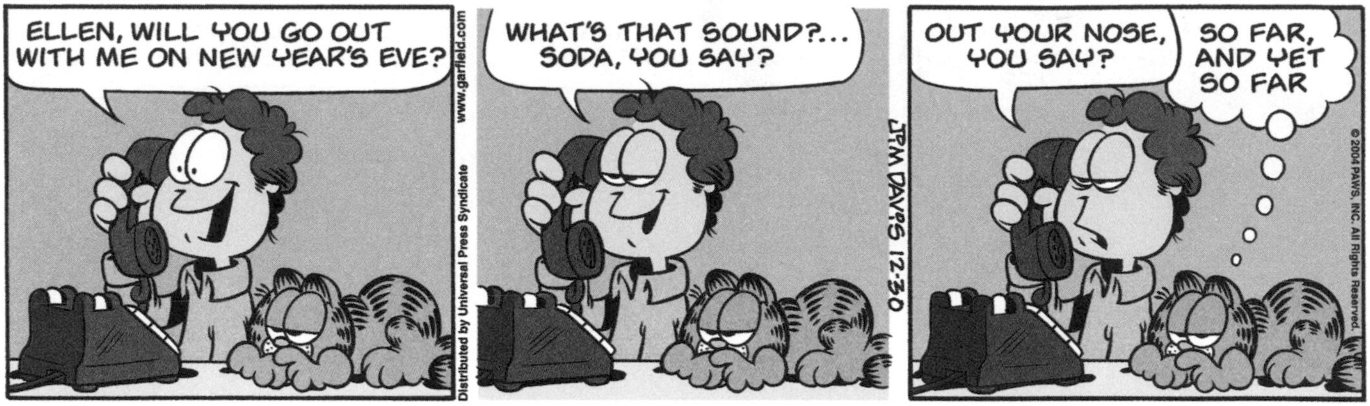
ELLEN, WILL YOU GO OUT WITH ME ON NEW YEAR'S EVE?
www.garfield.com
Distributed by Universal Press Syndicate
WHAT'S THAT SOUND?... SODA, YOU SAY?
JIM DAVIS 12-30
OUT YOUR NOSE, YOU SAY?
SO FAR, AND YET SO FAR
© 2004 PAWS, INC. All Rights Reserved.

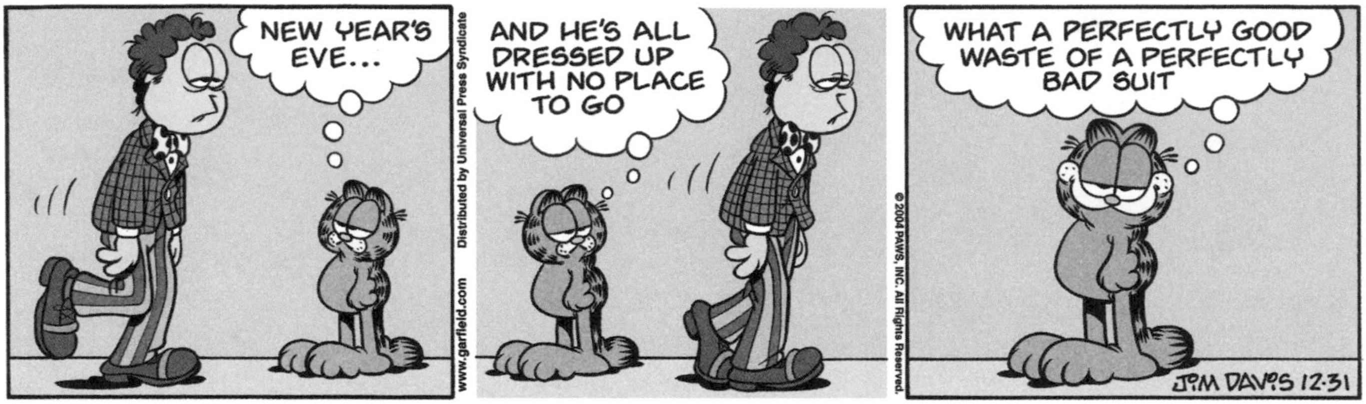
NEW YEAR'S EVE...
www.garfield.com
Distributed by Universal Press Syndicate
AND HE'S ALL DRESSED UP WITH NO PLACE TO GO
© 2004 PAWS, INC. All Rights Reserved.
WHAT A PERFECTLY GOOD WASTE OF A PERFECTLY BAD SUIT
JIM DAVIS 12-31

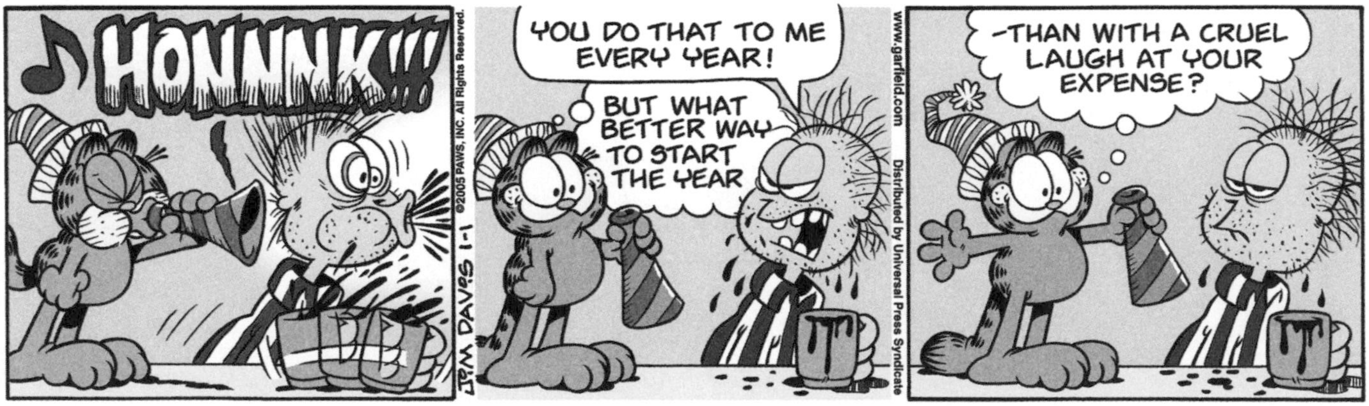
HONNNK!!!
© 2005 PAWS, INC. All Rights Reserved.
JIM DAVIS 1-1
YOU DO THAT TO ME EVERY YEAR!
BUT WHAT BETTER WAY TO START THE YEAR
www.garfield.com
Distributed by Universal Press Syndicate
-THAN WITH A CRUEL LAUGH AT YOUR EXPENSE?

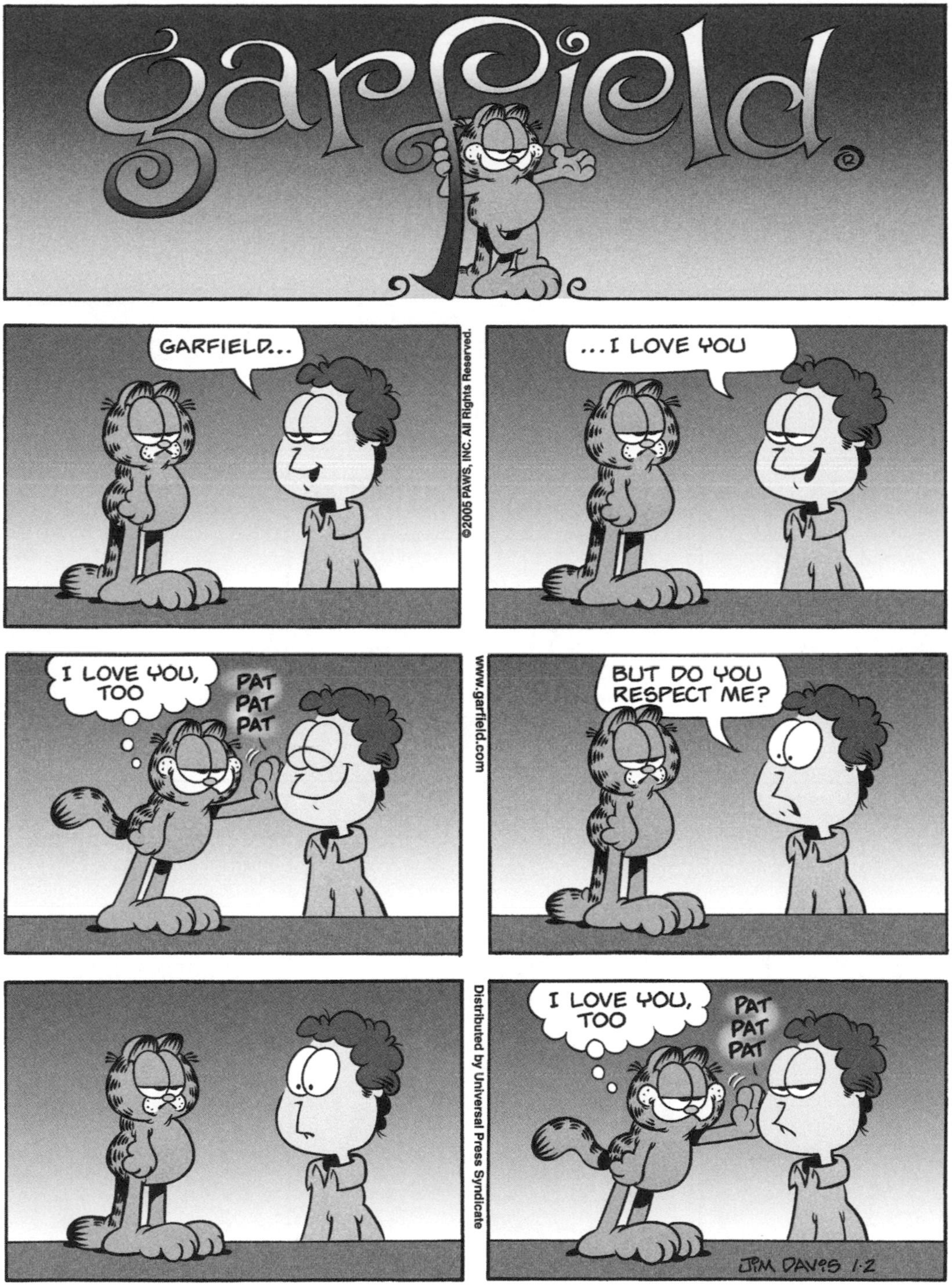
garfield
GARFIELD...
...I LOVE YOU
I LOVE YOU, TOO
PAT PAT PAT
BUT DO YOU RESPECT ME?
I LOVE YOU, TOO
PAT PAT PAT
JIM DAVIS 1·2
©2005 PAWS, INC. All Rights Reserved.
www.garfield.com
Distributed by Universal Press Syndicate

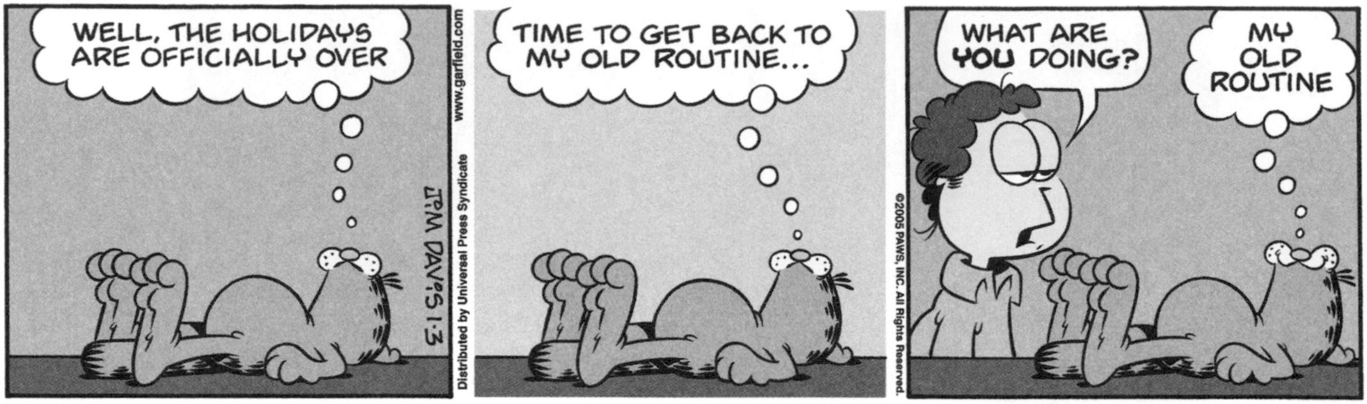
WELL, THE HOLIDAYS ARE OFFICIALLY OVER
JPM DAVIS 1-3
www.garfield.com
Distributed by Universal Press Syndicate
TIME TO GET BACK TO MY OLD ROUTINE...
©2005 PAWS, INC. All Rights Reserved.
WHAT ARE YOU DOING?
MY OLD ROUTINE

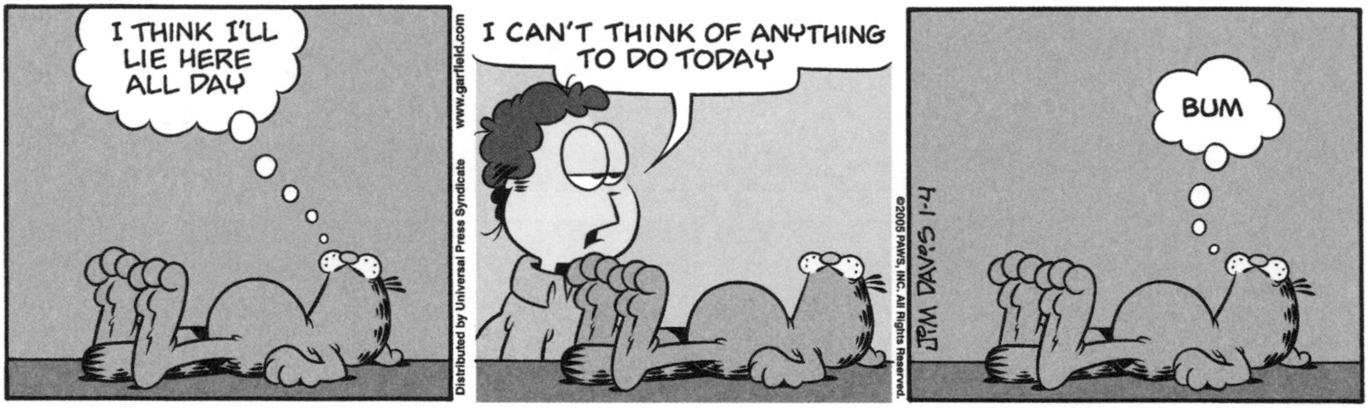
I THINK I'LL LIE HERE ALL DAY
www.garfield.com
Distributed by Universal Press Syndicate
I CAN'T THINK OF ANYTHING TO DO TODAY
©2005 PAWS, INC. All Rights Reserved.
JPM DAVIS 1-4
BUM

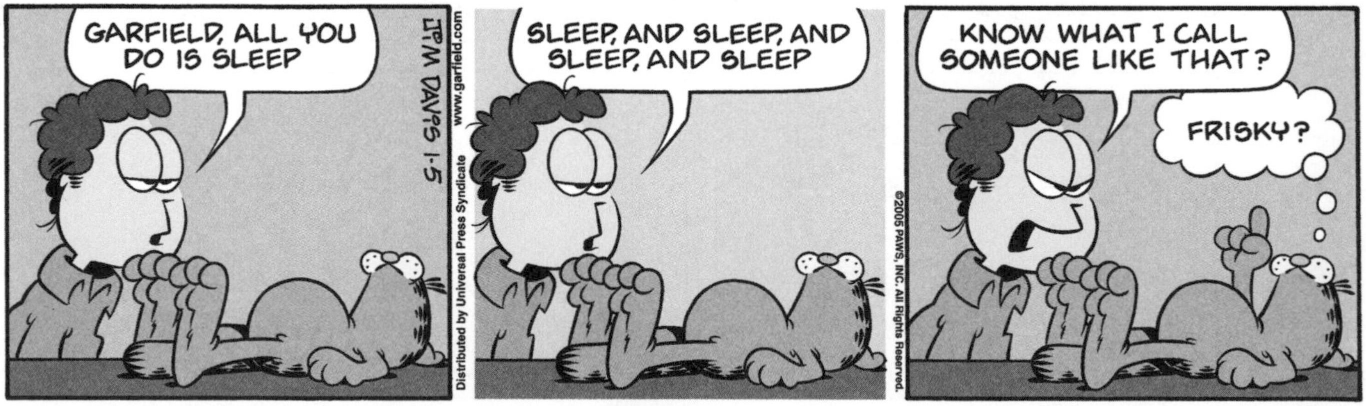
GARFIELD, ALL YOU DO IS SLEEP
JPM DAVIS 1-5
www.garfield.com
Distributed by Universal Press Syndicate
SLEEP, AND SLEEP, AND SLEEP, AND SLEEP
©2005 PAWS, INC. All Rights Reserved.
KNOW WHAT I CALL SOMEONE LIKE THAT?
FRISKY?

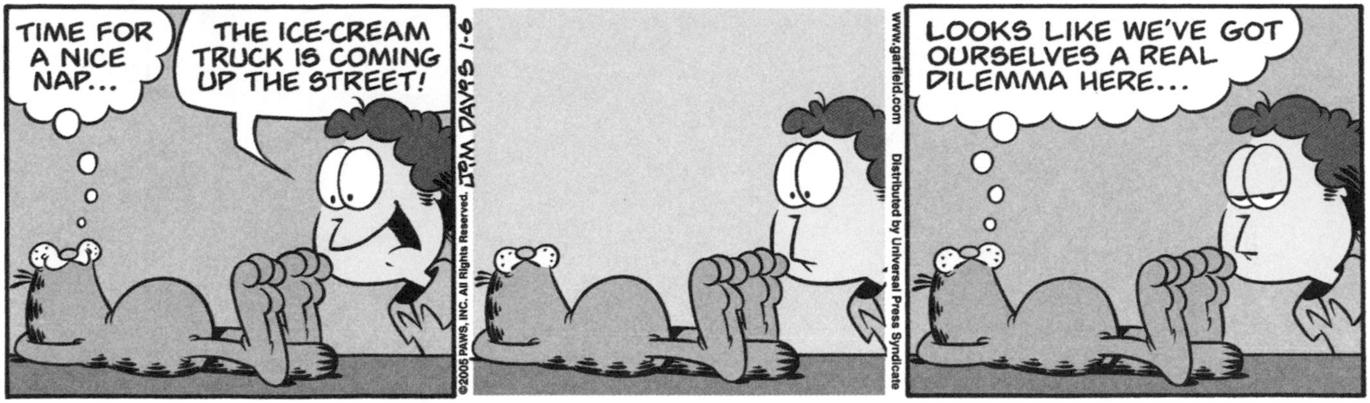
TIME FOR A NICE NAP...
THE ICE-CREAM TRUCK IS COMING UP THE STREET!
JPM DAVPS 1-6
©2005 PAWS, INC. All Rights Reserved.
www.garfield.com
Distributed by Universal Press Syndicate
LOOKS LIKE WE'VE GOT OURSELVES A REAL DILEMMA HERE...

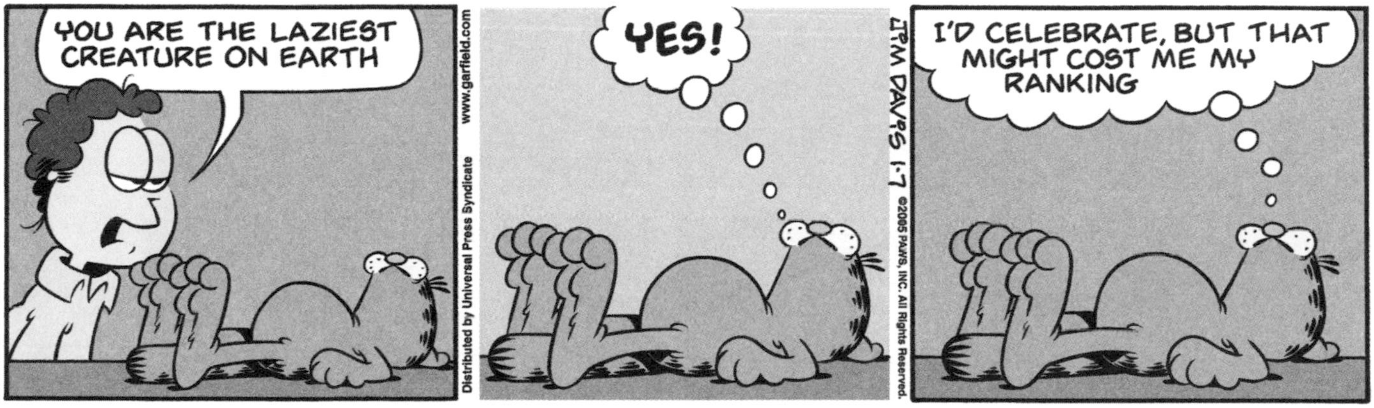
YOU ARE THE LAZIEST CREATURE ON EARTH
www.garfield.com
Distributed by Universal Press Syndicate
YES!
JPM DAVPS 1-7
©2005 PAWS, INC. All Rights Reserved.
I'D CELEBRATE, BUT THAT MIGHT COST ME MY RANKING

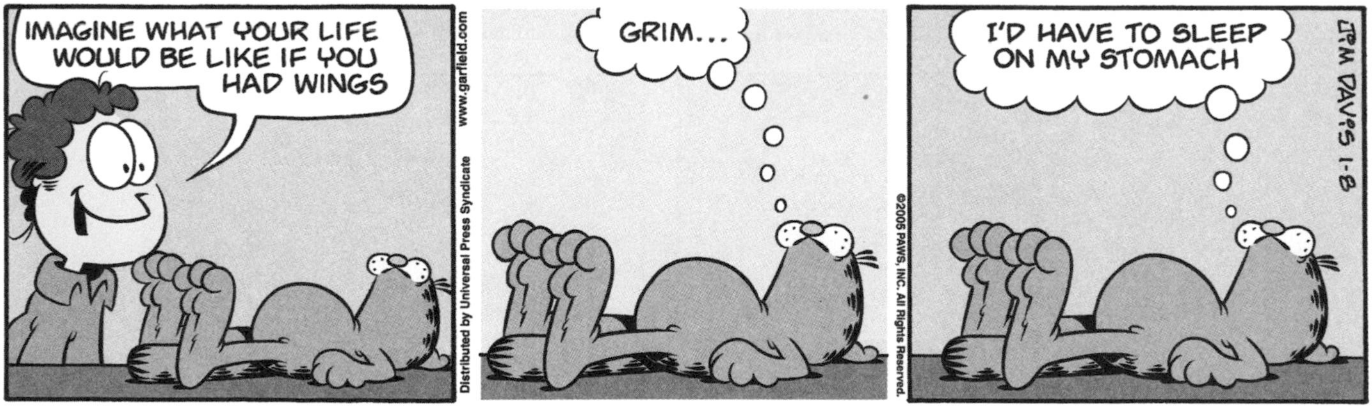
IMAGINE WHAT YOUR LIFE WOULD BE LIKE IF YOU HAD WINGS
www.garfield.com
Distributed by Universal Press Syndicate
GRIM...
©2005 PAWS, INC. All Rights Reserved.
I'D HAVE TO SLEEP ON MY STOMACH
JPM DAVPS 1-8

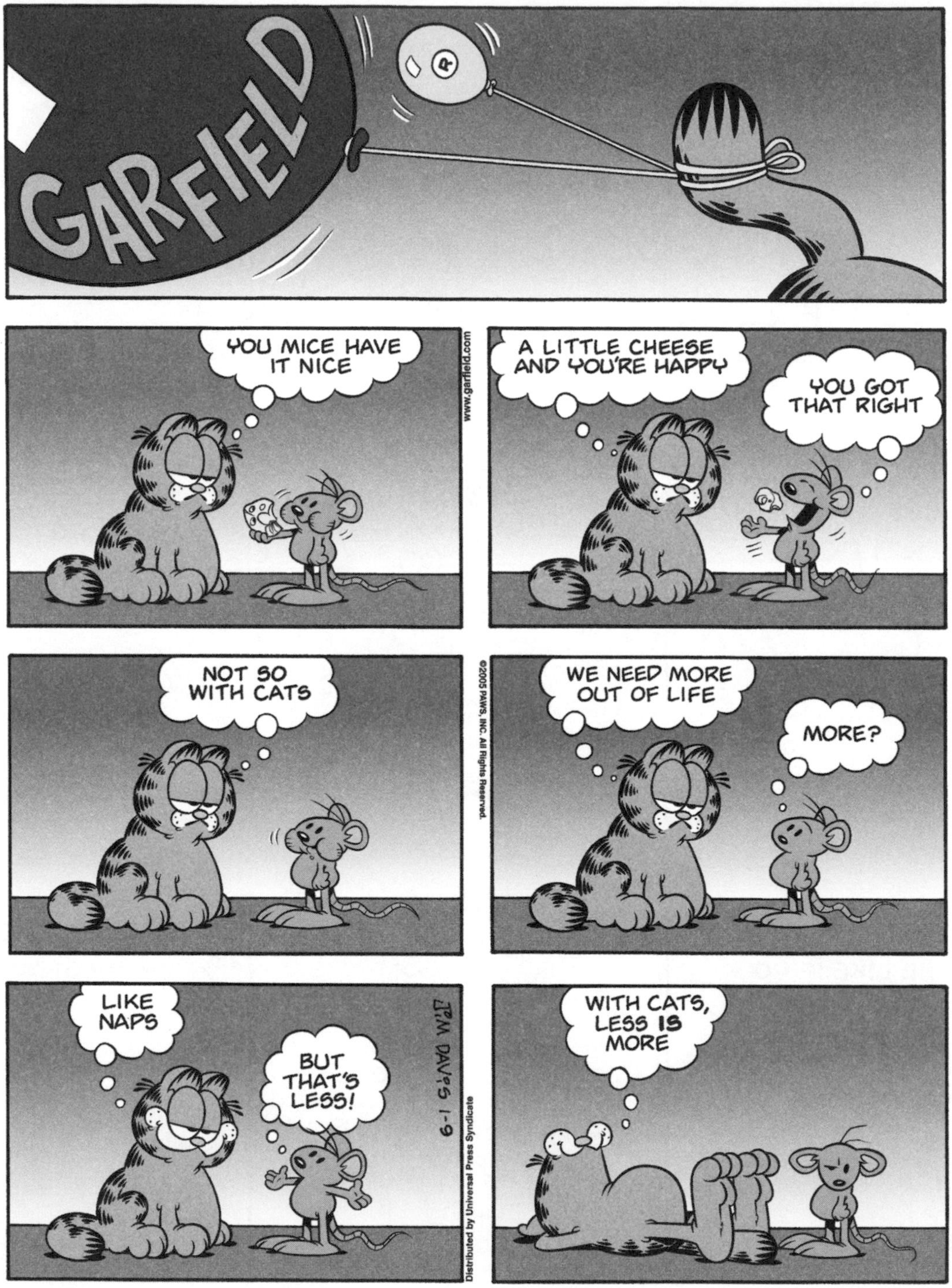
GARFIELD
YOU MICE HAVE IT NICE
www.garfield.com
A LITTLE CHEESE AND YOU'RE HAPPY
YOU GOT THAT RIGHT
NOT SO WITH CATS
©2005 PAWS, INC. All Rights Reserved.
WE NEED MORE OUT OF LIFE
MORE?
LIKE NAPS
BUT THAT'S LESS!
JPM DAVIS 1-9
Distributed by Universal Press Syndicate
WITH CATS, LESS **IS** MORE

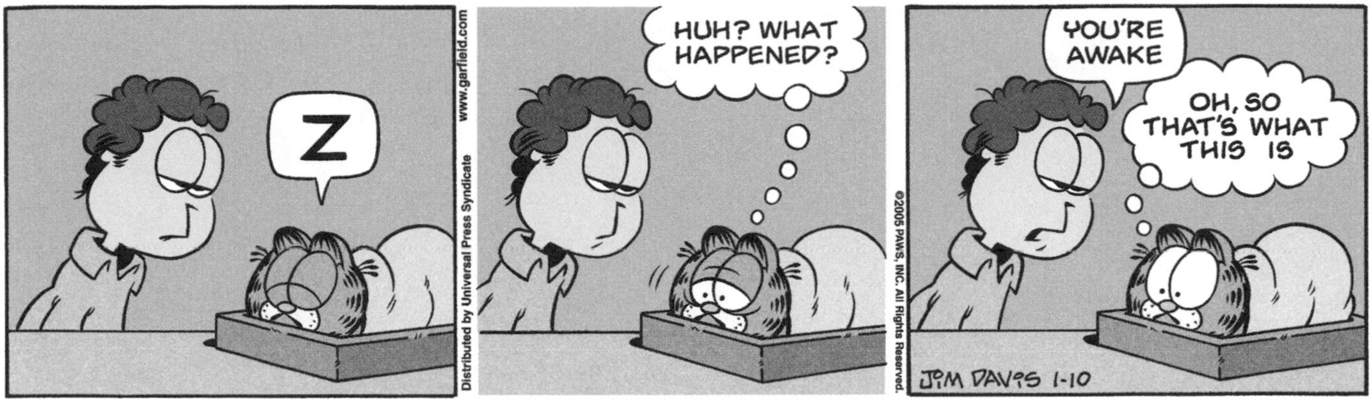
Z
HUH? WHAT HAPPENED?
YOU'RE AWAKE
OH, SO THAT'S WHAT THIS IS
JIM DAVIS 1-10
www.garfield.com
Distributed by Universal Press Syndicate
©2005 PAWS, INC. All Rights Reserved.

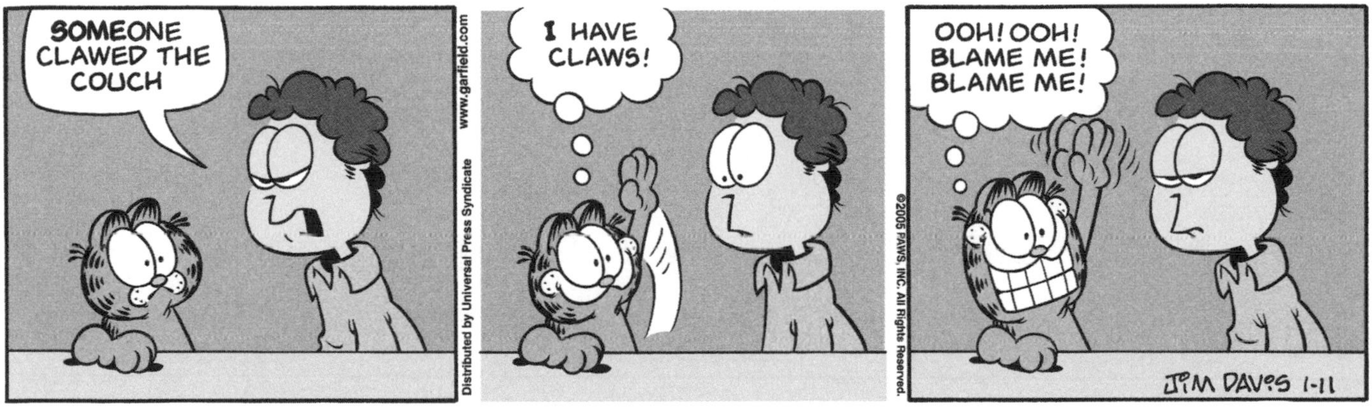
SOMEONE CLAWED THE COUCH
I HAVE CLAWS!
OOH! OOH! BLAME ME! BLAME ME!
JIM DAVIS 1-11
www.garfield.com
Distributed by Universal Press Syndicate
©2005 PAWS, INC. All Rights Reserved.

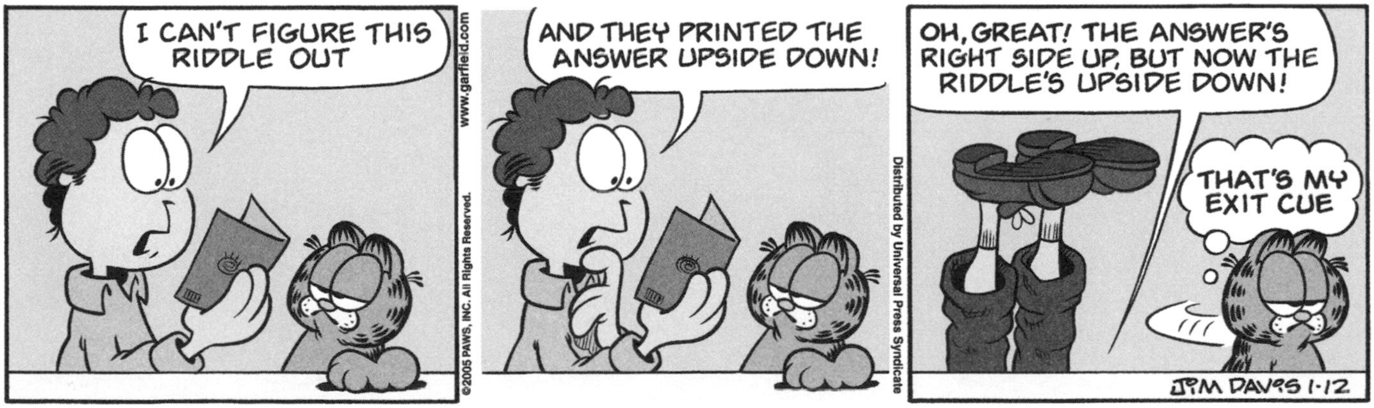
I CAN'T FIGURE THIS RIDDLE OUT
AND THEY PRINTED THE ANSWER UPSIDE DOWN!
OH, GREAT! THE ANSWER'S RIGHT SIDE UP, BUT NOW THE RIDDLE'S UPSIDE DOWN!
THAT'S MY EXIT CUE
JIM DAVIS 1-12
www.garfield.com
©2005 PAWS, INC. All Rights Reserved.
Distributed by Universal Press Syndicate

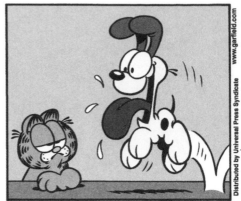

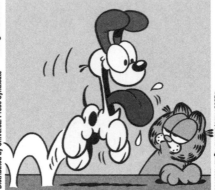

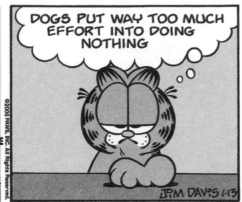

www.garfield.com
Distributed by Universal Press Syndicate
©2005 PAWS, INC. All Rights Reserved.
DOGS PUT WAY TOO MUCH EFFORT INTO DOING NOTHING
JIM DAVIS 1-13

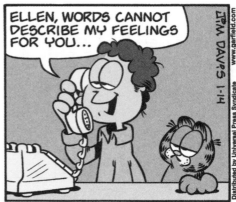

ELLEN, WORDS CANNOT DESCRIBE MY FEELINGS FOR YOU...
JIM DAVIS 1-14
www.garfield.com
Distributed by Universal Press Syndicate
-SO LET ME EXPRESS THEM WITH MUSIC INSTEAD
©2005 PAWS, INC. All Rights Reserved.
ANNA-ONE, ANNA-TWO...
ANNA BYE-BYE, ELLEN

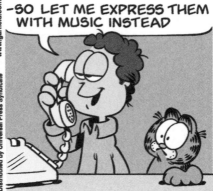

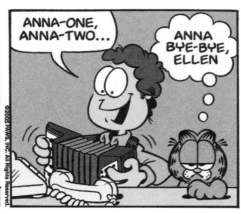

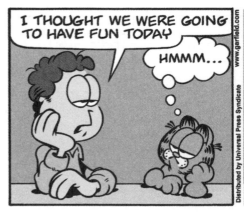

I THOUGHT WE WERE GOING TO HAVE FUN TODAY
HMMM...
www.garfield.com
Distributed by Universal Press Syndicate
REMEMBER THAT NAP WE TOOK?
©2005 PAWS, INC. All Rights Reserved.
JIM DAVIS 1-15
MAYBE IT HAPPENED THEN

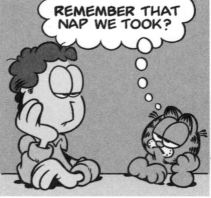

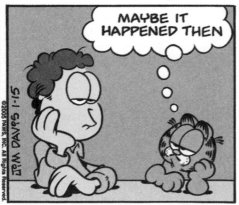

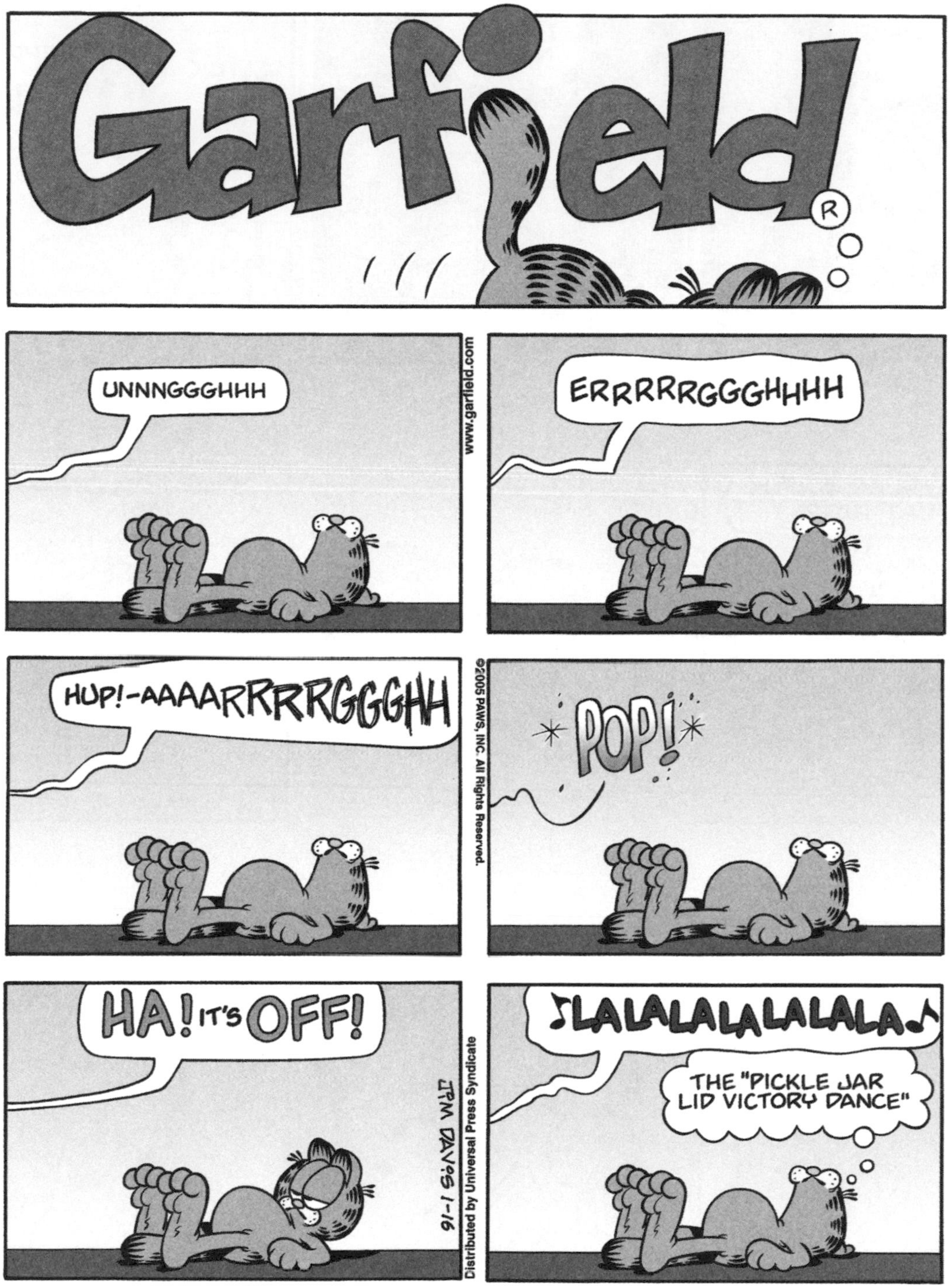
Garfield
UNNNGGGHHH
ERRRRRGGGHHHH
HUP!-AAAARRRRGGGHH
POP!
HA! IT'S OFF!
LALALALALALALALA
THE "PICKLE JAR LID VICTORY DANCE"
JIM DAVIS 1-16
www.garfield.com
©2005 PAWS, INC. All Rights Reserved.
Distributed by Universal Press Syndicate

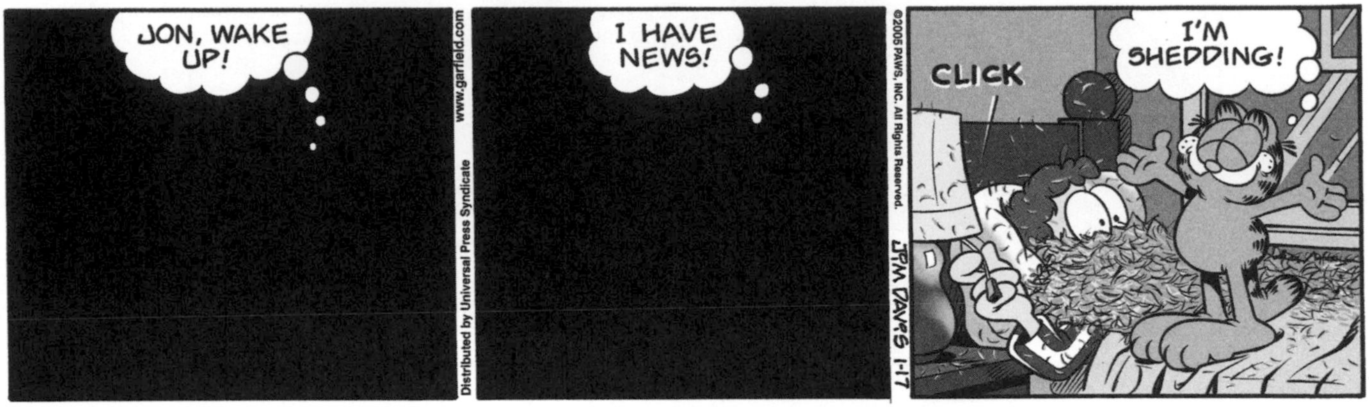
JON, WAKE UP!
I HAVE NEWS!
CLICK
I'M SHEDDING!
JPM DAVPS 1-17
©2005 PAWS, INC. All Rights Reserved.
Distributed by Universal Press Syndicate
www.garfield.com

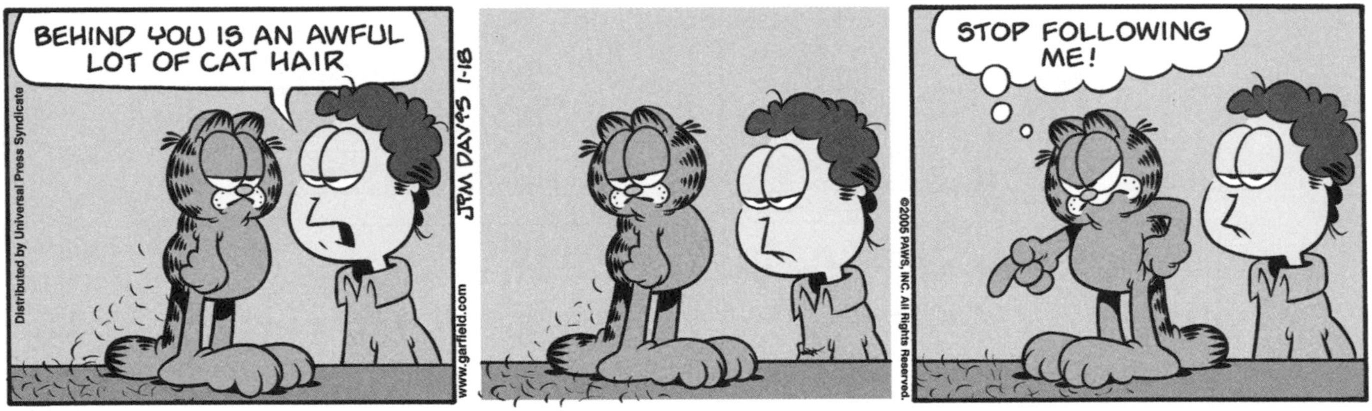
BEHIND YOU IS AN AWFUL LOT OF CAT HAIR
STOP FOLLOWING ME!
JPM DAVPS 1-18
©2005 PAWS, INC. All Rights Reserved.
Distributed by Universal Press Syndicate
www.garfield.com

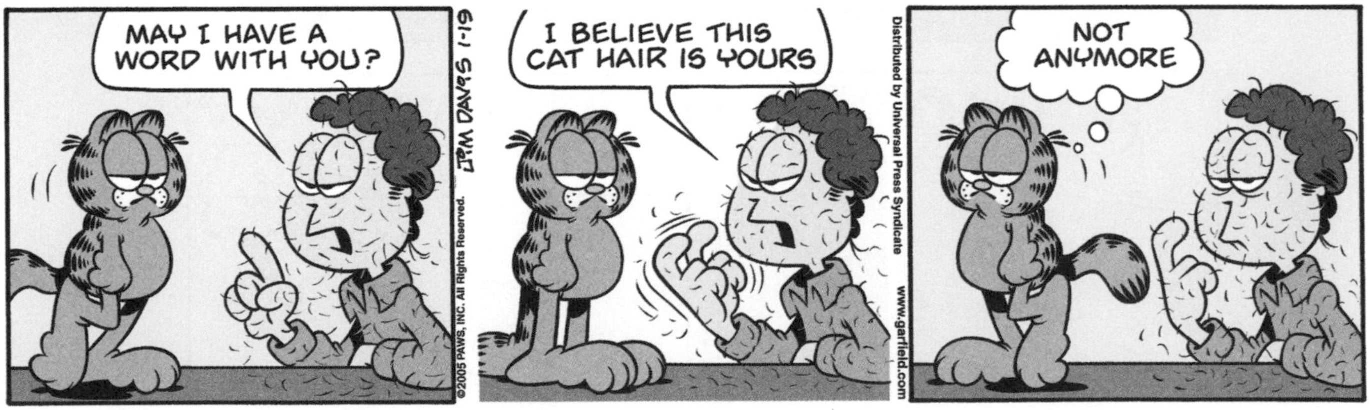
MAY I HAVE A WORD WITH YOU?
I BELIEVE THIS CAT HAIR IS YOURS
NOT ANYMORE
JPM DAVPS 1-19
©2005 PAWS, INC. All Rights Reserved.
Distributed by Universal Press Syndicate
www.garfield.com

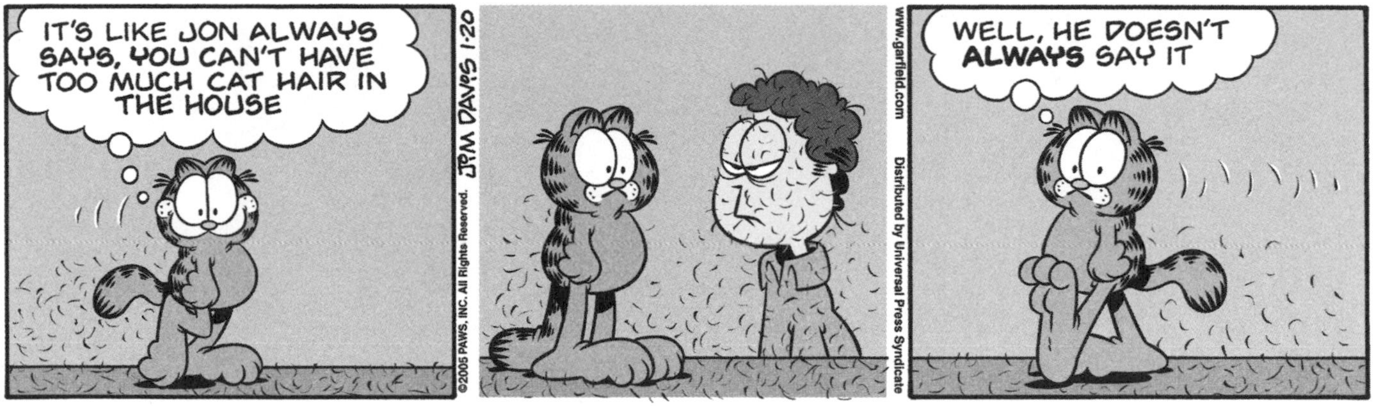
IT'S LIKE JON ALWAYS SAYS, YOU CAN'T HAVE TOO MUCH CAT HAIR IN THE HOUSE
JIM DAVIS 1-20
©2005 PAWS, INC. All Rights Reserved.
www.garfield.com Distributed by Universal Press Syndicate
WELL, HE DOESN'T **ALWAYS** SAY IT

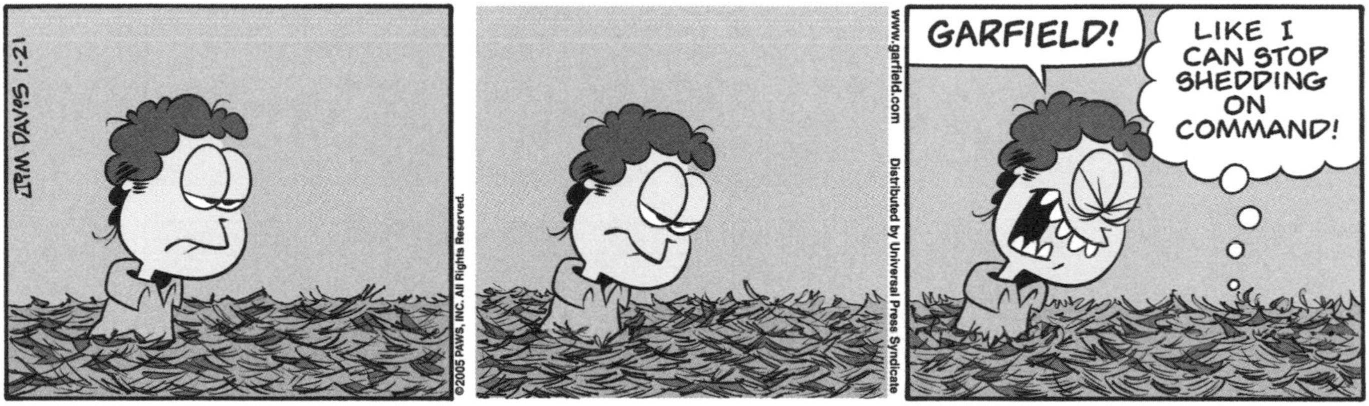
JIM DAVIS 1-21
©2005 PAWS, INC. All Rights Reserved.
www.garfield.com Distributed by Universal Press Syndicate
GARFIELD!
LIKE I CAN STOP SHEDDING ON COMMAND!

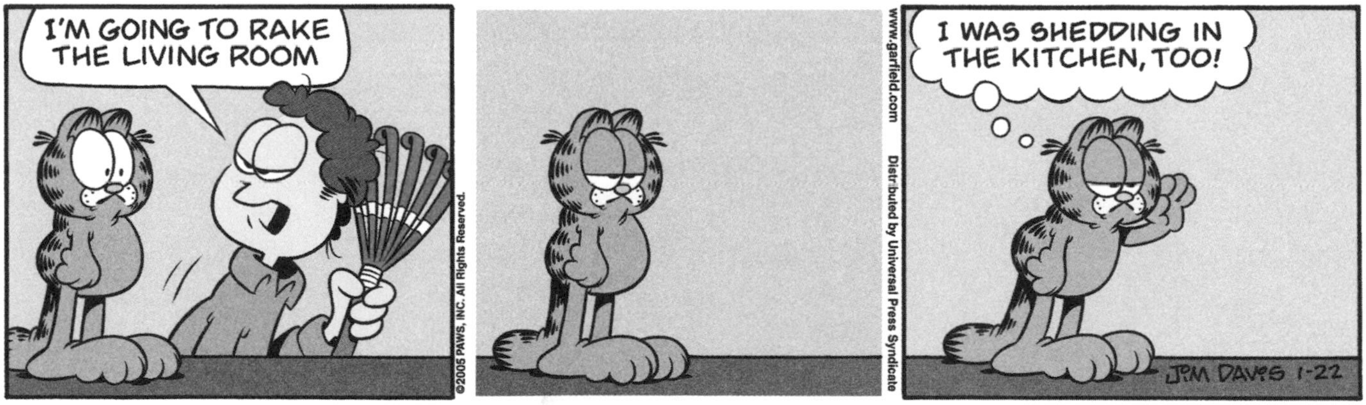
I'M GOING TO RAKE THE LIVING ROOM
©2005 PAWS, INC. All Rights Reserved.
www.garfield.com Distributed by Universal Press Syndicate
I WAS SHEDDING IN THE KITCHEN, TOO!
JIM DAVIS 1-22

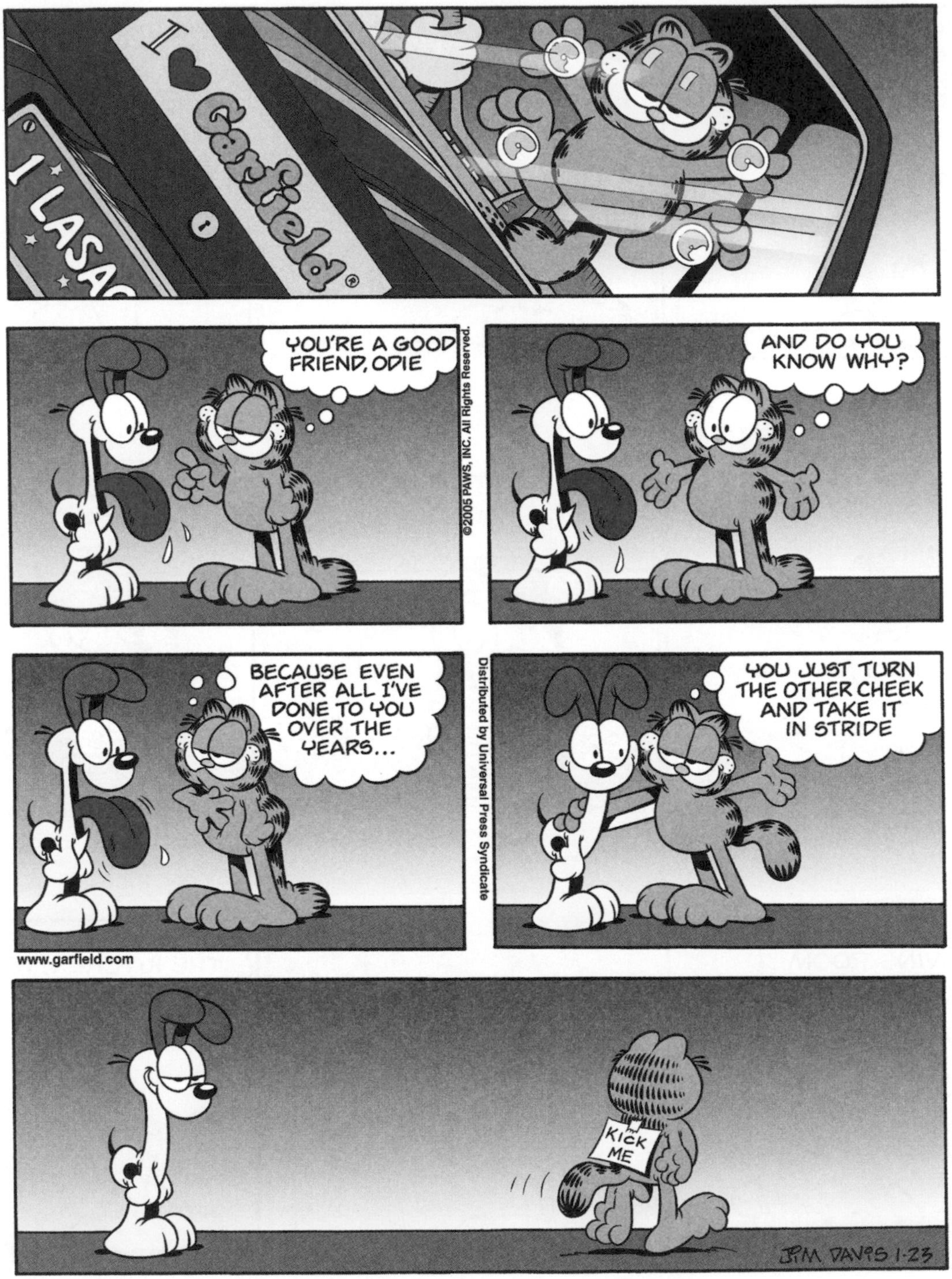
I ♥ Garfield®
YOU'RE A GOOD FRIEND, ODIE
AND DO YOU KNOW WHY?
BECAUSE EVEN AFTER ALL I'VE DONE TO YOU OVER THE YEARS...
YOU JUST TURN THE OTHER CHEEK AND TAKE IT IN STRIDE
KICK ME
JIM DAVIS 1-23
©2005 PAWS, INC. All Rights Reserved.
Distributed by Universal Press Syndicate
www.garfield.com

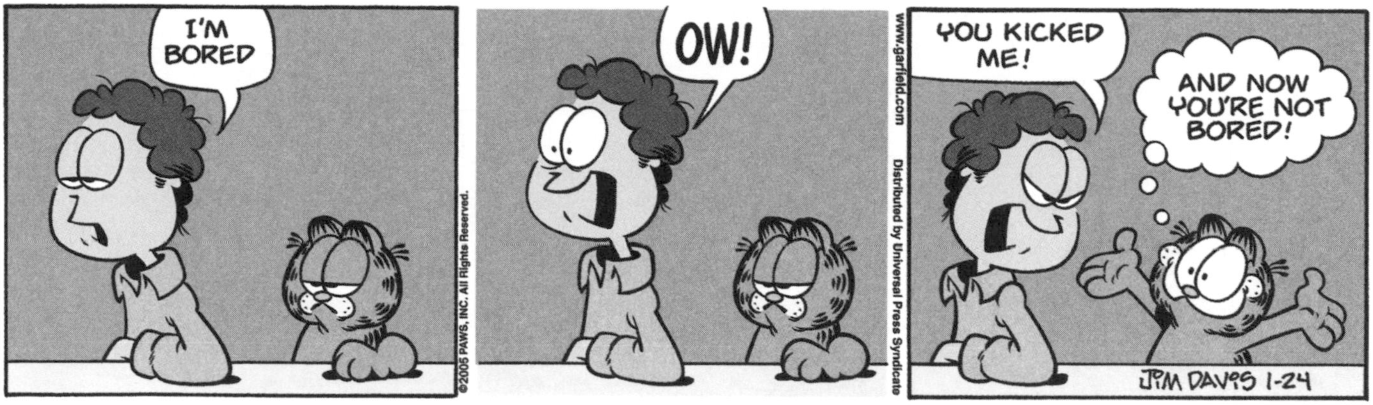
I'M BORED
OW!
YOU KICKED ME!
AND NOW YOU'RE NOT BORED!
JPM DAVPS 1-24
©2005 PAWS, INC. All Rights Reserved.
www.garfield.com
Distributed by Universal Press Syndicate

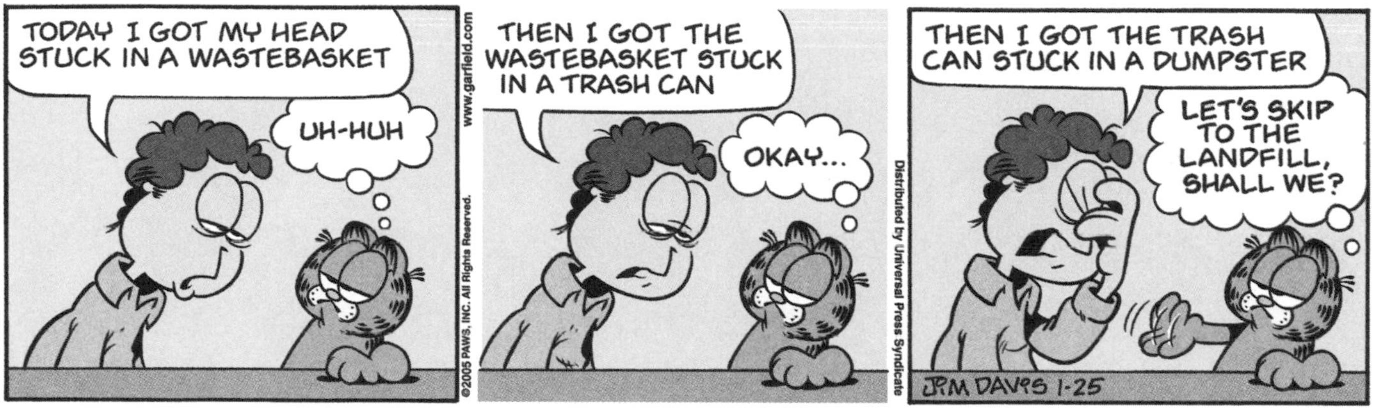
TODAY I GOT MY HEAD STUCK IN A WASTEBASKET
UH-HUH
THEN I GOT THE WASTEBASKET STUCK IN A TRASH CAN
OKAY...
THEN I GOT THE TRASH CAN STUCK IN A DUMPSTER
LET'S SKIP TO THE LANDFILL, SHALL WE?
JPM DAVPS 1-25
©2005 PAWS, INC. All Rights Reserved.
www.garfield.com
Distributed by Universal Press Syndicate

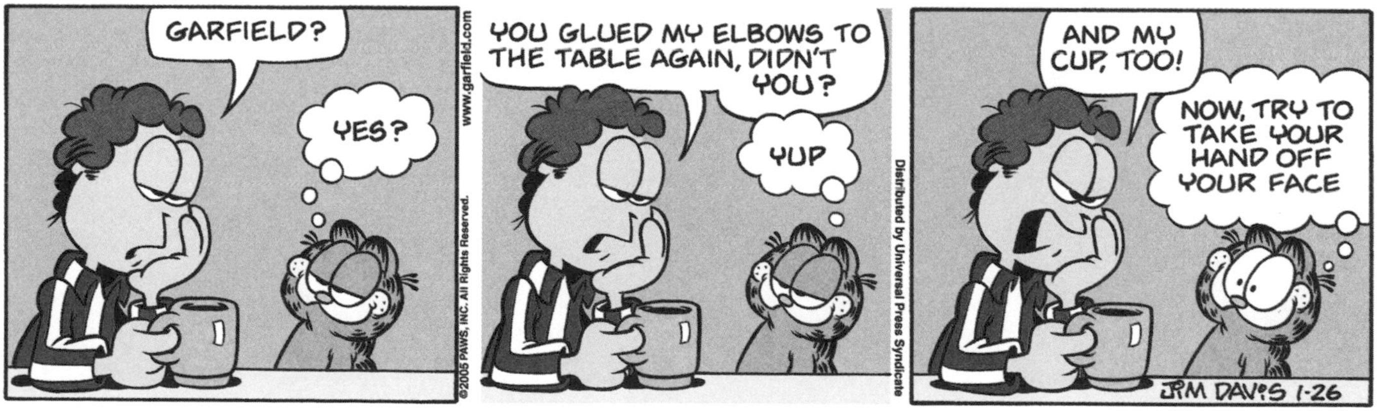
GARFIELD?
YES?
YOU GLUED MY ELBOWS TO THE TABLE AGAIN, DIDN'T YOU?
YUP
AND MY CUP, TOO!
NOW, TRY TO TAKE YOUR HAND OFF YOUR FACE
JPM DAVPS 1-26
©2005 PAWS, INC. All Rights Reserved.
www.garfield.com
Distributed by Universal Press Syndicate

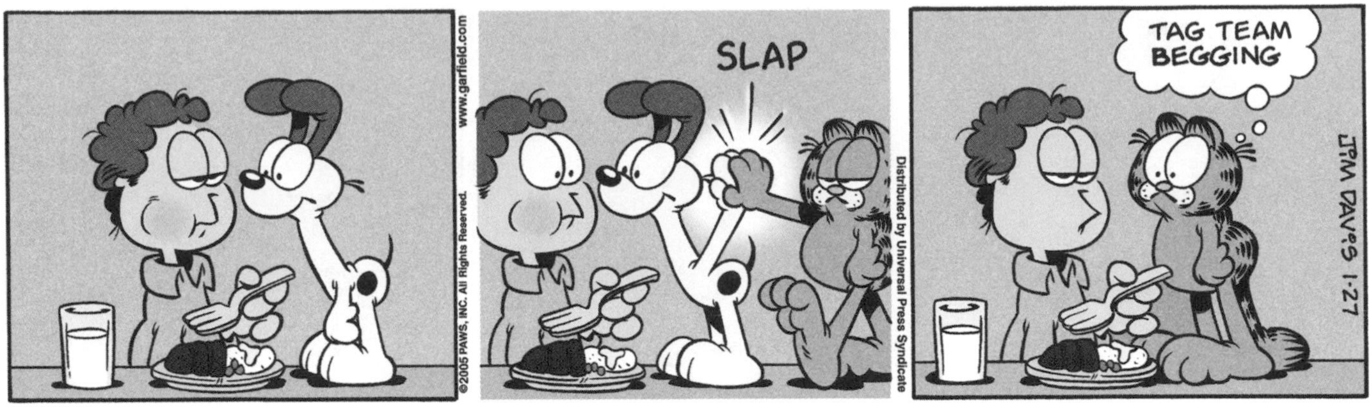
©2005 PAWS, INC. All Rights Reserved.
www.garfield.com
SLAP
Distributed by Universal Press Syndicate
TAG TEAM BEGGING
JIM DAVIS 1-27

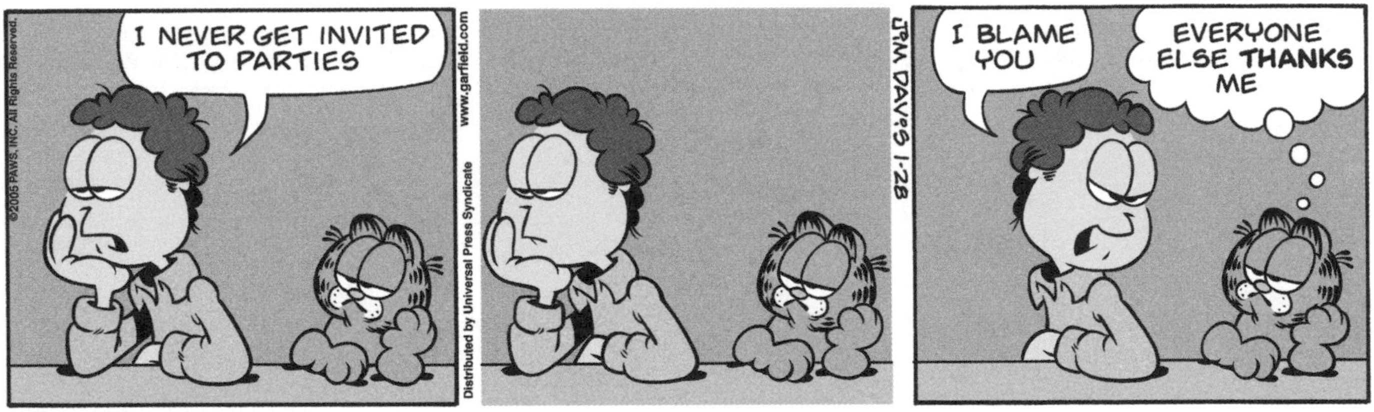
©2005 PAWS, INC. All Rights Reserved.
I NEVER GET INVITED TO PARTIES
Distributed by Universal Press Syndicate
www.garfield.com
JIM DAVIS 1-28
I BLAME YOU
EVERYONE ELSE THANKS ME

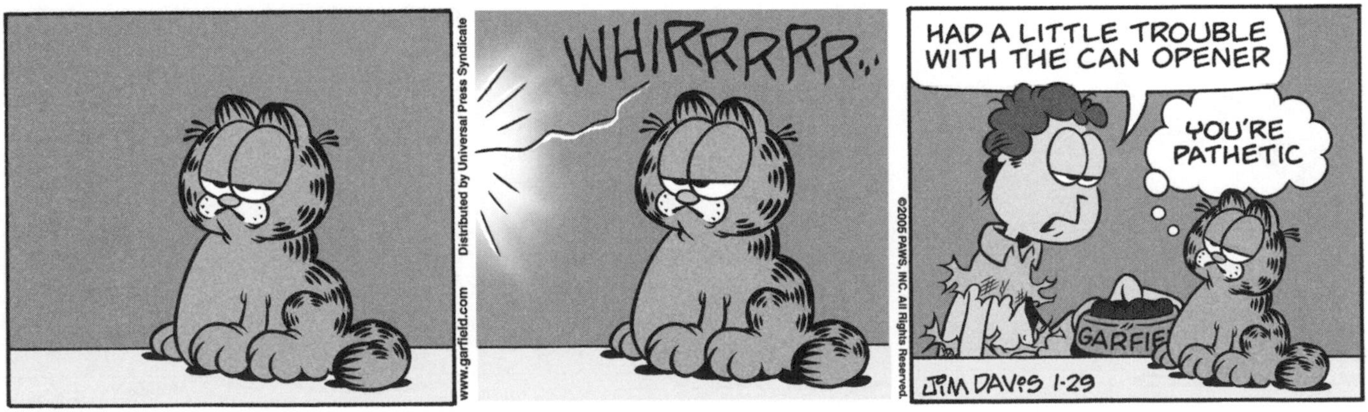
www.garfield.com
Distributed by Universal Press Syndicate
WHIRRRRR..
HAD A LITTLE TROUBLE WITH THE CAN OPENER
YOU'RE PATHETIC
GARFIE
©2005 PAWS, INC. All Rights Reserved.
JIM DAVIS 1-29

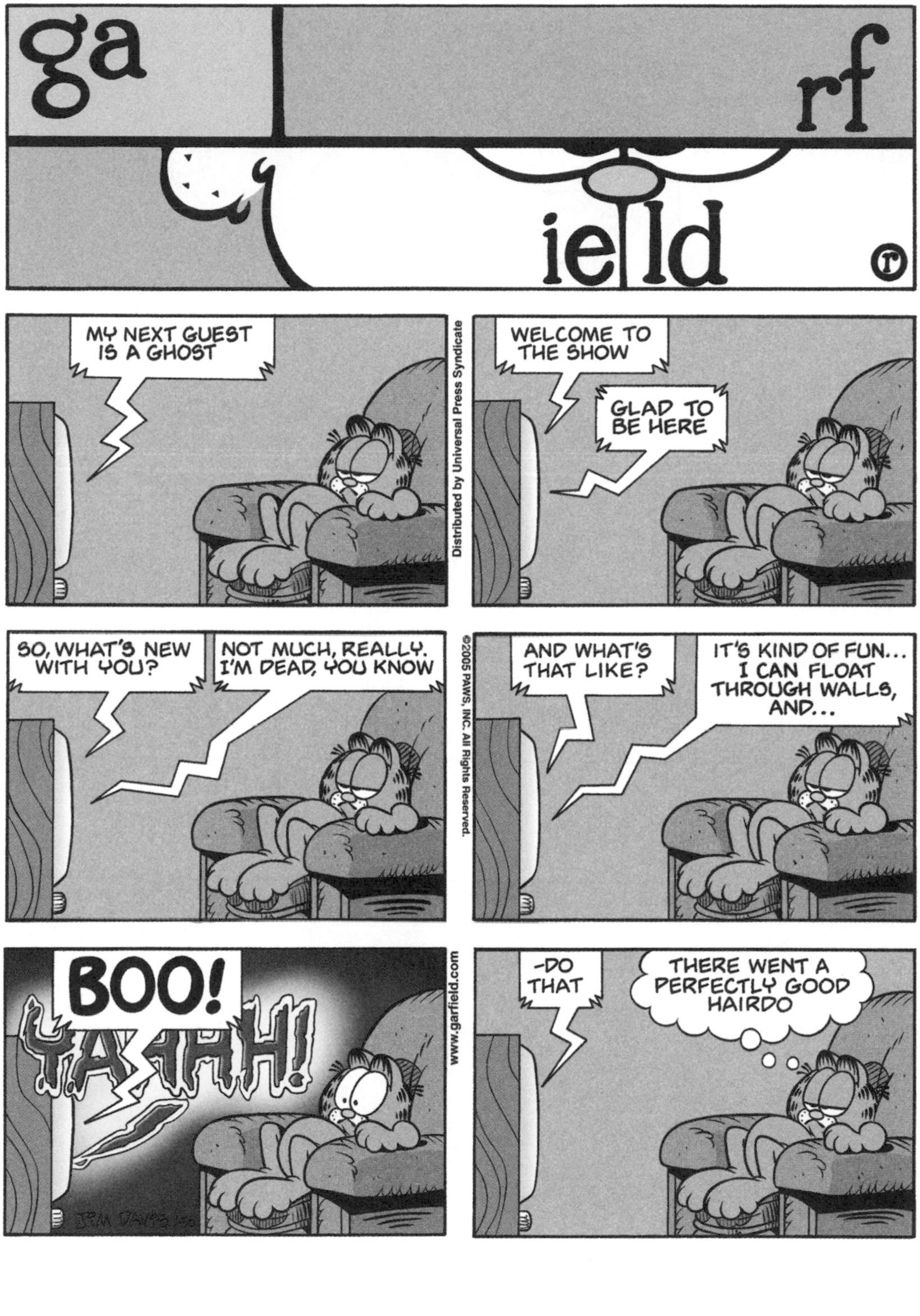
ga
rf
ield
MY NEXT GUEST IS A GHOST
Distributed by Universal Press Syndicate
WELCOME TO THE SHOW
GLAD TO BE HERE
SO, WHAT'S NEW WITH YOU?
NOT MUCH, REALLY. I'M DEAD, YOU KNOW
©2005 PAWS, INC. All Rights Reserved.
AND WHAT'S THAT LIKE?
IT'S KIND OF FUN... I CAN FLOAT THROUGH WALLS, AND...
BOO!
YAAHH!
www.garfield.com
-DO THAT
THERE WENT A PERFECTLY GOOD HAIRDO

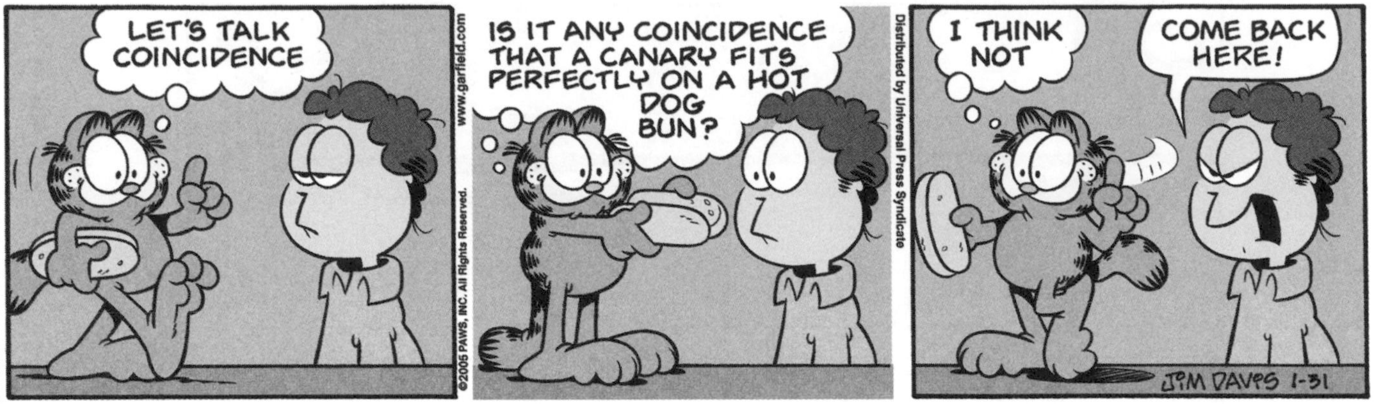
LET'S TALK COINCIDENCE
©2005 PAWS, INC. All Rights Reserved. www.garfield.com
IS IT ANY COINCIDENCE THAT A CANARY FITS PERFECTLY ON A HOT DOG BUN?
Distributed by Universal Press Syndicate
I THINK NOT
COME BACK HERE!
JIM DAVIS 1-31

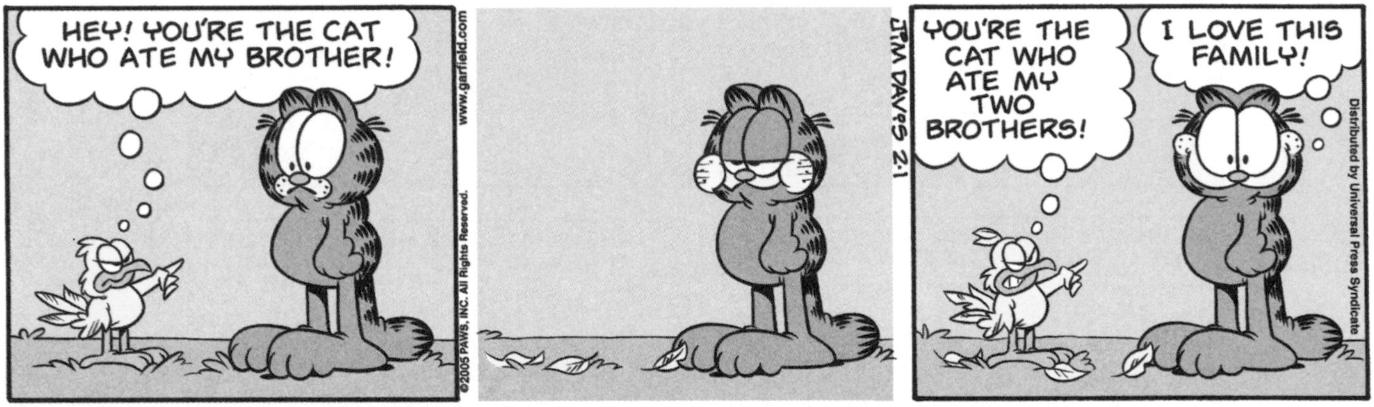
HEY! YOU'RE THE CAT WHO ATE MY BROTHER!
©2005 PAWS, INC. All Rights Reserved. www.garfield.com
JIM DAVIS 2-1
YOU'RE THE CAT WHO ATE MY TWO BROTHERS!
I LOVE THIS FAMILY!
Distributed by Universal Press Syndicate

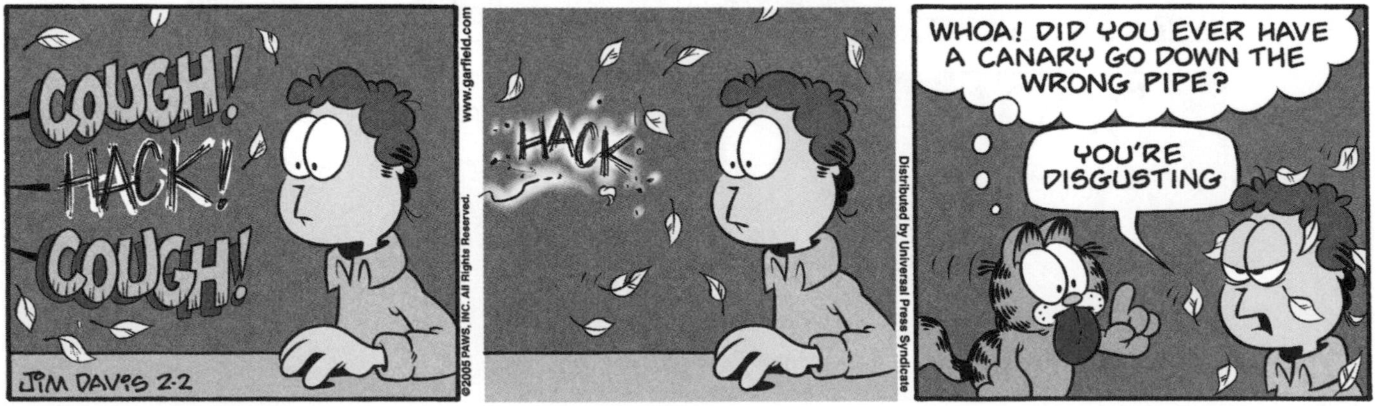
COUGH! HACK! COUGH!
JIM DAVIS 2-2
©2005 PAWS, INC. All Rights Reserved. www.garfield.com
HACK
Distributed by Universal Press Syndicate
WHOA! DID YOU EVER HAVE A CANARY GO DOWN THE WRONG PIPE?
YOU'RE DISGUSTING

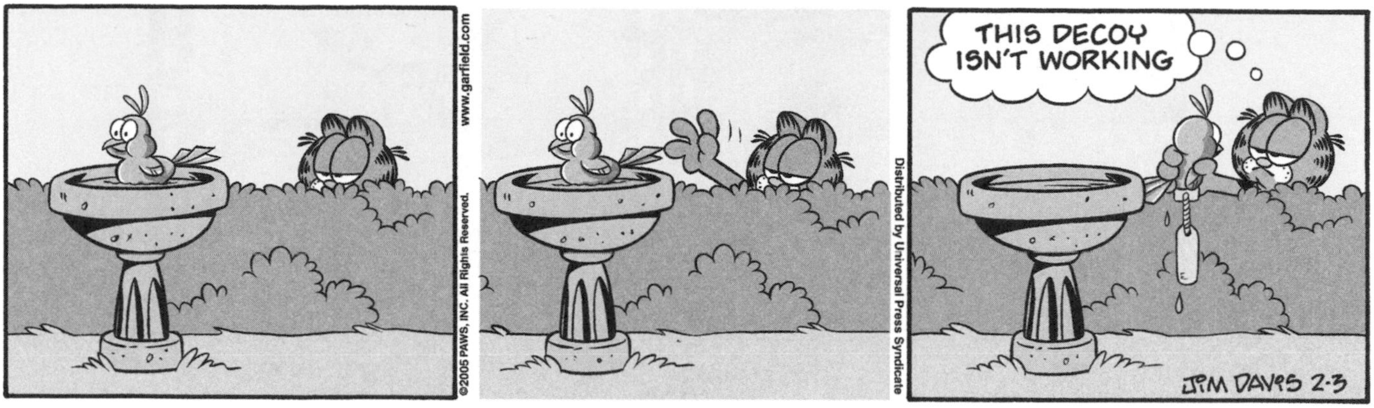
©2005 PAWS, INC. All Rights Reserved.
www.garfield.com
Distributed by Universal Press Syndicate
THIS DECOY ISN'T WORKING
JIM DAVIS 2-3

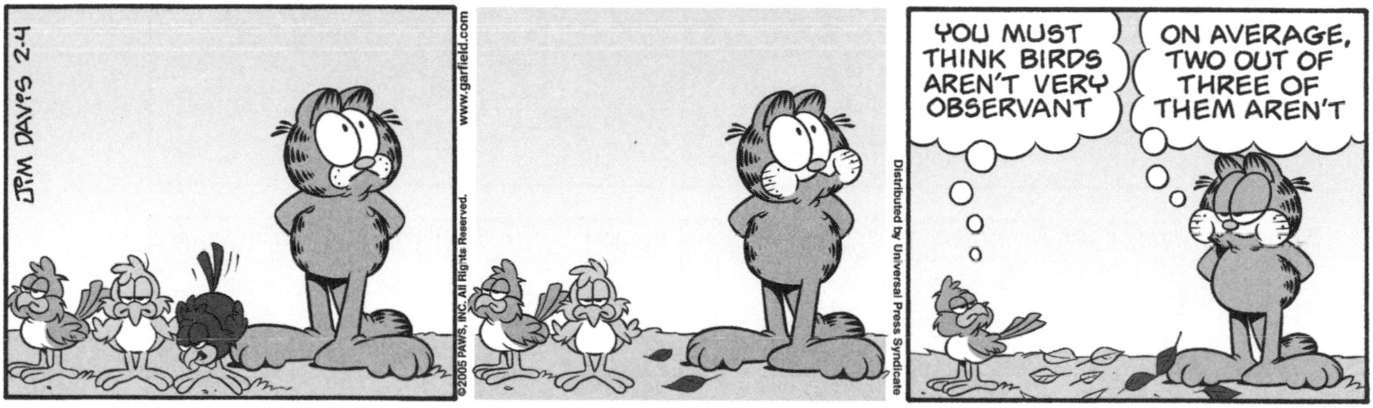
JIM DAVIS 2-4
©2005 PAWS, INC. All Rights Reserved.
www.garfield.com
Distributed by Universal Press Syndicate
YOU MUST THINK BIRDS AREN'T VERY OBSERVANT
ON AVERAGE, TWO OUT OF THREE OF THEM AREN'T

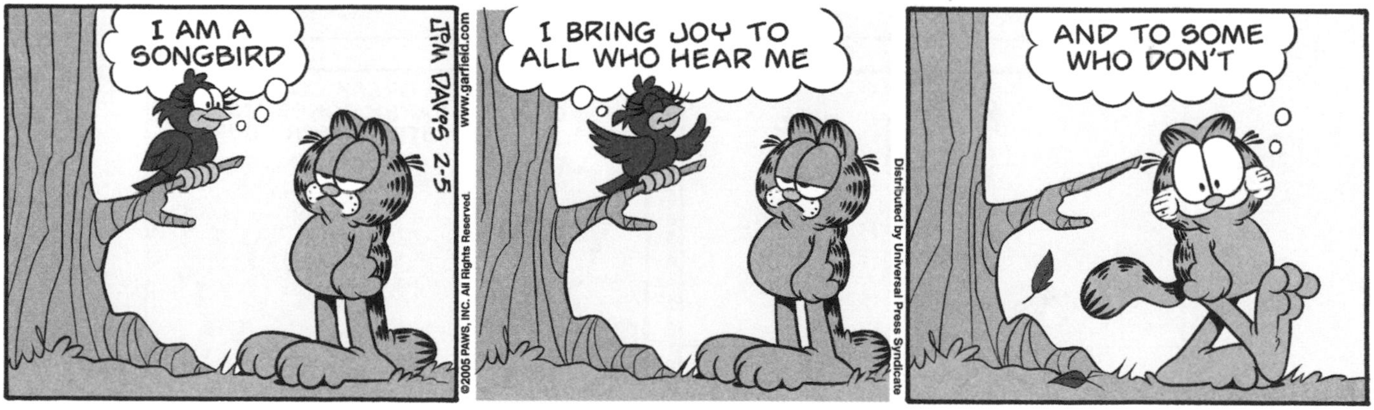
I AM A SONGBIRD
JIM DAVIS 2-5
©2005 PAWS, INC. All Rights Reserved.
www.garfield.com
I BRING JOY TO ALL WHO HEAR ME
Distributed by Universal Press Syndicate
AND TO SOME WHO DON'T

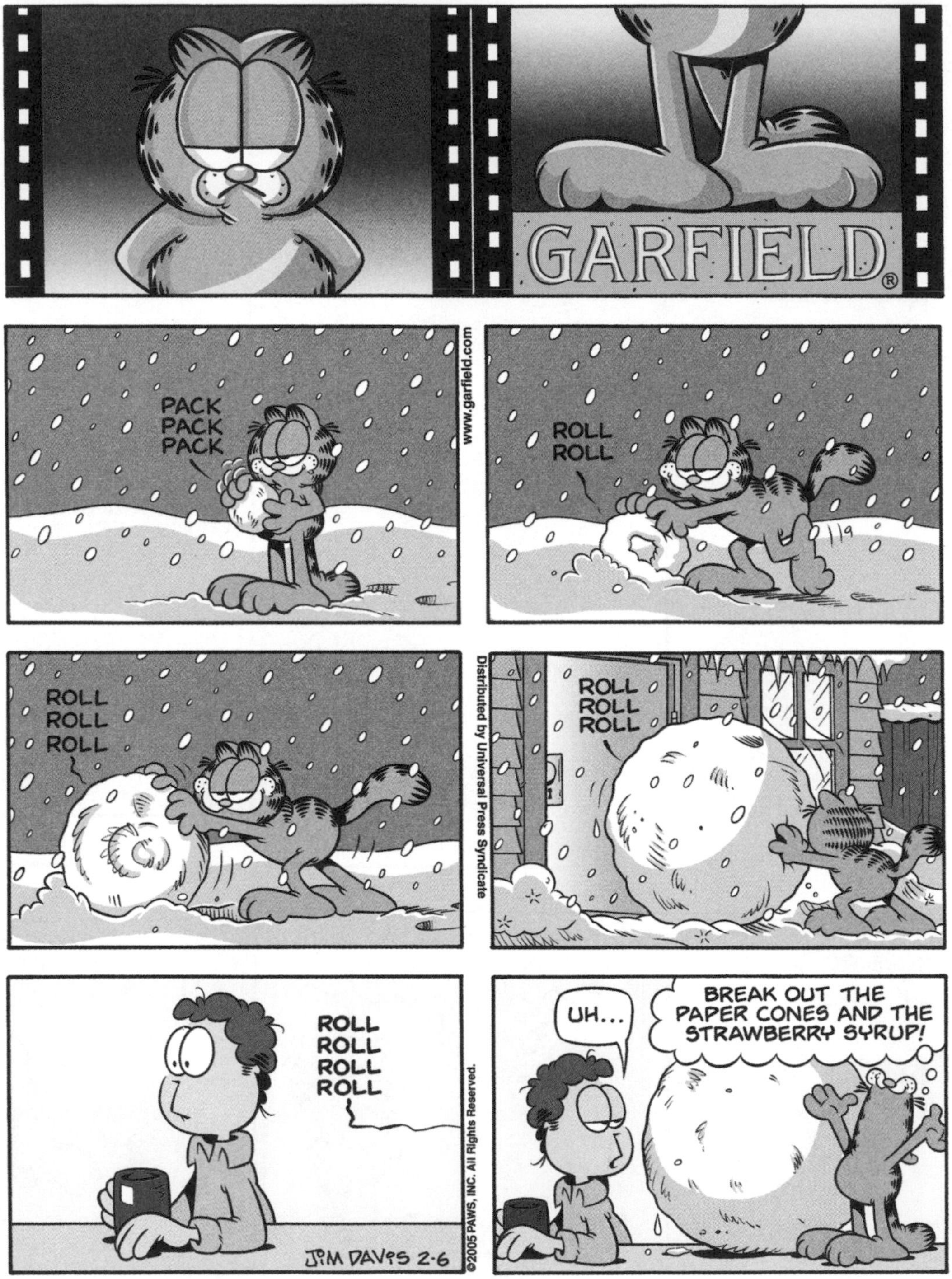
GARFIELD®
PACK PACK PACK
www.garfield.com
ROLL ROLL
ROLL ROLL ROLL
Distributed by Universal Press Syndicate
ROLL ROLL ROLL
ROLL ROLL ROLL ROLL
JIM DAVIS 2-6
©2005 PAWS, INC. All Rights Reserved.
UH...
BREAK OUT THE PAPER CONES AND THE STRAWBERRY SYRUP!

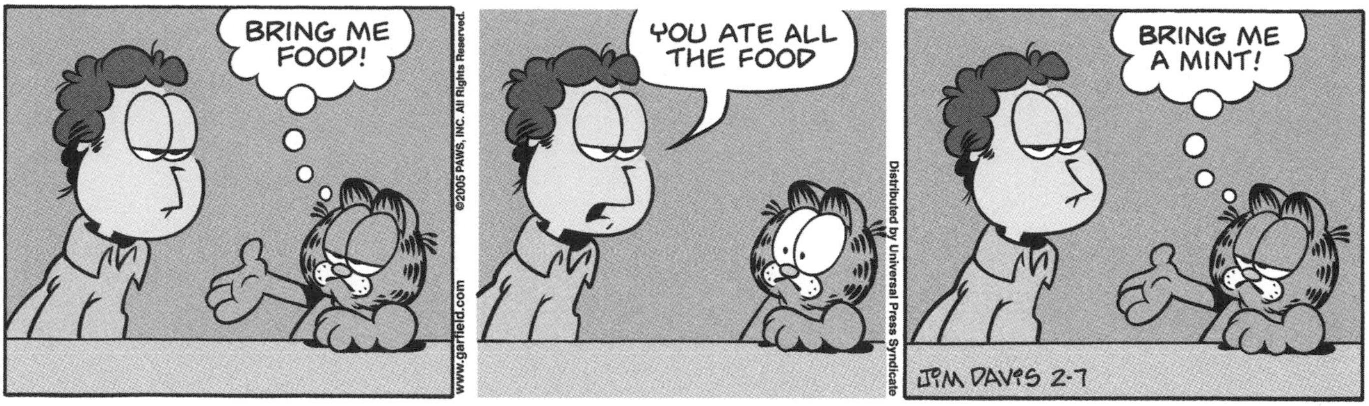
BRING ME FOOD!
©2005 PAWS, INC. All Rights Reserved.
www.garfield.com
YOU ATE ALL THE FOOD
Distributed by Universal Press Syndicate
BRING ME A MINT!
JIM DAVIS 2-7

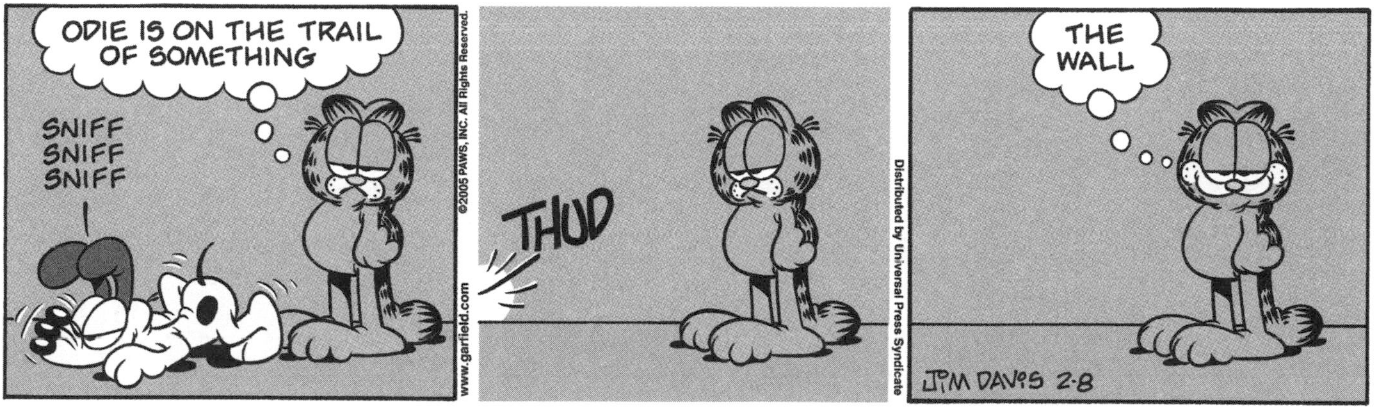
ODIE IS ON THE TRAIL OF SOMETHING
SNIFF SNIFF SNIFF
©2005 PAWS, INC. All Rights Reserved.
www.garfield.com
THUD
Distributed by Universal Press Syndicate
THE WALL
JIM DAVIS 2-8

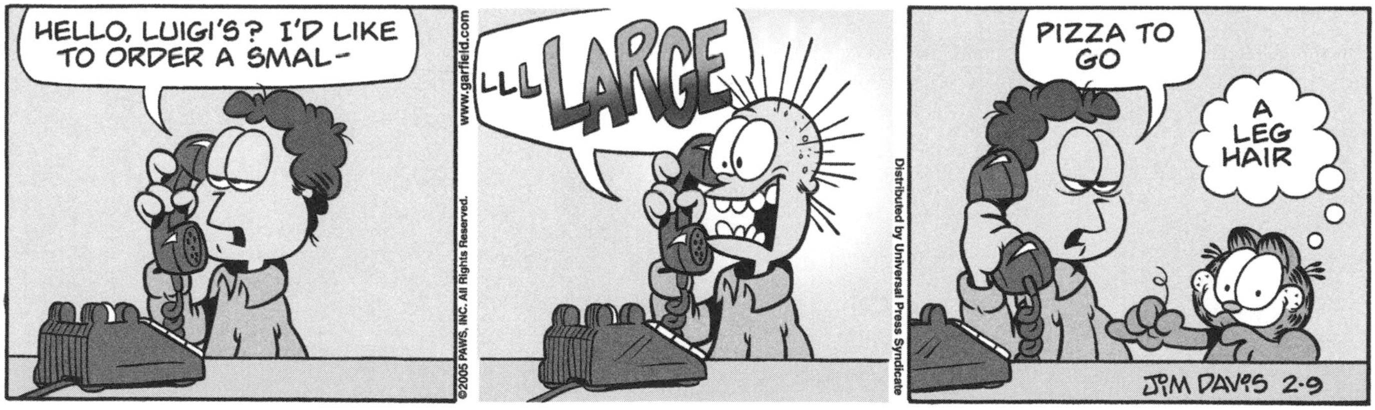
HELLO, LUIGI'S? I'D LIKE TO ORDER A SMAL-
www.garfield.com
©2005 PAWS, INC. All Rights Reserved.
LLL LARGE
Distributed by Universal Press Syndicate
PIZZA TO GO
A LEG HAIR
JIM DAVIS 2-9

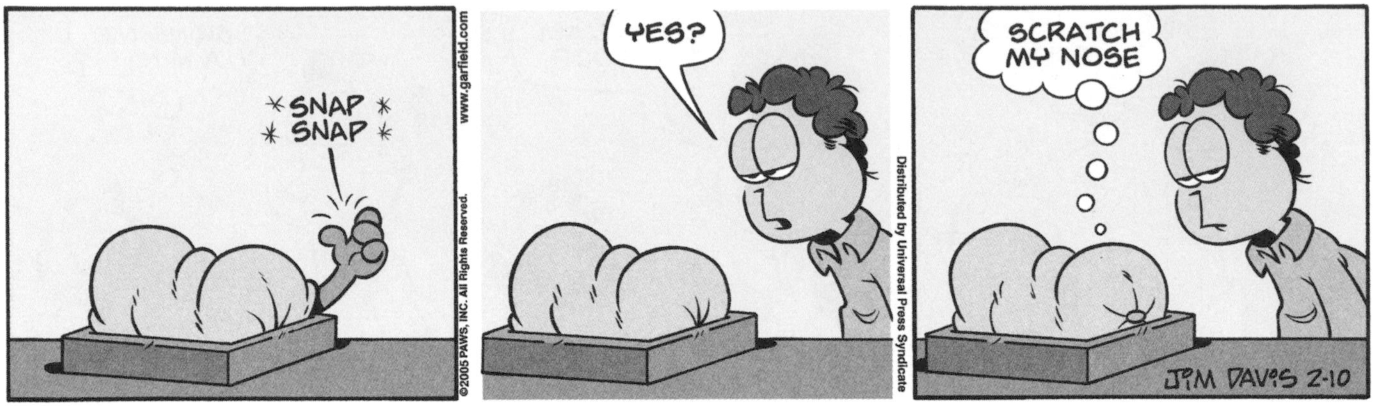
SNAP SNAP
YES?
SCRATCH MY NOSE
JIM DAVIS 2-10
©2005 PAWS, INC. All Rights Reserved.
www.garfield.com
Distributed by Universal Press Syndicate

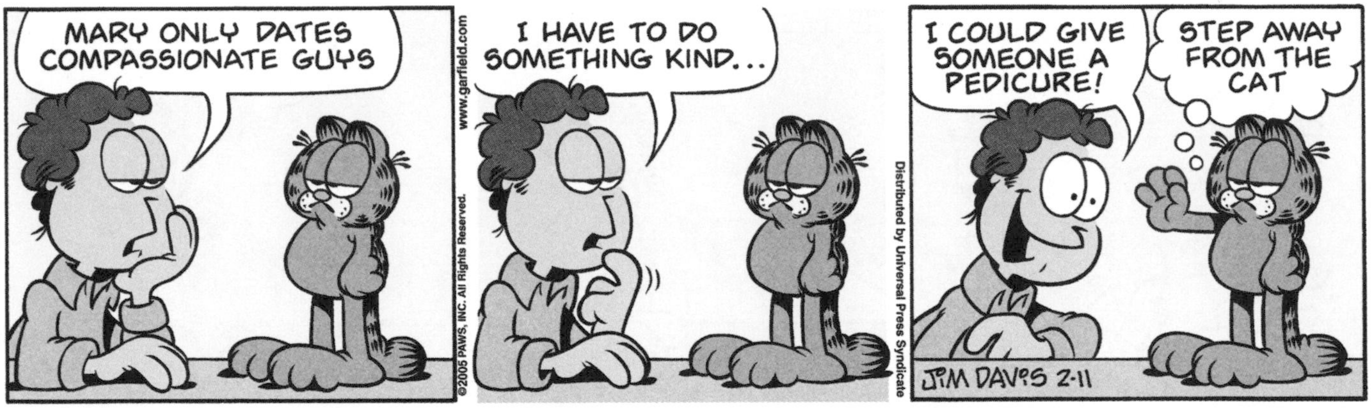
MARY ONLY DATES COMPASSIONATE GUYS
I HAVE TO DO SOMETHING KIND...
I COULD GIVE SOMEONE A PEDICURE!
STEP AWAY FROM THE CAT
JIM DAVIS 2-11
©2005 PAWS, INC. All Rights Reserved.
www.garfield.com
Distributed by Universal Press Syndicate

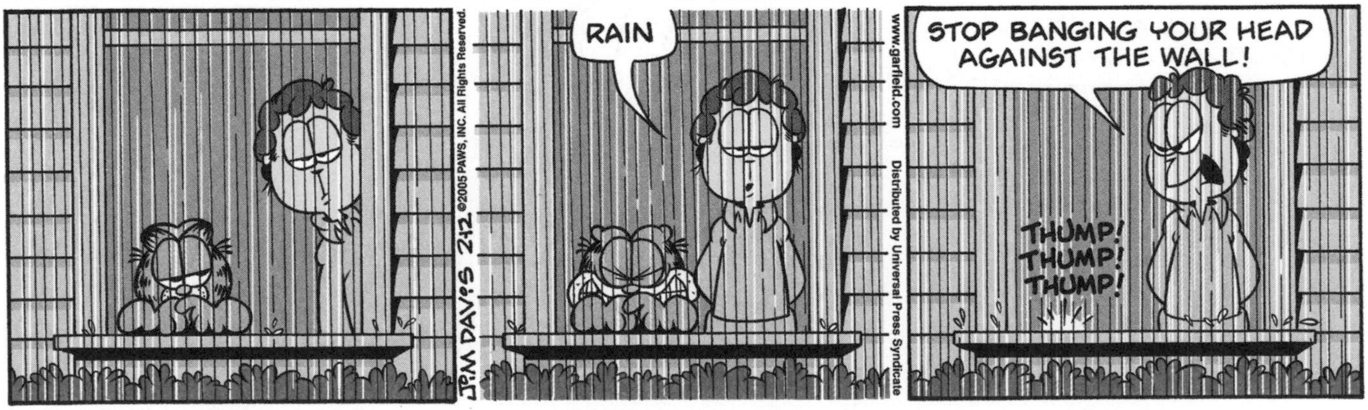
JIM DAVIS 2-12
©2005 PAWS, INC. All Rights Reserved.
RAIN
STOP BANGING YOUR HEAD AGAINST THE WALL!
THUMP! THUMP! THUMP!
www.garfield.com
Distributed by Universal Press Syndicate

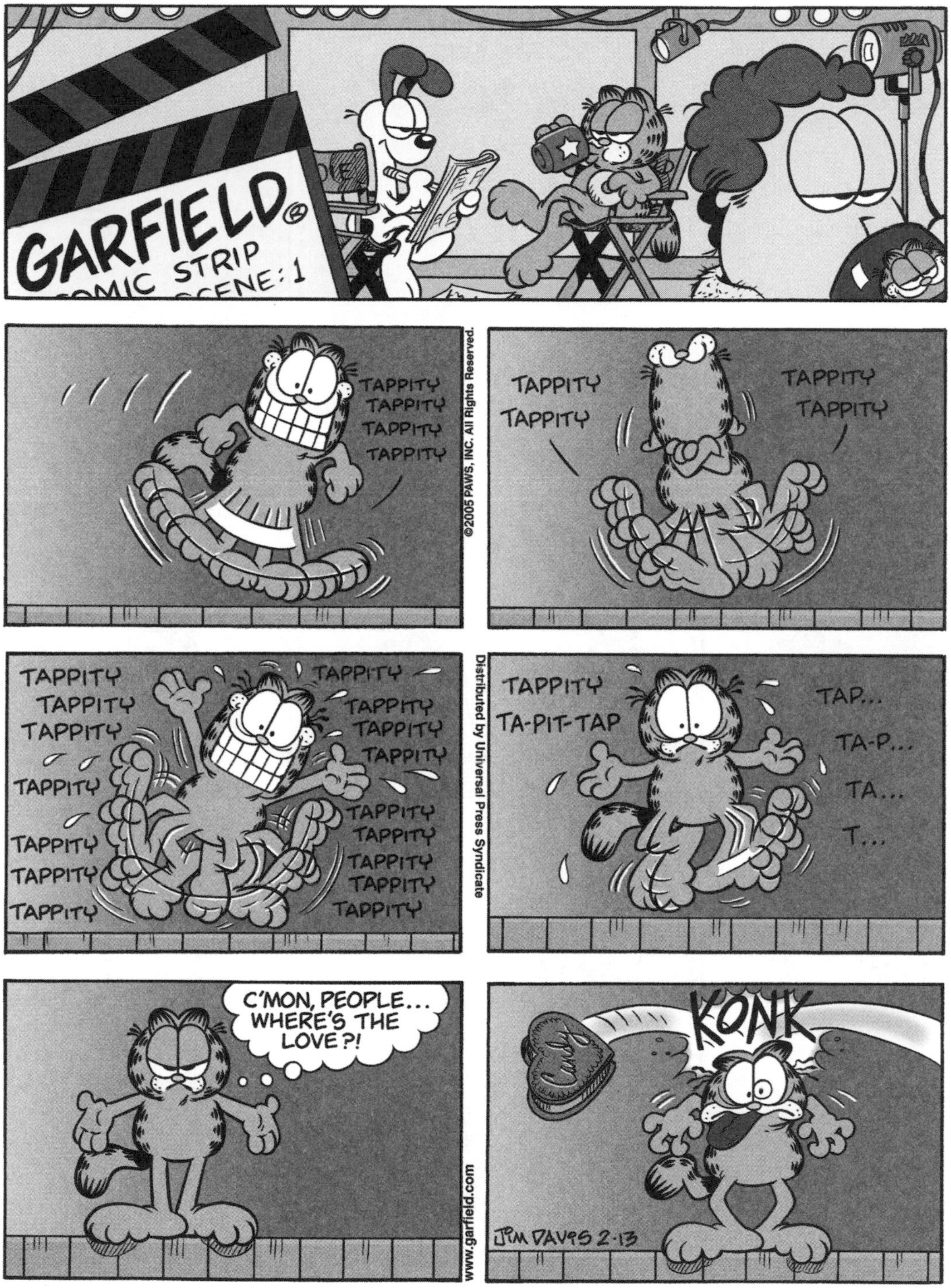
GARFIELD®
OMIC STRIP
CENE: 1
TAPPITY TAPPITY TAPPITY TAPPITY
TAPPITY TAPPITY
TAPPITY TAPPITY
TAPPITY TAPPITY TAPPITY
TAPPITY TAPPITY TAPPITY TAPPITY
TAPPITY
TAPPITY TAPPITY TAPPITY
TAPPITY TAPPITY TAPPITY TAPPITY TAPPITY
TAPPITY
TA-PIT-TAP
TAP...
TA-P...
TA...
T...
C'MON, PEOPLE... WHERE'S THE LOVE?!
Candy
KONK
JIM DAVIS 2-13
©2005 PAWS, INC. All Rights Reserved.
Distributed by Universal Press Syndicate
www.garfield.com

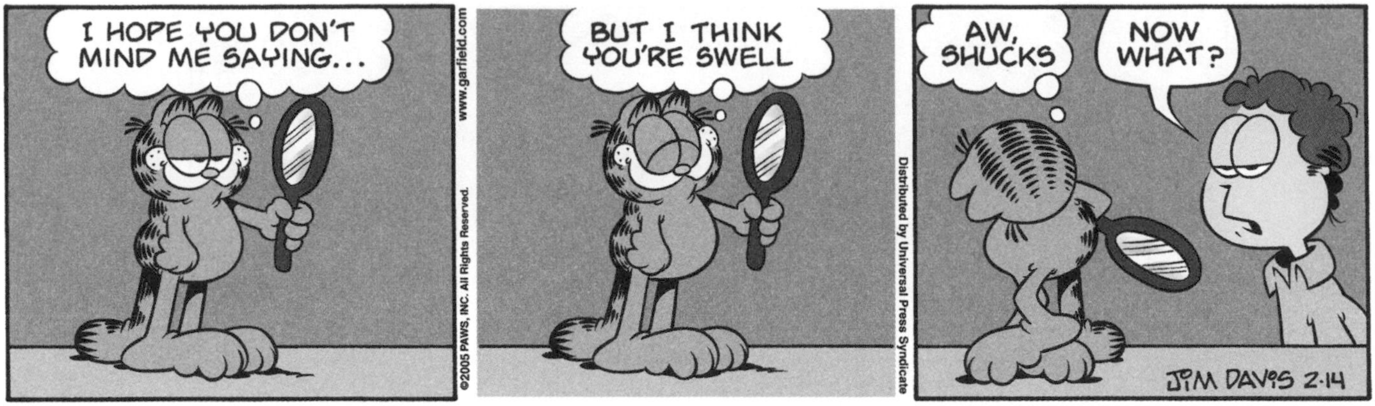
I HOPE YOU DON'T MIND ME SAYING...
BUT I THINK YOU'RE SWELL
AW, SHUCKS
NOW WHAT?
JIM DAVIS 2·14
©2005 PAWS, INC. All Rights Reserved. www.garfield.com
Distributed by Universal Press Syndicate

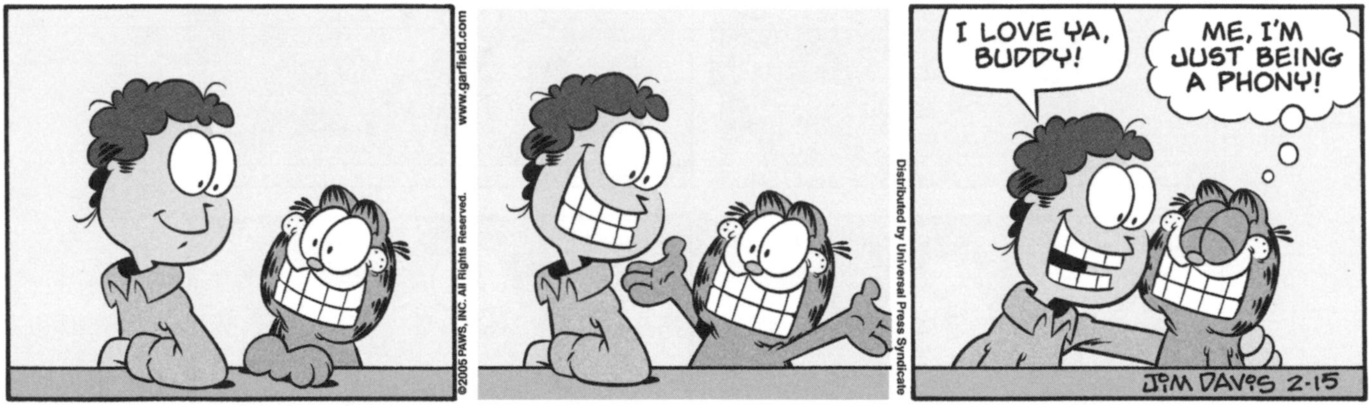
I LOVE YA, BUDDY!
ME, I'M JUST BEING A PHONY!
JIM DAVIS 2·15
©2005 PAWS, INC. All Rights Reserved. www.garfield.com
Distributed by Universal Press Syndicate

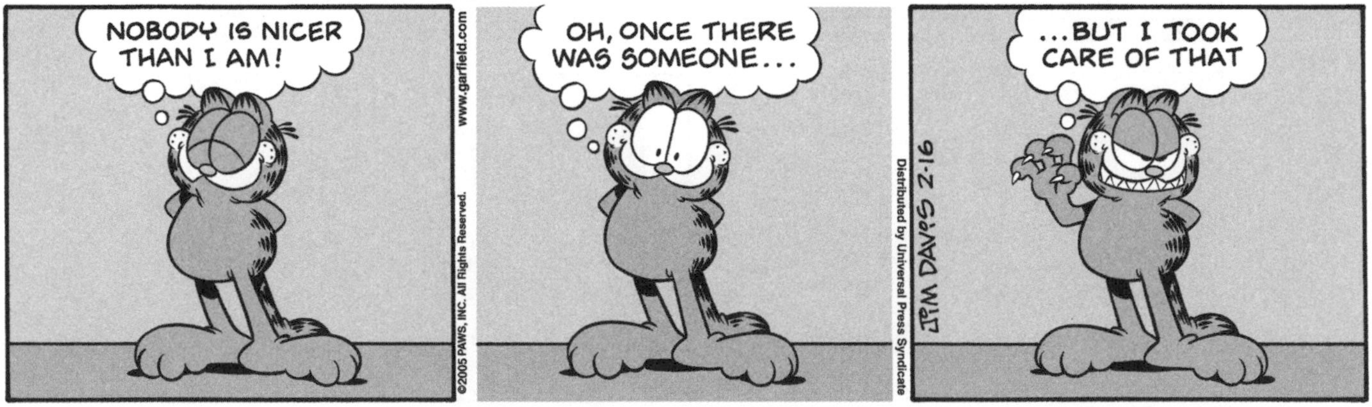
NOBODY IS NICER THAN I AM!
OH, ONCE THERE WAS SOMEONE...
...BUT I TOOK CARE OF THAT
JIM DAVIS 2·16
©2005 PAWS, INC. All Rights Reserved. www.garfield.com
Distributed by Universal Press Syndicate

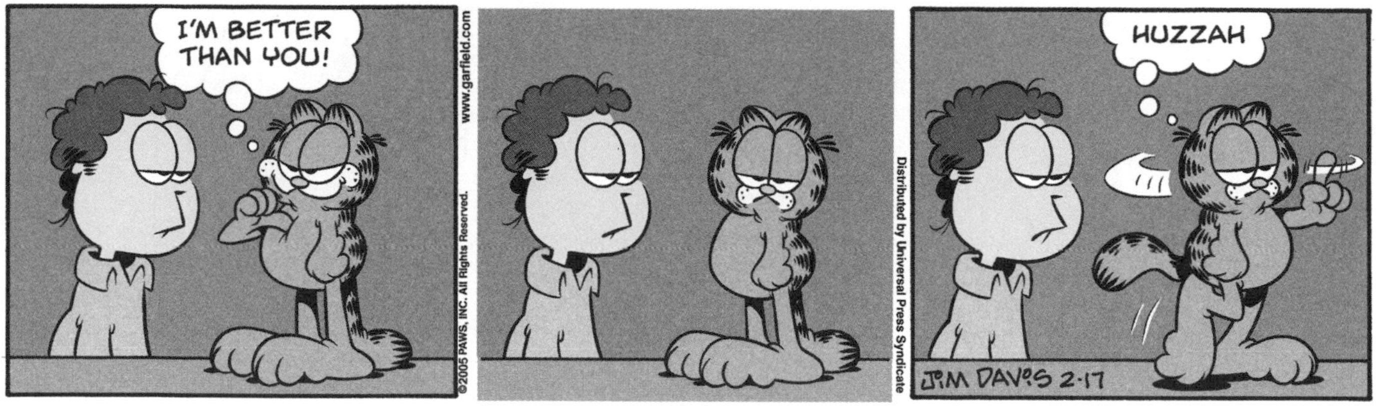
I'M BETTER THAN YOU!
HUZZAH
©2005 PAWS, INC. All Rights Reserved. www.garfield.com
Distributed by Universal Press Syndicate
JIM DAVIS 2·17

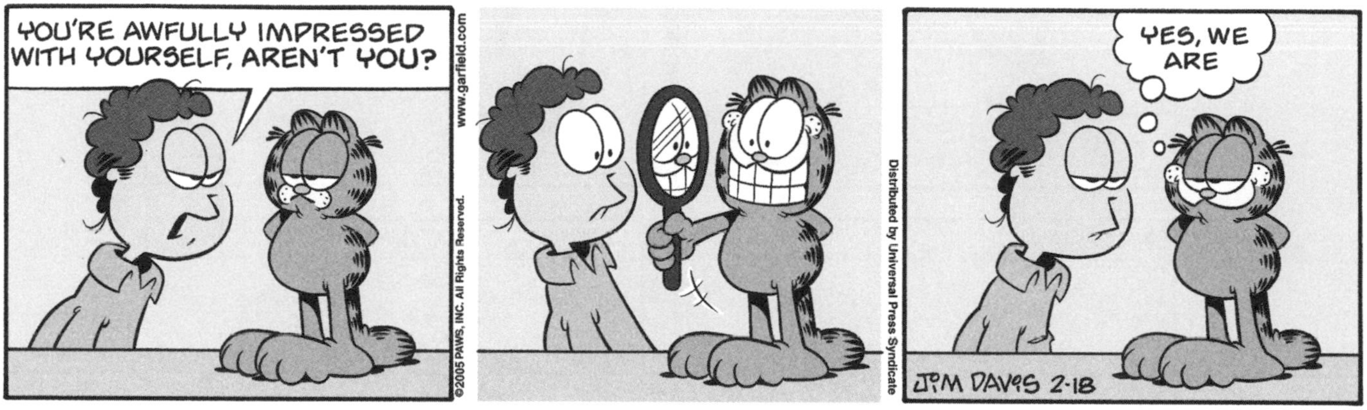
YOU'RE AWFULLY IMPRESSED WITH YOURSELF, AREN'T YOU?
YES, WE ARE
©2005 PAWS, INC. All Rights Reserved. www.garfield.com
Distributed by Universal Press Syndicate
JIM DAVIS 2·18

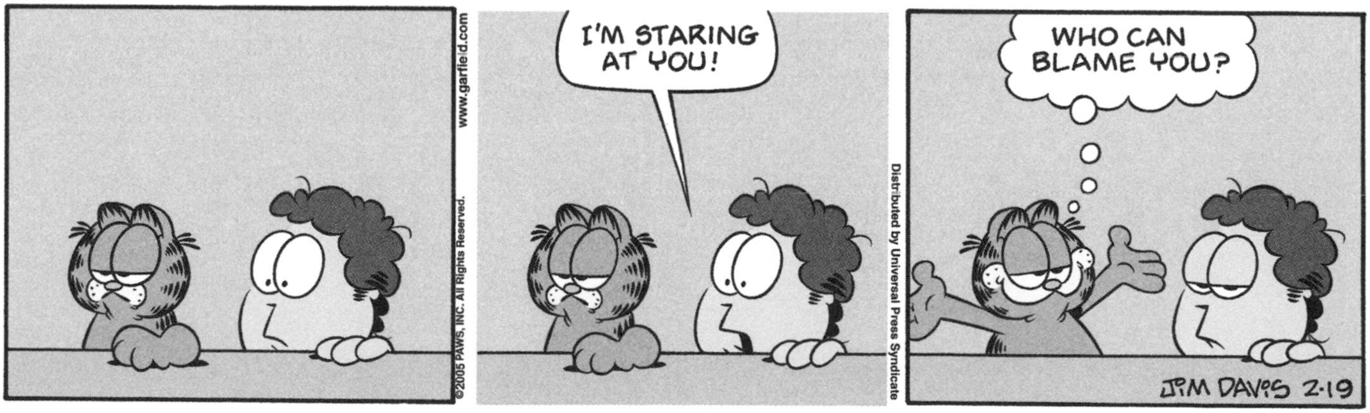
I'M STARING AT YOU!
WHO CAN BLAME YOU?
©2005 PAWS, INC. All Rights Reserved. www.garfield.com
Distributed by Universal Press Syndicate
JIM DAVIS 2·19

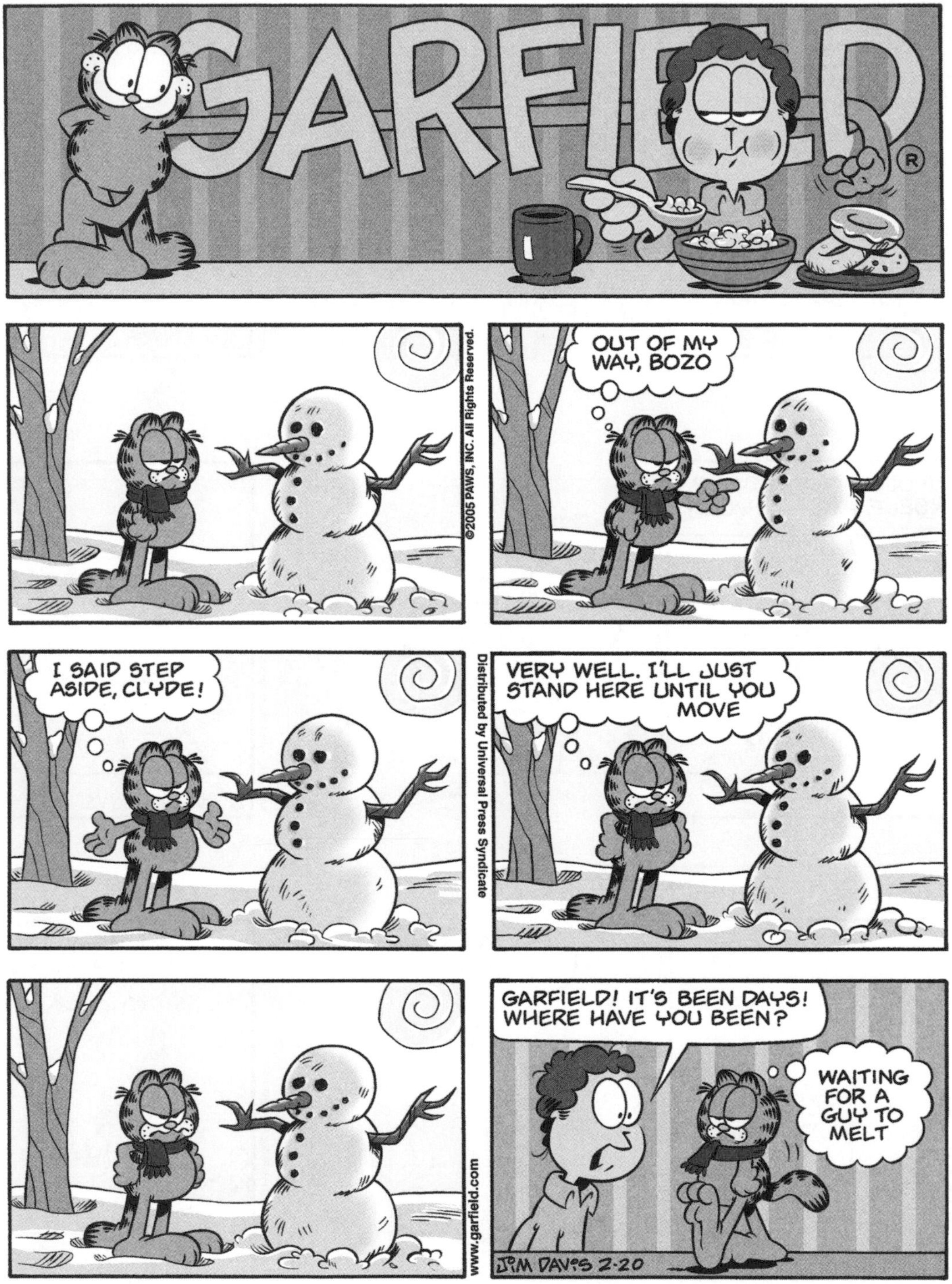
GARFIELD
©2005 PAWS, INC. All Rights Reserved.
OUT OF MY WAY, BOZO
I SAID STEP ASIDE, CLYDE!
Distributed by Universal Press Syndicate
VERY WELL. I'LL JUST STAND HERE UNTIL YOU MOVE
www.garfield.com
GARFIELD! IT'S BEEN DAYS! WHERE HAVE YOU BEEN?
WAITING FOR A GUY TO MELT
JIM DAVIS 2-20

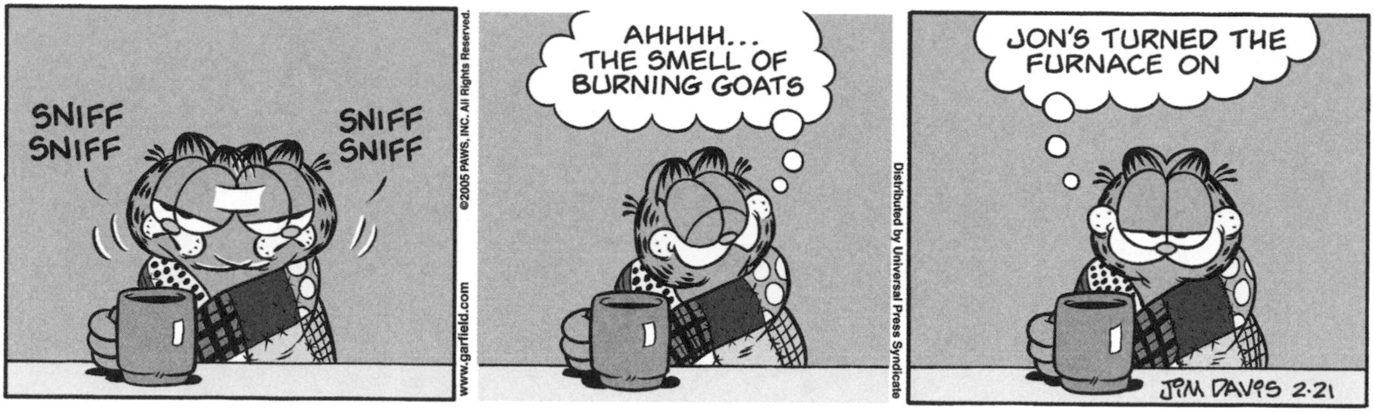
SNIFF SNIFF
SNIFF SNIFF
©2005 PAWS, INC. All Rights Reserved.
www.garfield.com
AHHHH... THE SMELL OF BURNING GOATS
Distributed by Universal Press Syndicate
JON'S TURNED THE FURNACE ON
JIM DAVIS 2·21

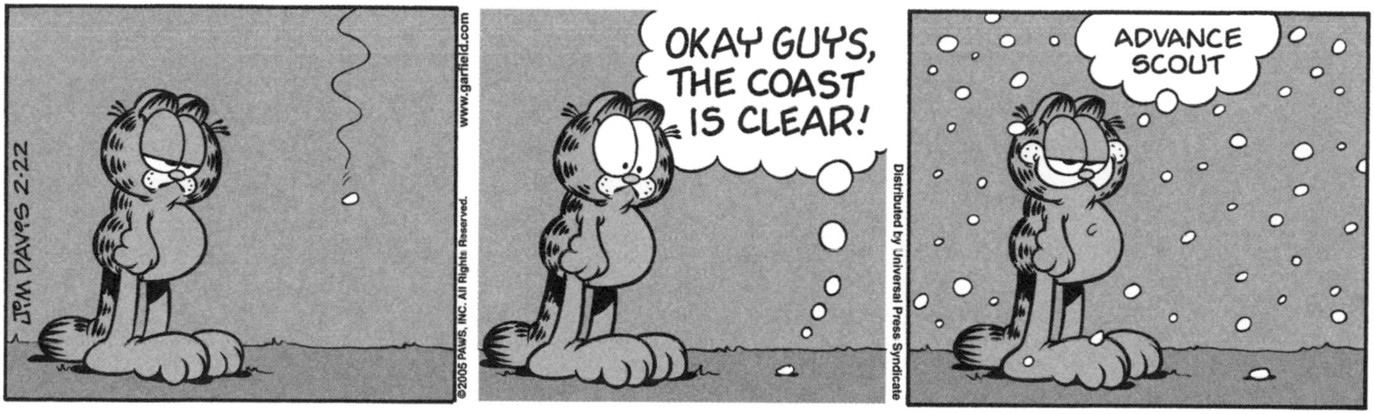
JIM DAVIS 2·22
www.garfield.com
©2005 PAWS, INC. All Rights Reserved.
OKAY GUYS, THE COAST IS CLEAR!
Distributed by Universal Press Syndicate
ADVANCE SCOUT

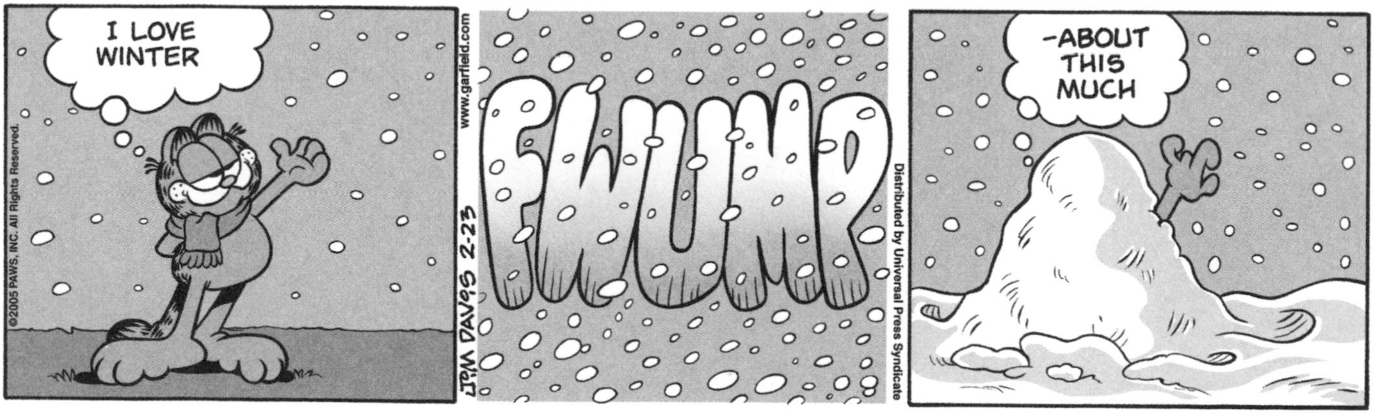
I LOVE WINTER
©2005 PAWS, INC. All Rights Reserved.
www.garfield.com
JIM DAVIS 2·23
FWUMP
Distributed by Universal Press Syndicate
-ABOUT THIS MUCH

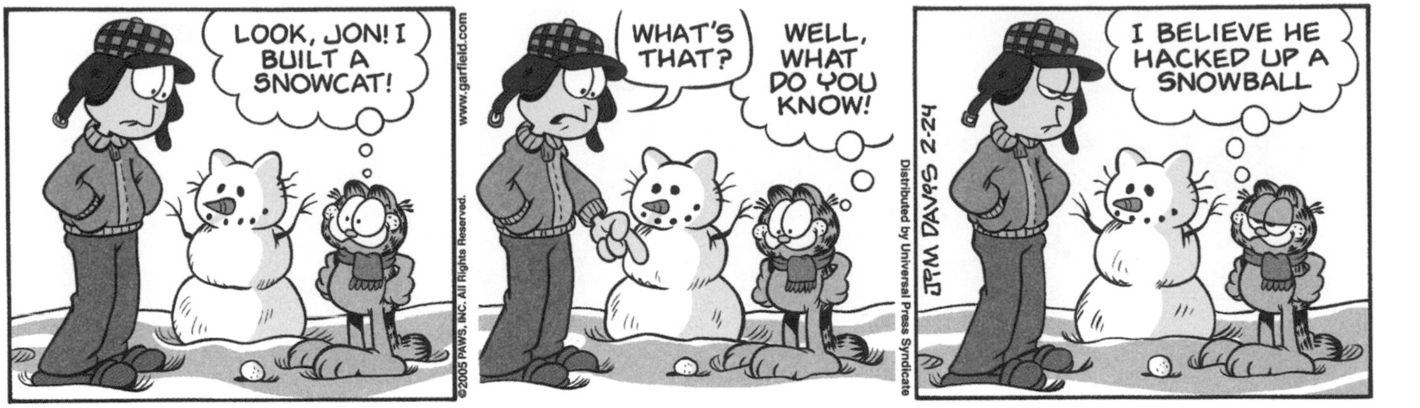
LOOK, JON! I BUILT A SNOWCAT!
WHAT'S THAT?
WELL, WHAT DO YOU KNOW!
I BELIEVE HE HACKED UP A SNOWBALL
JIM DAVIS 2·24

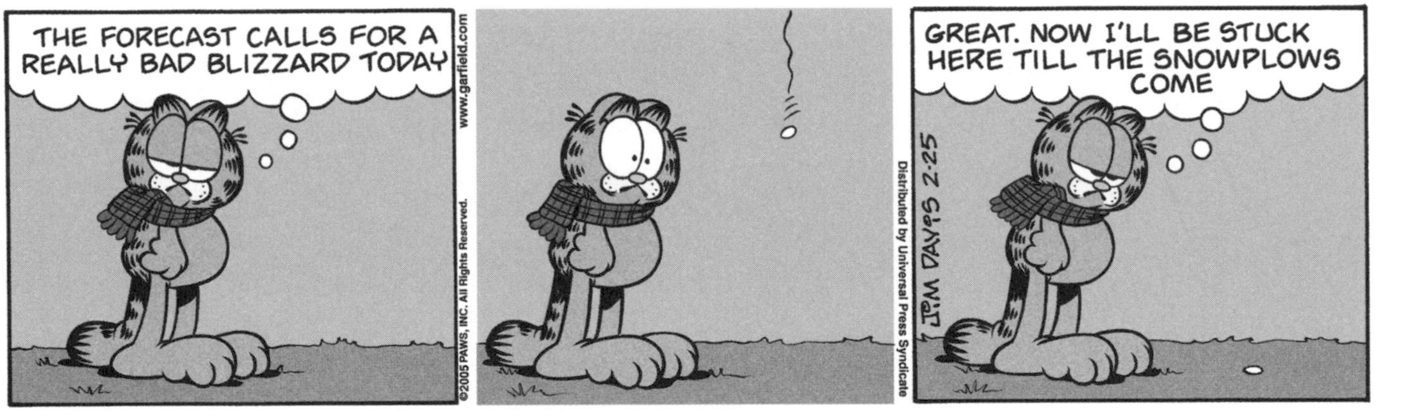
THE FORECAST CALLS FOR A REALLY BAD BLIZZARD TODAY
GREAT. NOW I'LL BE STUCK HERE TILL THE SNOWPLOWS COME
JIM DAVIS 2·25

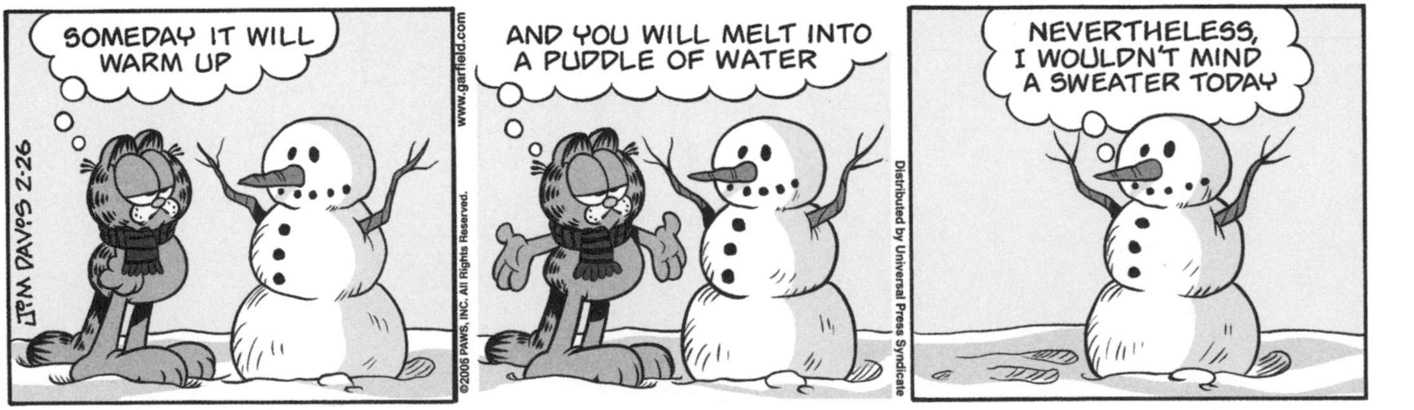
SOMEDAY IT WILL WARM UP
AND YOU WILL MELT INTO A PUDDLE OF WATER
NEVERTHELESS, I WOULDN'T MIND A SWEATER TODAY
JIM DAVIS 2·26

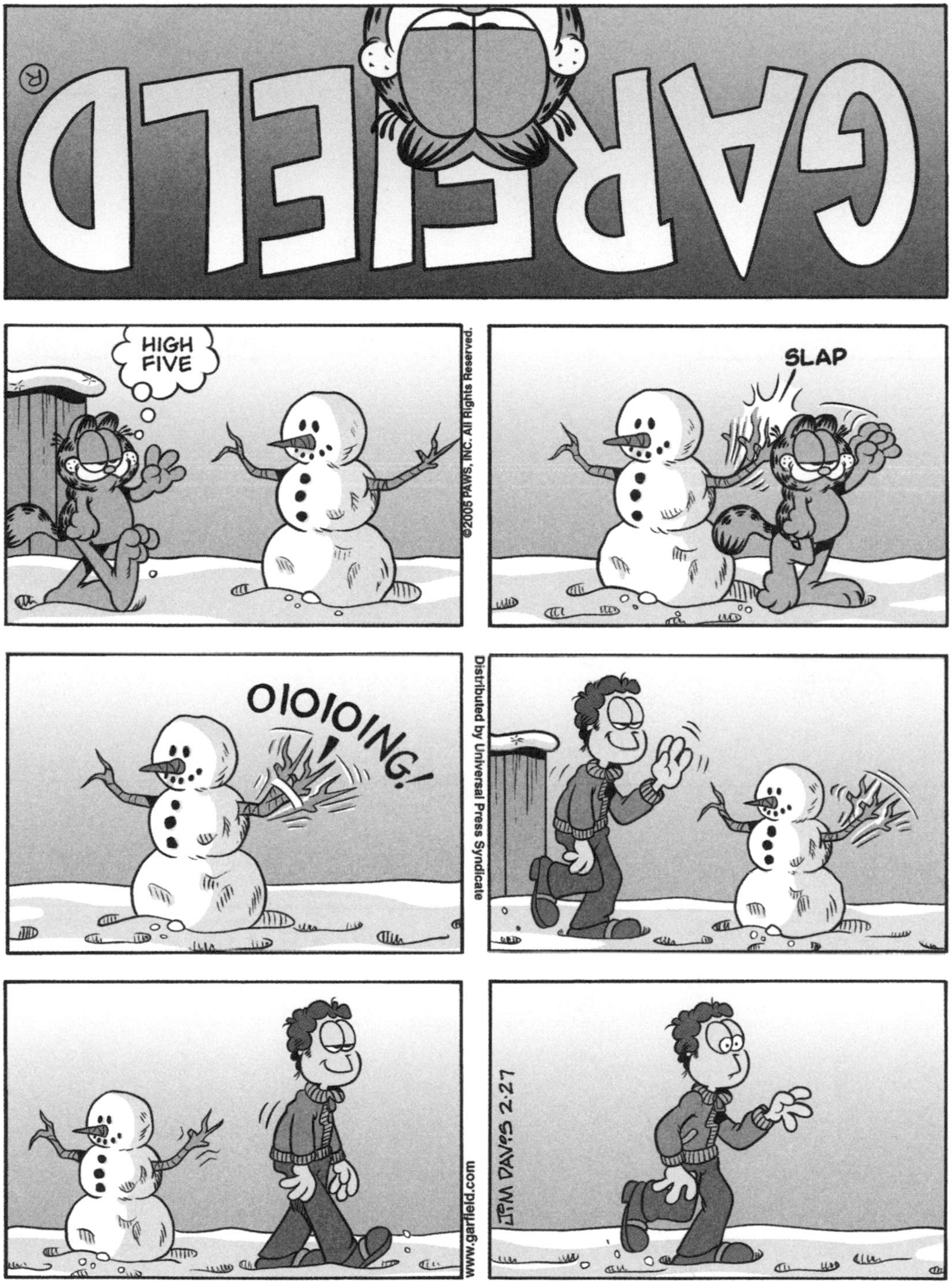
GARFIELD
HIGH FIVE
SLAP
OIOIOING!
JIM DAVIS 2-27
©2005 PAWS, INC. All Rights Reserved.
Distributed by Universal Press Syndicate
www.garfield.com

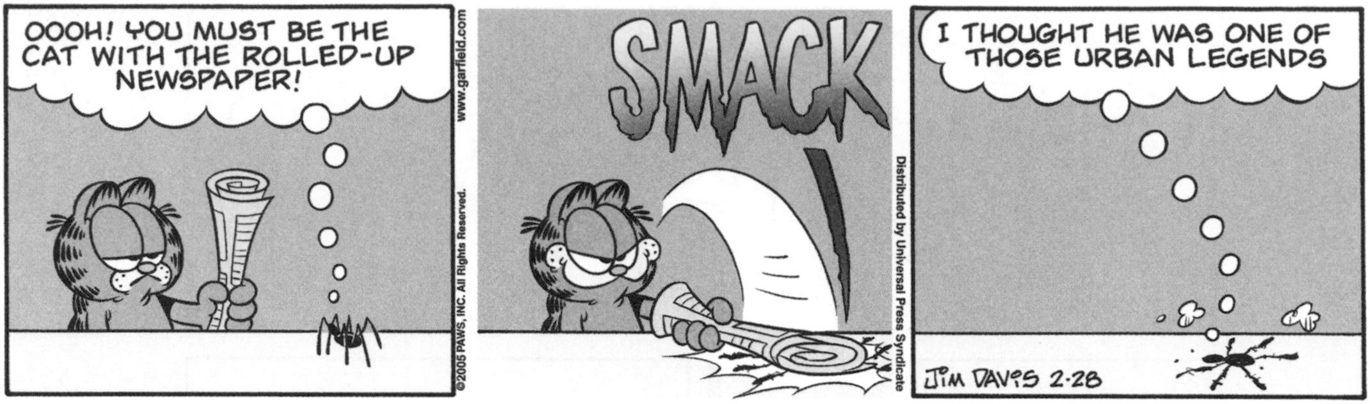
OOOH! YOU MUST BE THE CAT WITH THE ROLLED-UP NEWSPAPER!
©2005 PAWS, INC. All Rights Reserved.
www.garfield.com
SMACK
Distributed by Universal Press Syndicate
I THOUGHT HE WAS ONE OF THOSE URBAN LEGENDS
JIM DAVIS 2-28

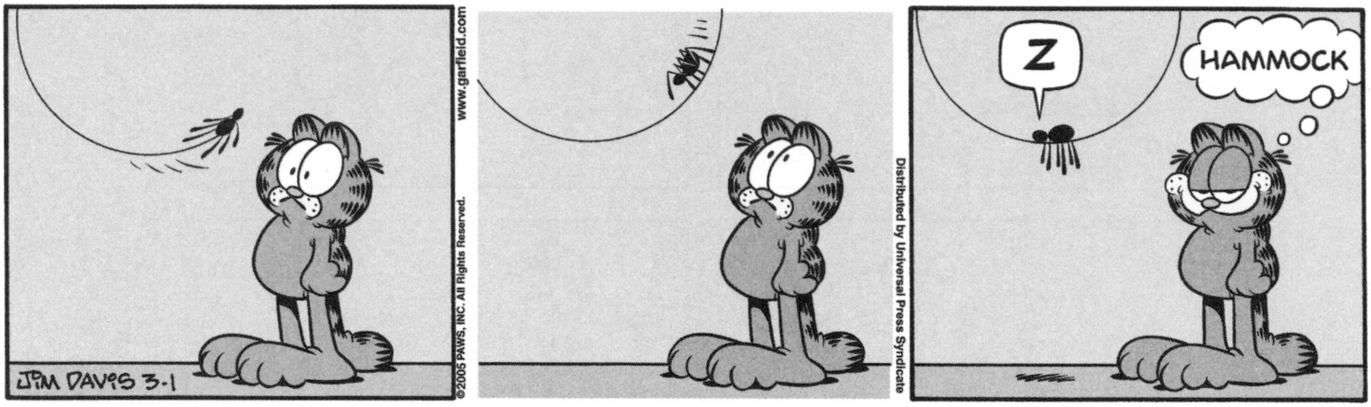
JIM DAVIS 3-1
©2005 PAWS, INC. All Rights Reserved.
www.garfield.com
Distributed by Universal Press Syndicate
Z
HAMMOCK

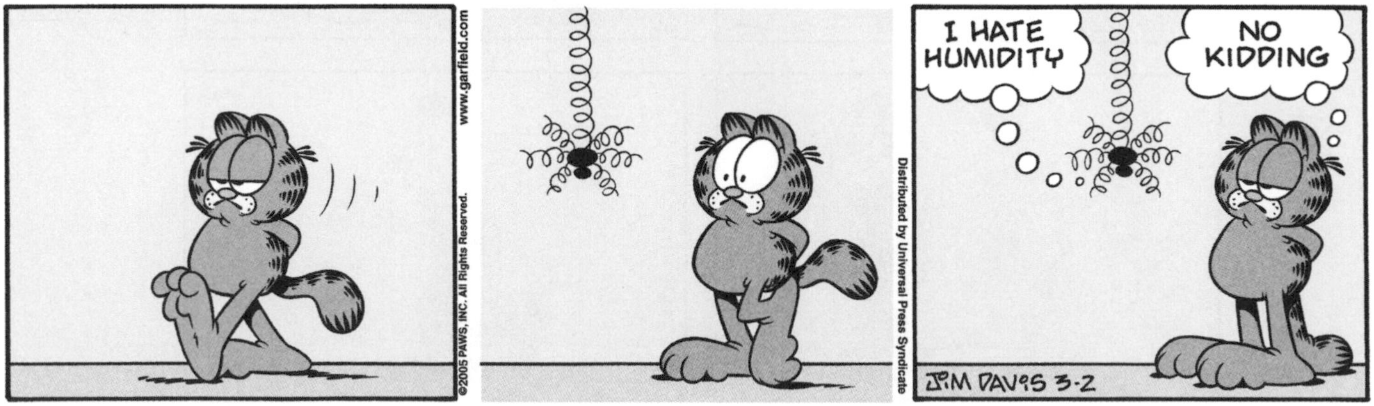
©2005 PAWS, INC. All Rights Reserved.
www.garfield.com
Distributed by Universal Press Syndicate
I HATE HUMIDITY
NO KIDDING
JIM DAVIS 3-2

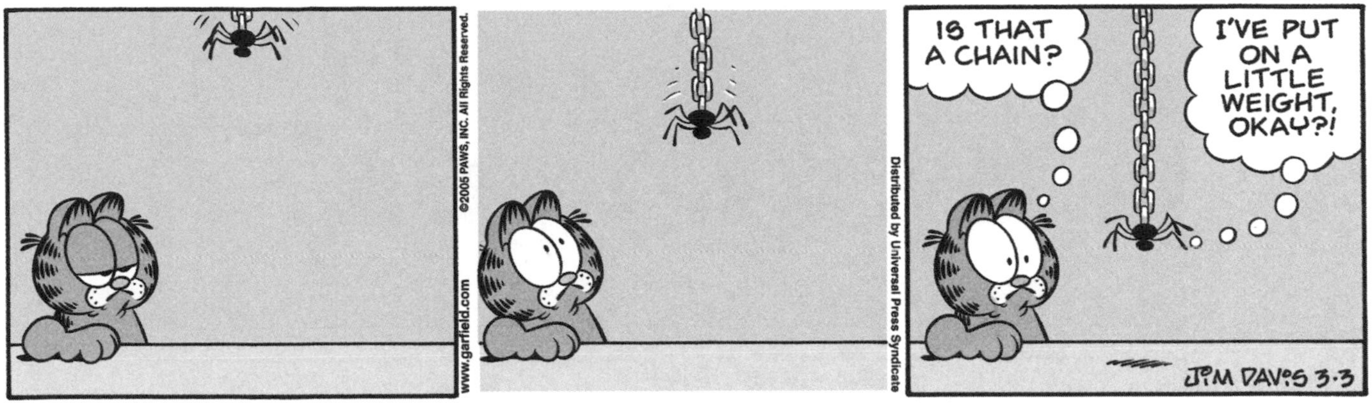
©2005 PAWS, INC. All Rights Reserved.
www.garfield.com
Distributed by Universal Press Syndicate
IS THAT A CHAIN?
I'VE PUT ON A LITTLE WEIGHT, OKAY?!
JIM DAVIS 3-3

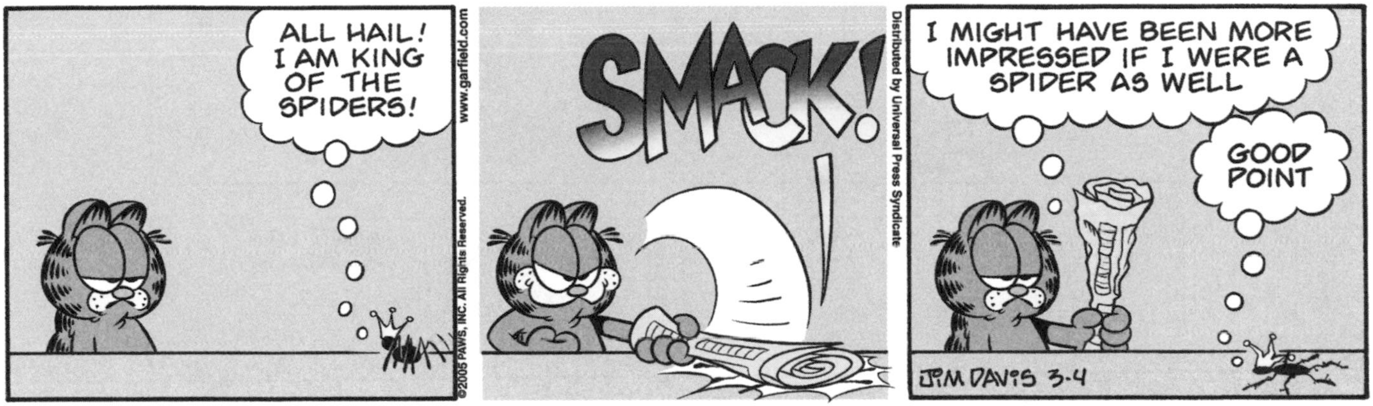
ALL HAIL! I AM KING OF THE SPIDERS!
www.garfield.com
©2005 PAWS, INC. All Rights Reserved.
SMACK!
Distributed by Universal Press Syndicate
I MIGHT HAVE BEEN MORE IMPRESSED IF I WERE A SPIDER AS WELL
GOOD POINT
JIM DAVIS 3-4

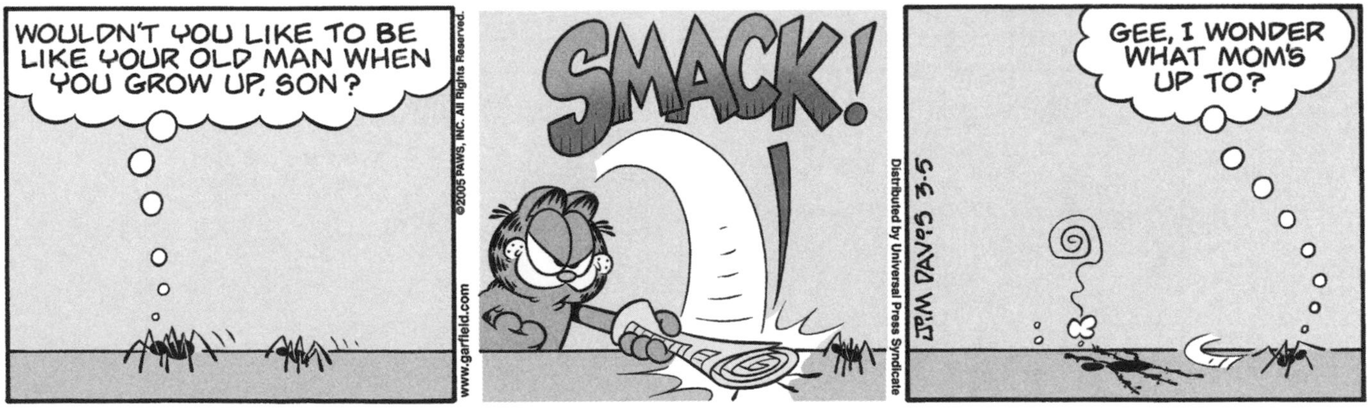
WOULDN'T YOU LIKE TO BE LIKE YOUR OLD MAN WHEN YOU GROW UP, SON?
©2005 PAWS, INC. All Rights Reserved.
www.garfield.com
SMACK!
Distributed by Universal Press Syndicate
JIM DAVIS 3-5
GEE, I WONDER WHAT MOM'S UP TO?

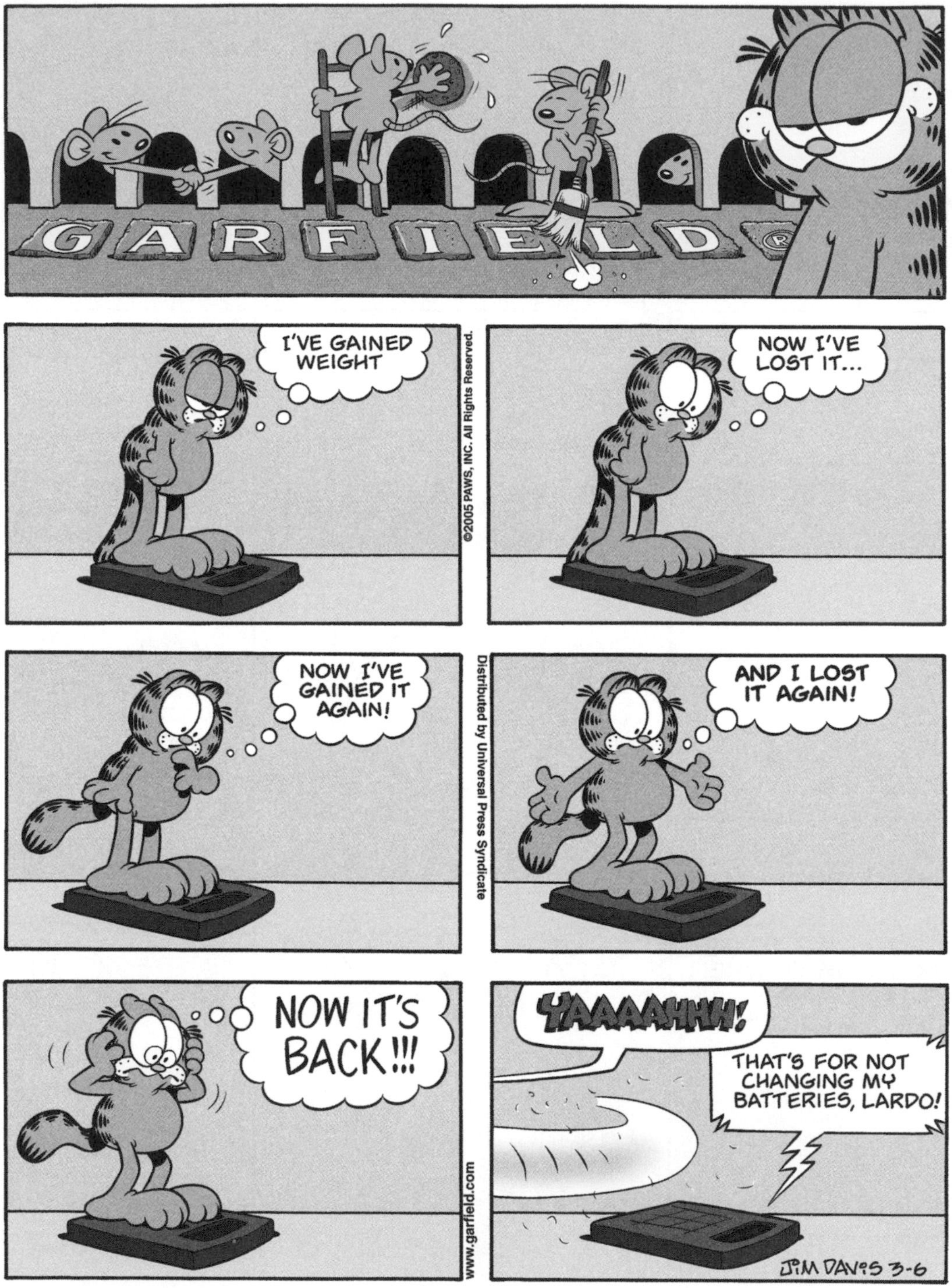
GARFIELD
I'VE GAINED WEIGHT
NOW I'VE LOST IT...
NOW I'VE GAINED IT AGAIN!
AND I LOST IT AGAIN!
NOW IT'S BACK!!!
YAAAAHHH!
THAT'S FOR NOT CHANGING MY BATTERIES, LARDO!
JIM DAVIS 3-6
©2005 PAWS, INC. All Rights Reserved.
Distributed by Universal Press Syndicate
www.garfield.com

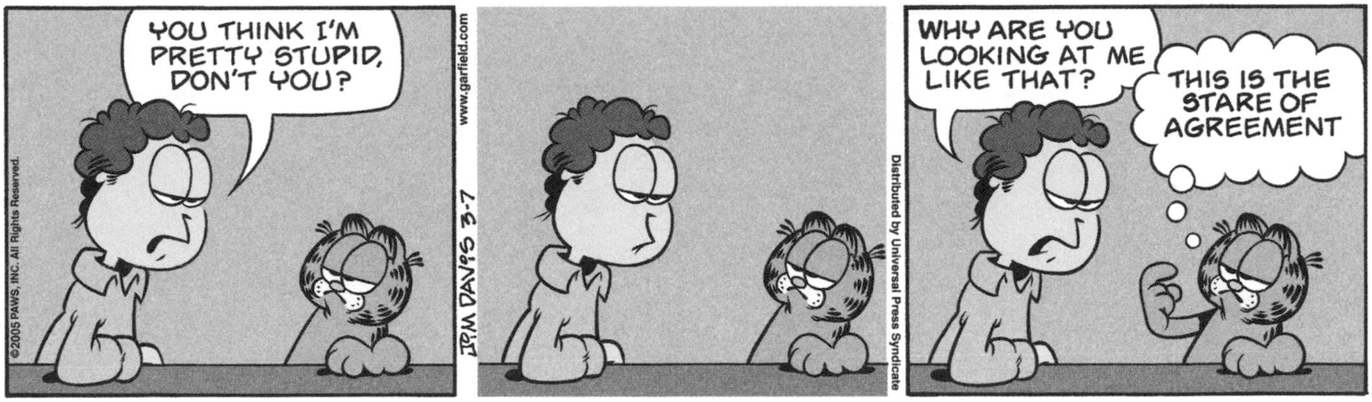
YOU THINK I'M PRETTY STUPID, DON'T YOU?
WHY ARE YOU LOOKING AT ME LIKE THAT?
THIS IS THE STARE OF AGREEMENT
©2005 PAWS, INC. All Rights Reserved.
www.garfield.com
JIM DAVIS 3-7
Distributed by Universal Press Syndicate

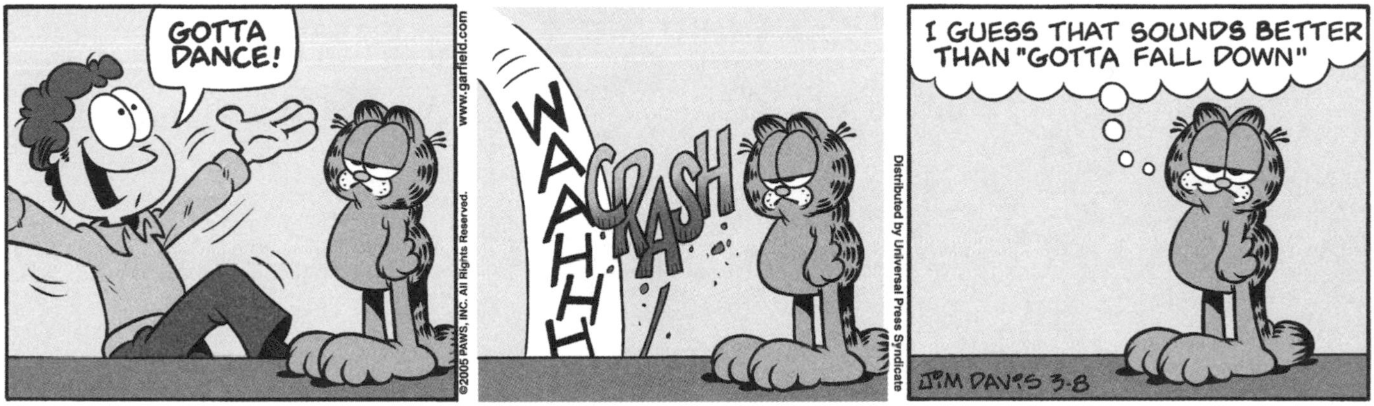
GOTTA DANCE!
WAAHHH
CRASH
I GUESS THAT SOUNDS BETTER THAN "GOTTA FALL DOWN"
©2005 PAWS, INC. All Rights Reserved.
www.garfield.com
Distributed by Universal Press Syndicate
JIM DAVIS 3-8

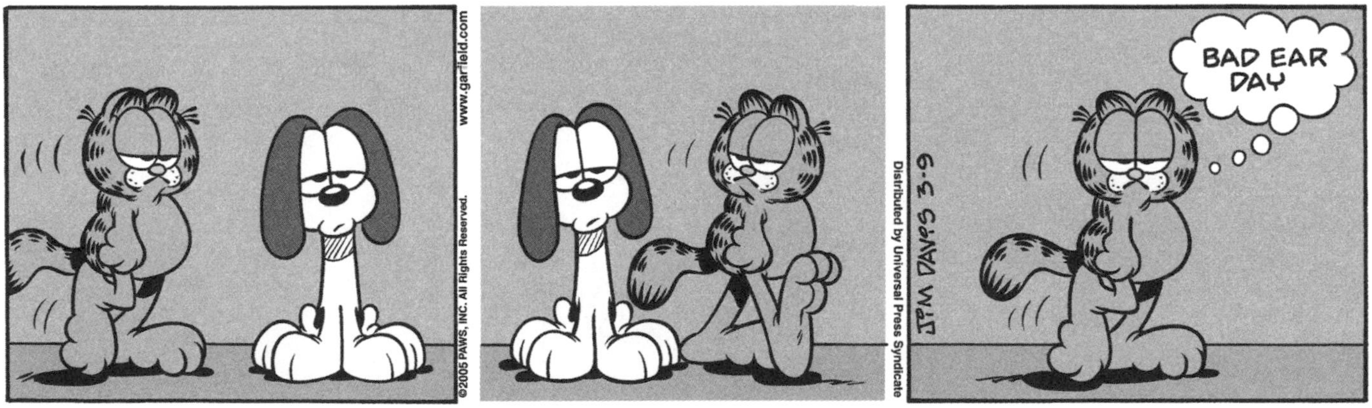
BAD EAR DAY
©2005 PAWS, INC. All Rights Reserved.
www.garfield.com
JIM DAVIS 3-9
Distributed by Universal Press Syndicate

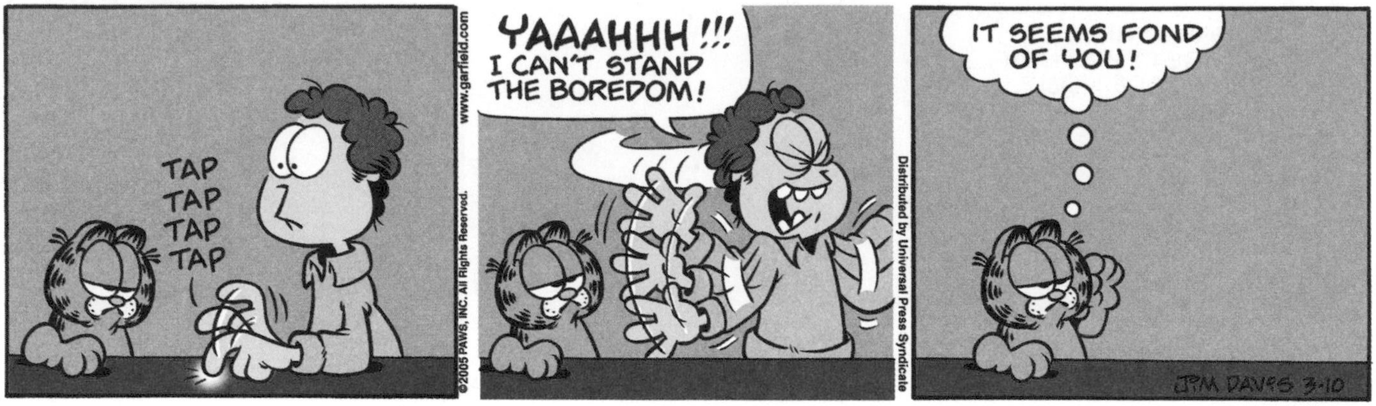
TAP
TAP
TAP
TAP
www.garfield.com
©2005 PAWS, INC. All Rights Reserved.
YAAAHHH!!!
I CAN'T STAND
THE BOREDOM!
Distributed by Universal Press Syndicate
IT SEEMS FOND
OF YOU!
JIM DAVIS 3-10

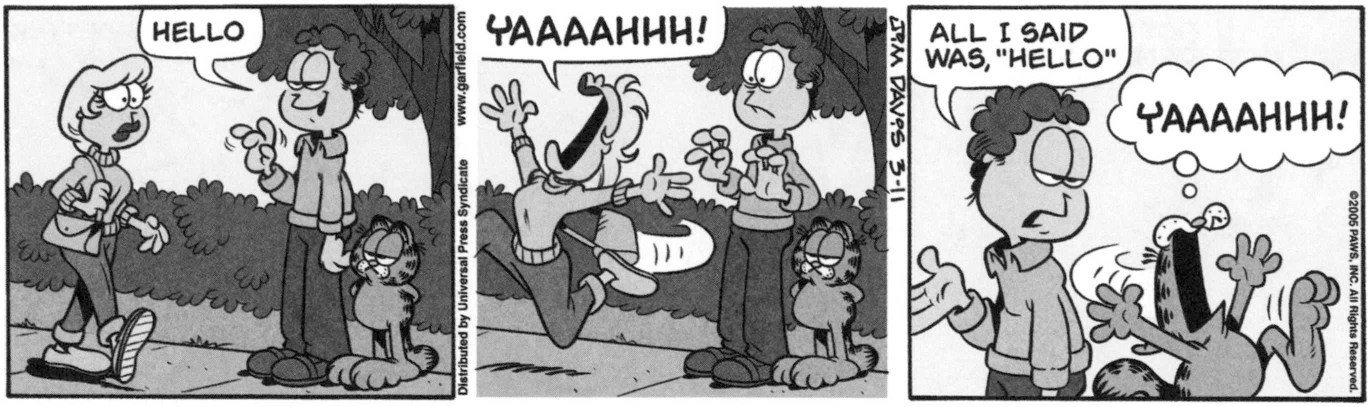
HELLO
www.garfield.com
Distributed by Universal Press Syndicate
YAAAAHHH!
JIM DAVIS 3-11
ALL I SAID
WAS, "HELLO"
YAAAAHHH!
©2005 PAWS, INC. All Rights Reserved.

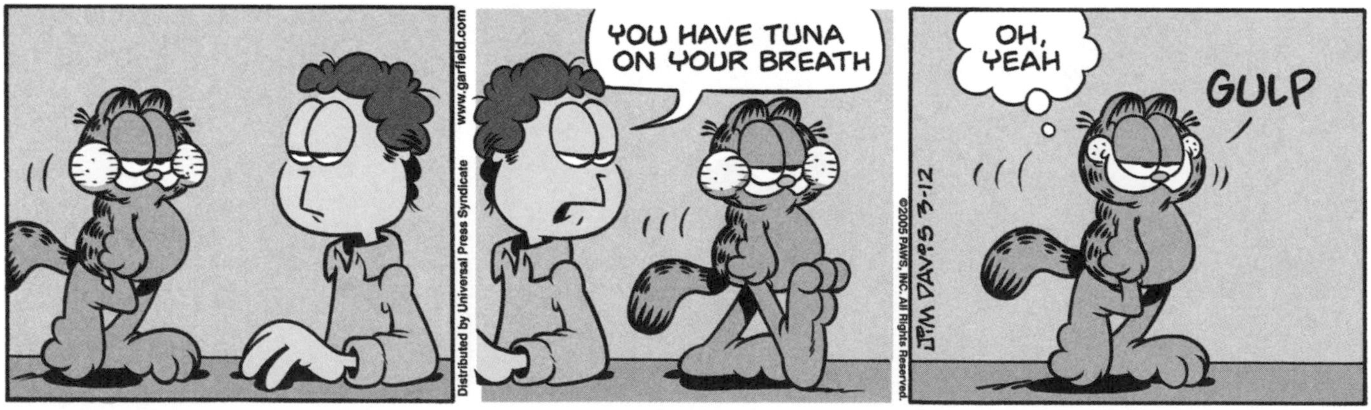
www.garfield.com
Distributed by Universal Press Syndicate
YOU HAVE TUNA
ON YOUR BREATH
JIM DAVIS 3-12
©2005 PAWS, INC. All Rights Reserved.
OH,
YEAH
GULP

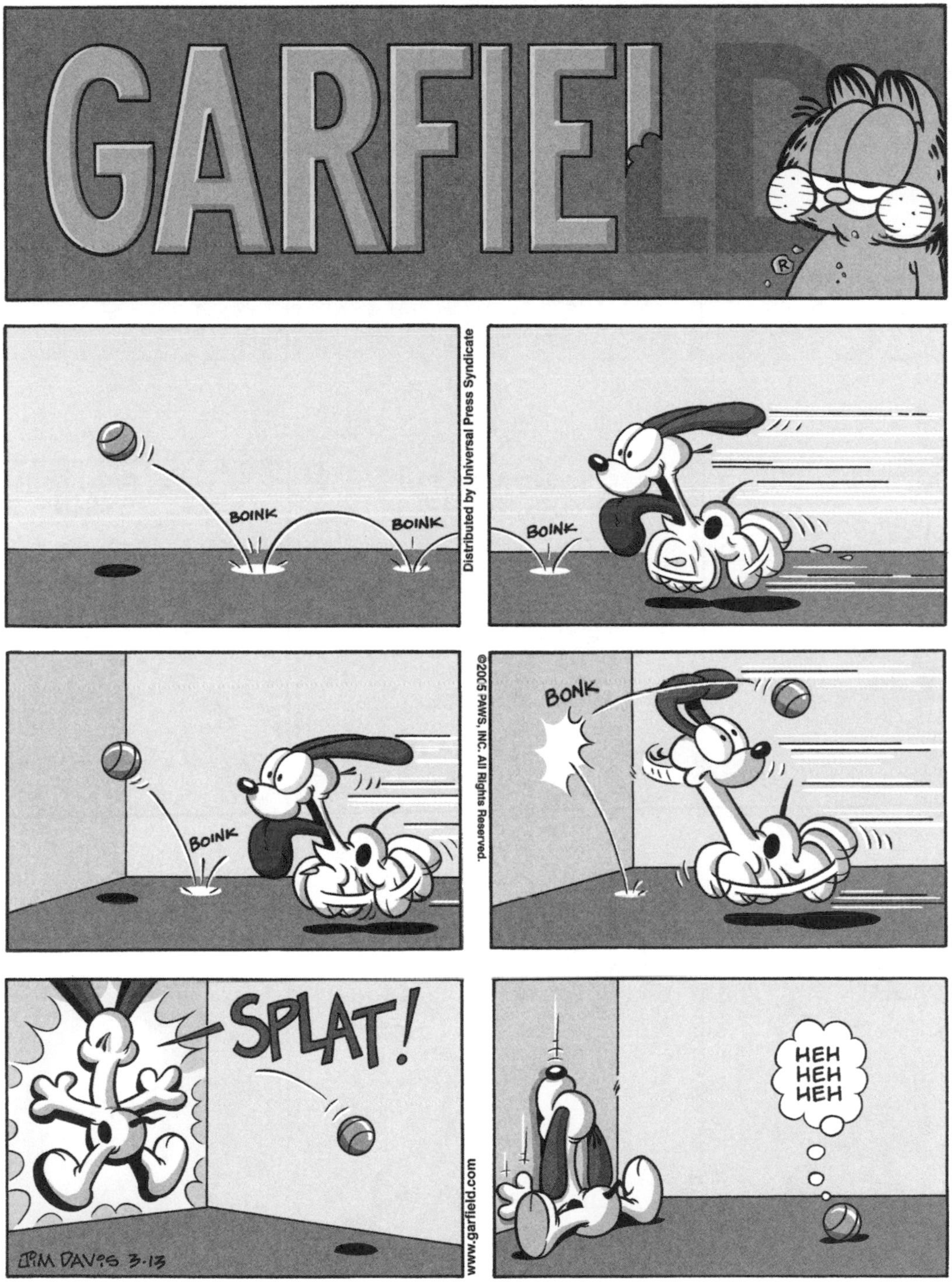
GARFIELD
BOINK
BOINK
Distributed by Universal Press Syndicate
BOINK
BOINK
©2005 PAWS, INC. All Rights Reserved.
BONK
SPLAT!
JIM DAVIS 3-13
www.garfield.com
HEH
HEH
HEH

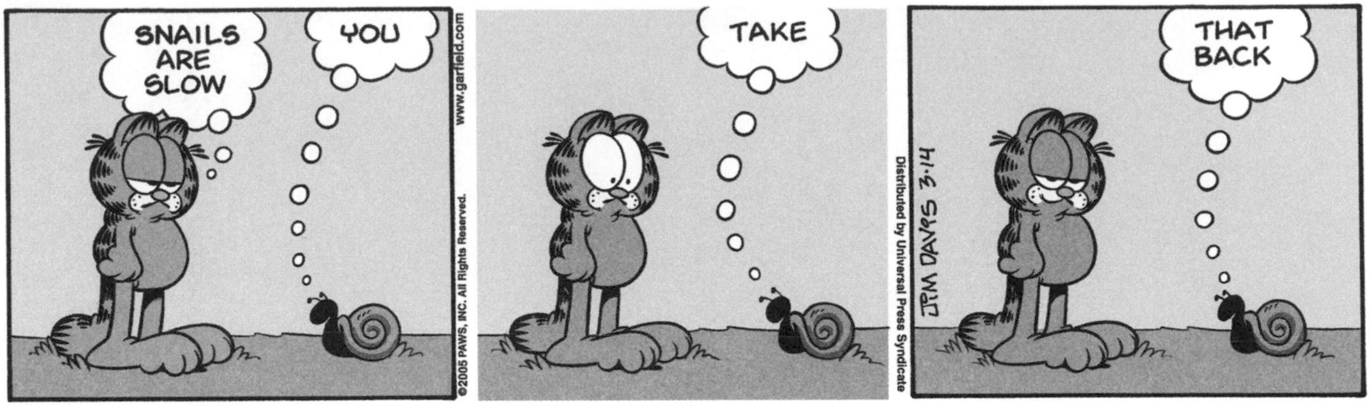
SNAILS ARE SLOW
YOU
TAKE
THAT BACK
©2005 PAWS, INC. All Rights Reserved. www.garfield.com
Distributed by Universal Press Syndicate

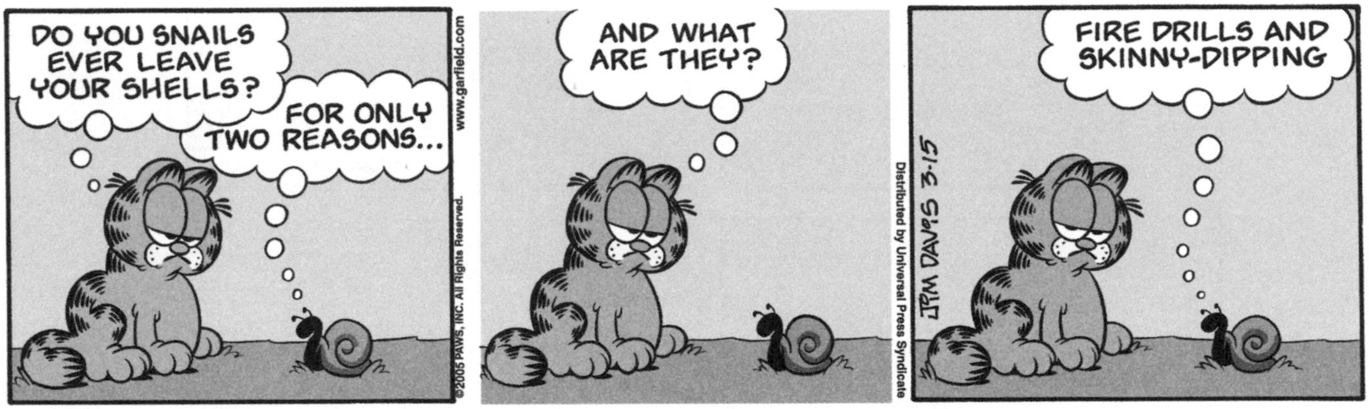
DO YOU SNAILS EVER LEAVE YOUR SHELLS?
FOR ONLY TWO REASONS...
AND WHAT ARE THEY?
FIRE DRILLS AND SKINNY-DIPPING
©2005 PAWS, INC. All Rights Reserved. www.garfield.com
Distributed by Universal Press Syndicate

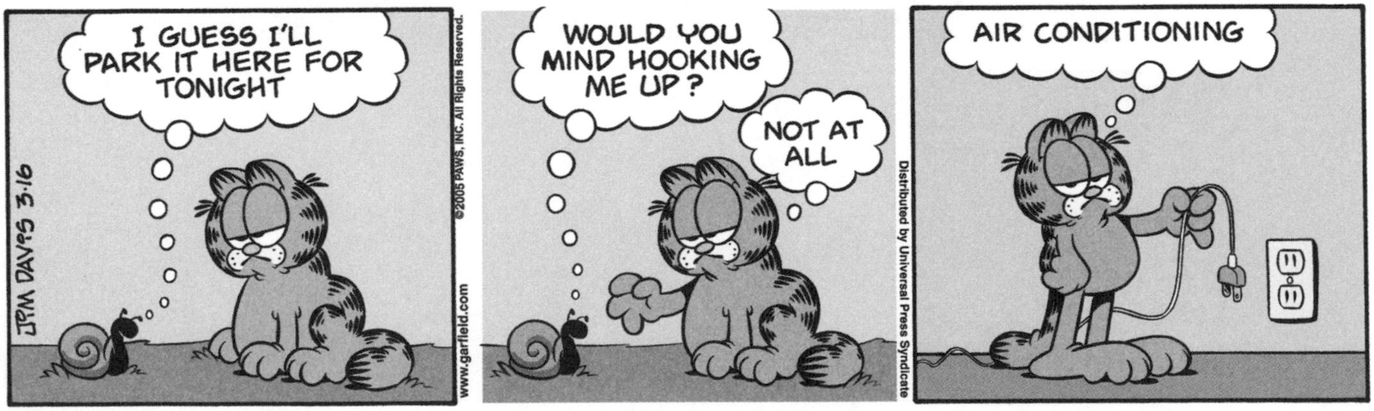
I GUESS I'LL PARK IT HERE FOR TONIGHT
WOULD YOU MIND HOOKING ME UP?
NOT AT ALL
AIR CONDITIONING
©2005 PAWS, INC. All Rights Reserved. www.garfield.com
Distributed by Universal Press Syndicate

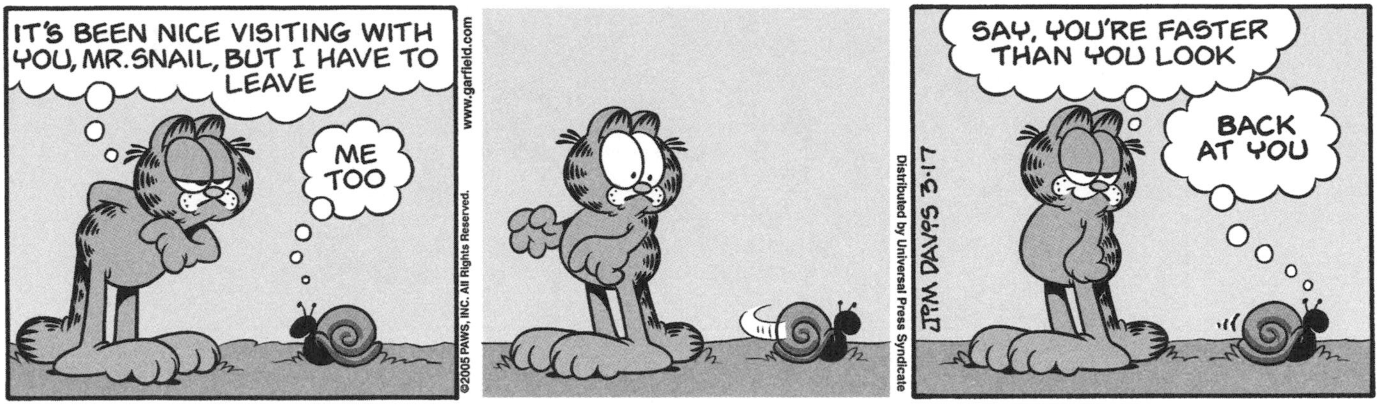
IT'S BEEN NICE VISITING WITH YOU, MR. SNAIL, BUT I HAVE TO LEAVE
ME TOO
©2005 PAWS, INC. All Rights Reserved. www.garfield.com
SAY, YOU'RE FASTER THAN YOU LOOK
BACK AT YOU
Distributed by Universal Press Syndicate
JPM DAVPS 3·17

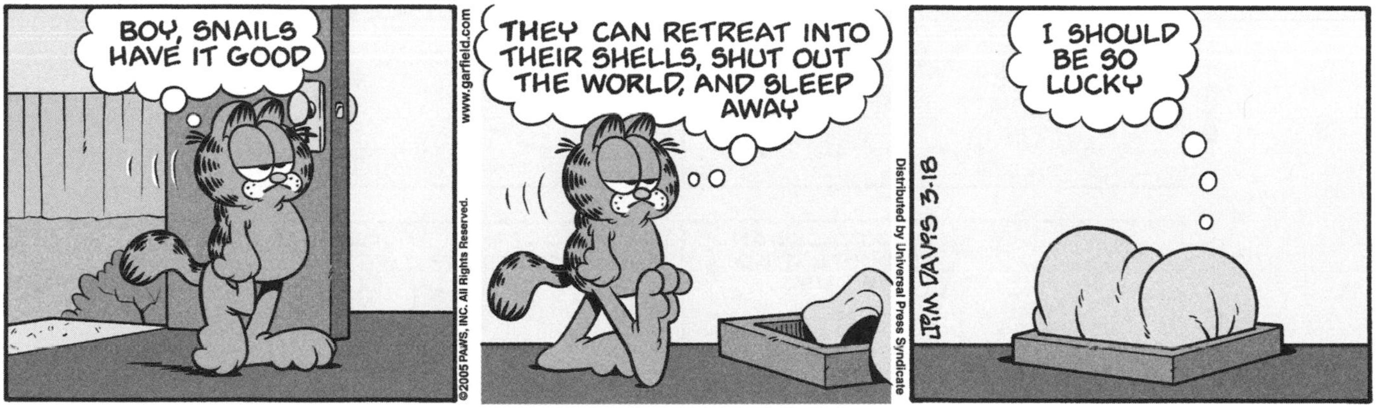
BOY, SNAILS HAVE IT GOOD
©2005 PAWS, INC. All Rights Reserved. www.garfield.com
THEY CAN RETREAT INTO THEIR SHELLS, SHUT OUT THE WORLD, AND SLEEP AWAY
Distributed by Universal Press Syndicate
I SHOULD BE SO LUCKY
JPM DAVPS 3·18

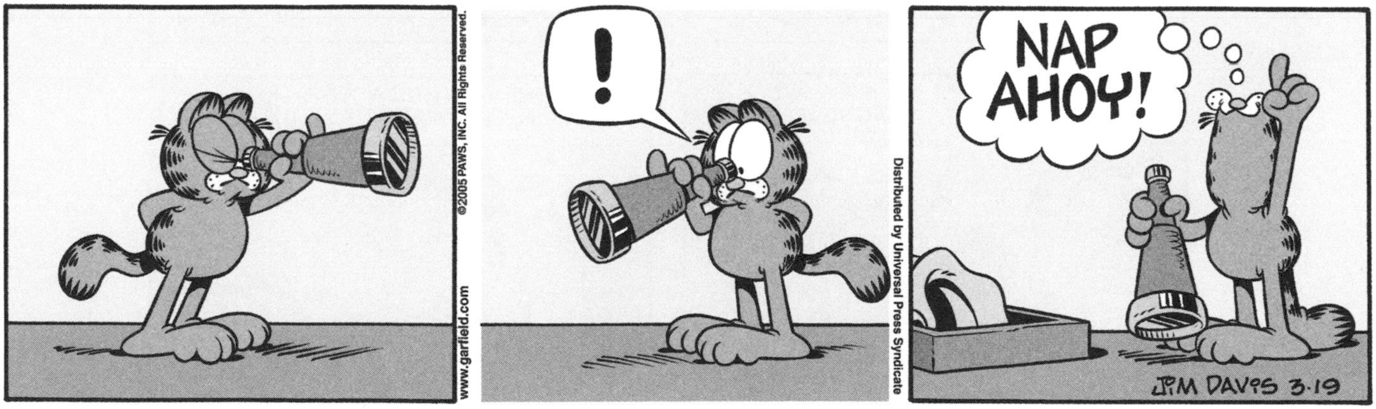
©2005 PAWS, INC. All Rights Reserved. www.garfield.com
!
Distributed by Universal Press Syndicate
NAP AHOY!
JPM DAVPS 3·19

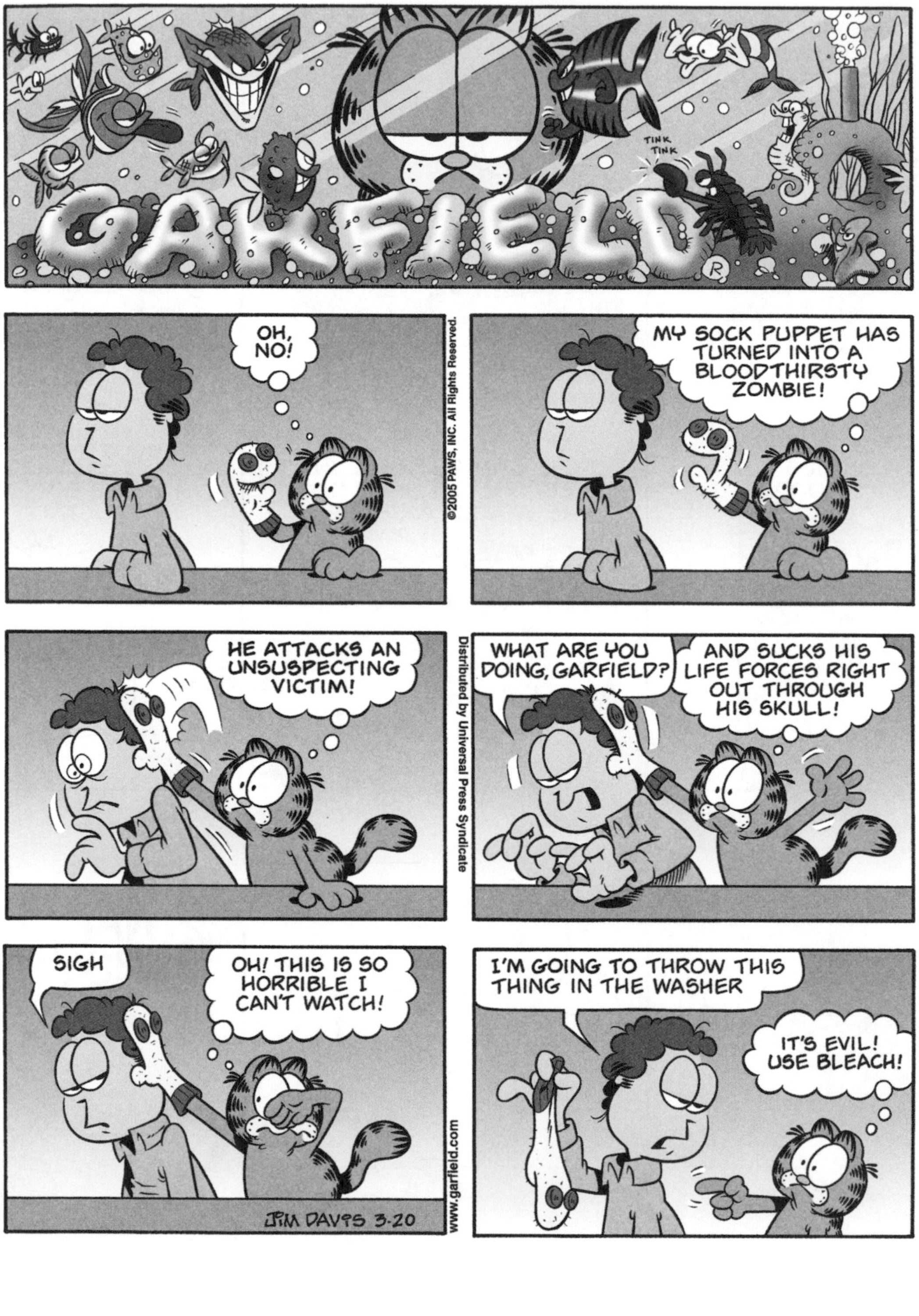
GARFIELD
TINK TINK
OH, NO!
MY SOCK PUPPET HAS TURNED INTO A BLOODTHIRSTY ZOMBIE!
HE ATTACKS AN UNSUSPECTING VICTIM!
WHAT ARE YOU DOING, GARFIELD?
AND SUCKS HIS LIFE FORCES RIGHT OUT THROUGH HIS SKULL!
SIGH
OH! THIS IS SO HORRIBLE I CAN'T WATCH!
I'M GOING TO THROW THIS THING IN THE WASHER
IT'S EVIL! USE BLEACH!
JIM DAVIS 3-20
©2005 PAWS, INC. All Rights Reserved.
Distributed by Universal Press Syndicate
www.garfield.com

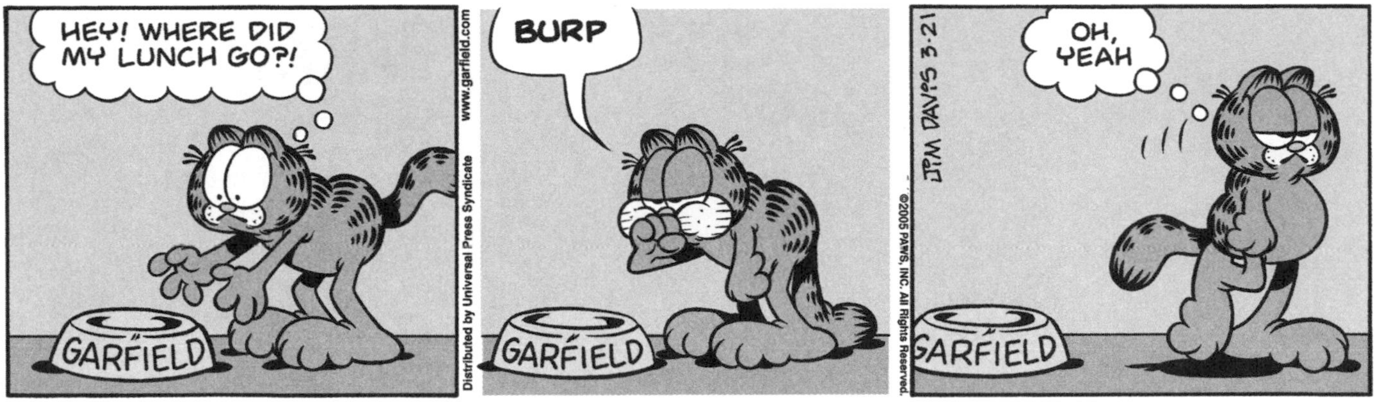
HEY! WHERE DID MY LUNCH GO?!
GARFIELD
www.garfield.com
Distributed by Universal Press Syndicate
BURP
GARFIELD
©2005 PAWS, INC. All Rights Reserved.
JIM DAVIS 3-21
OH, YEAH
GARFIELD

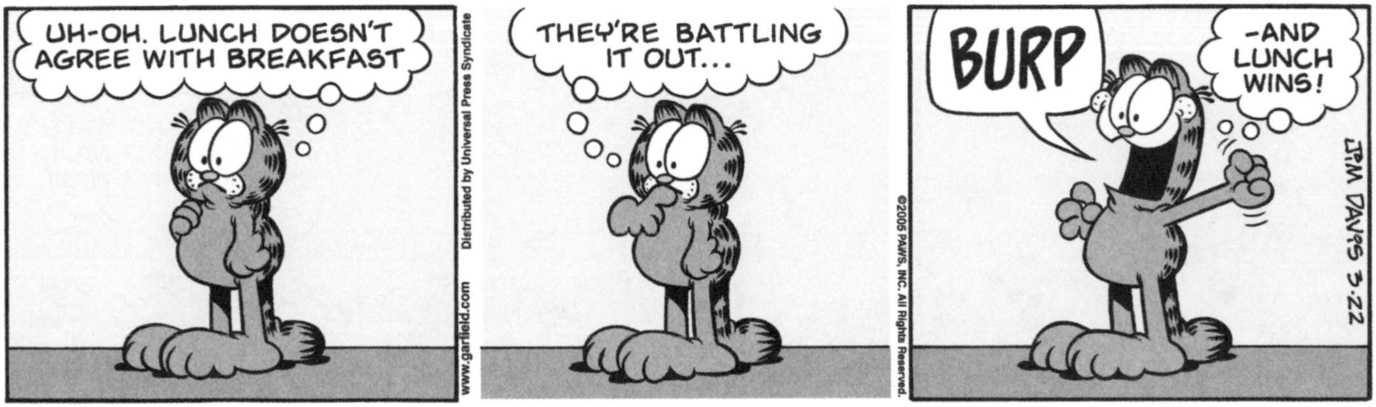
UH-OH. LUNCH DOESN'T AGREE WITH BREAKFAST
www.garfield.com
Distributed by Universal Press Syndicate
THEY'RE BATTLING IT OUT...
©2005 PAWS, INC. All Rights Reserved.
BURP
-AND LUNCH WINS!
JIM DAVIS 3-22

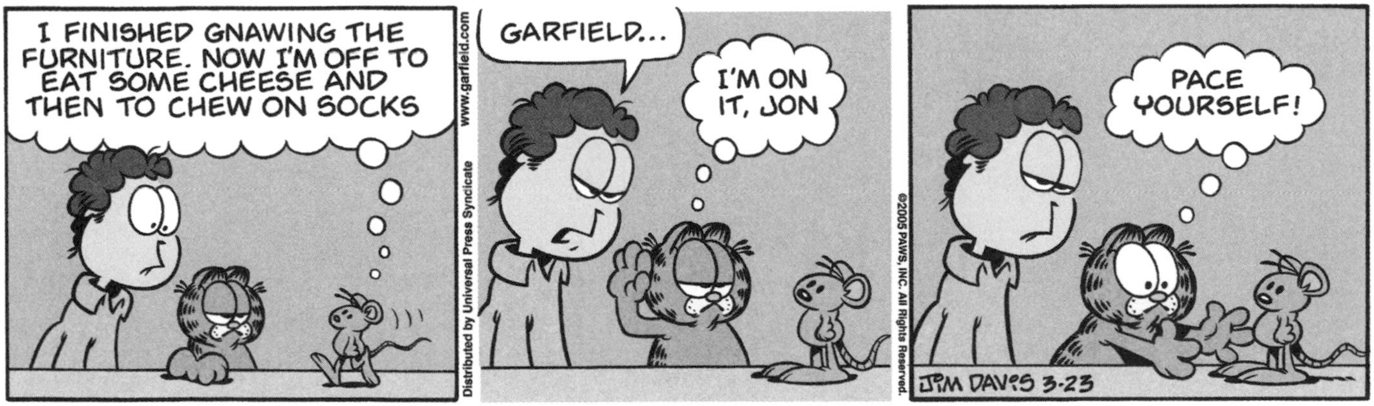
I FINISHED GNAWING THE FURNITURE. NOW I'M OFF TO EAT SOME CHEESE AND THEN TO CHEW ON SOCKS
www.garfield.com
Distributed by Universal Press Syndicate
GARFIELD...
I'M ON IT, JON
©2005 PAWS, INC. All Rights Reserved.
PACE YOURSELF!
JIM DAVIS 3-23

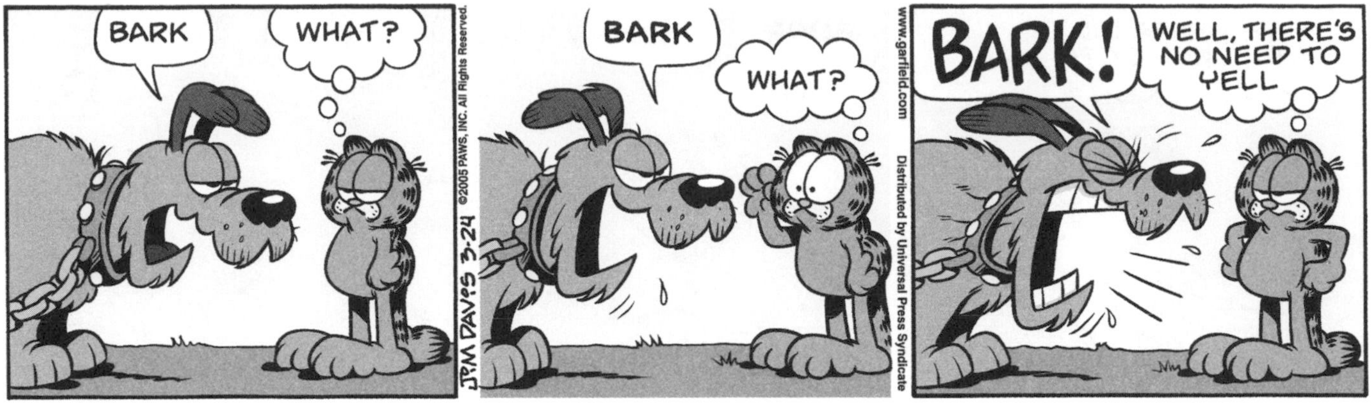
BARK
WHAT?
BARK
WHAT?
BARK!
WELL, THERE'S NO NEED TO YELL
JPM DAVIS 3-24
©2005 PAWS, INC. All Rights Reserved.
www.garfield.com
Distributed by Universal Press Syndicate

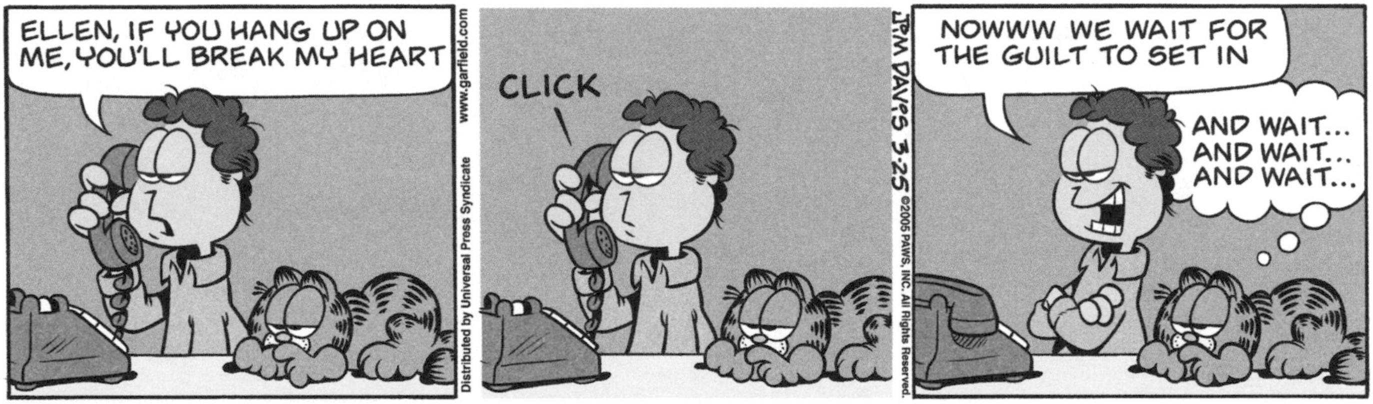
ELLEN, IF YOU HANG UP ON ME, YOU'LL BREAK MY HEART
www.garfield.com
Distributed by Universal Press Syndicate
CLICK
JPM DAVIS 3-25
©2005 PAWS, INC. All Rights Reserved.
NOWWW WE WAIT FOR THE GUILT TO SET IN
AND WAIT... AND WAIT... AND WAIT...

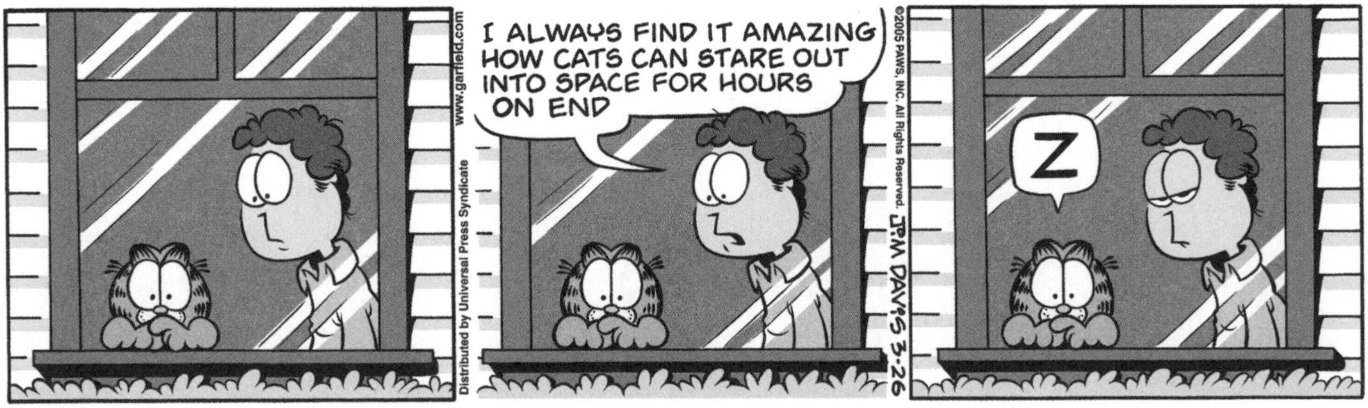
www.garfield.com
Distributed by Universal Press Syndicate
I ALWAYS FIND IT AMAZING HOW CATS CAN STARE OUT INTO SPACE FOR HOURS ON END
©2005 PAWS, INC. All Rights Reserved.
JPM DAVIS 3-26
Z

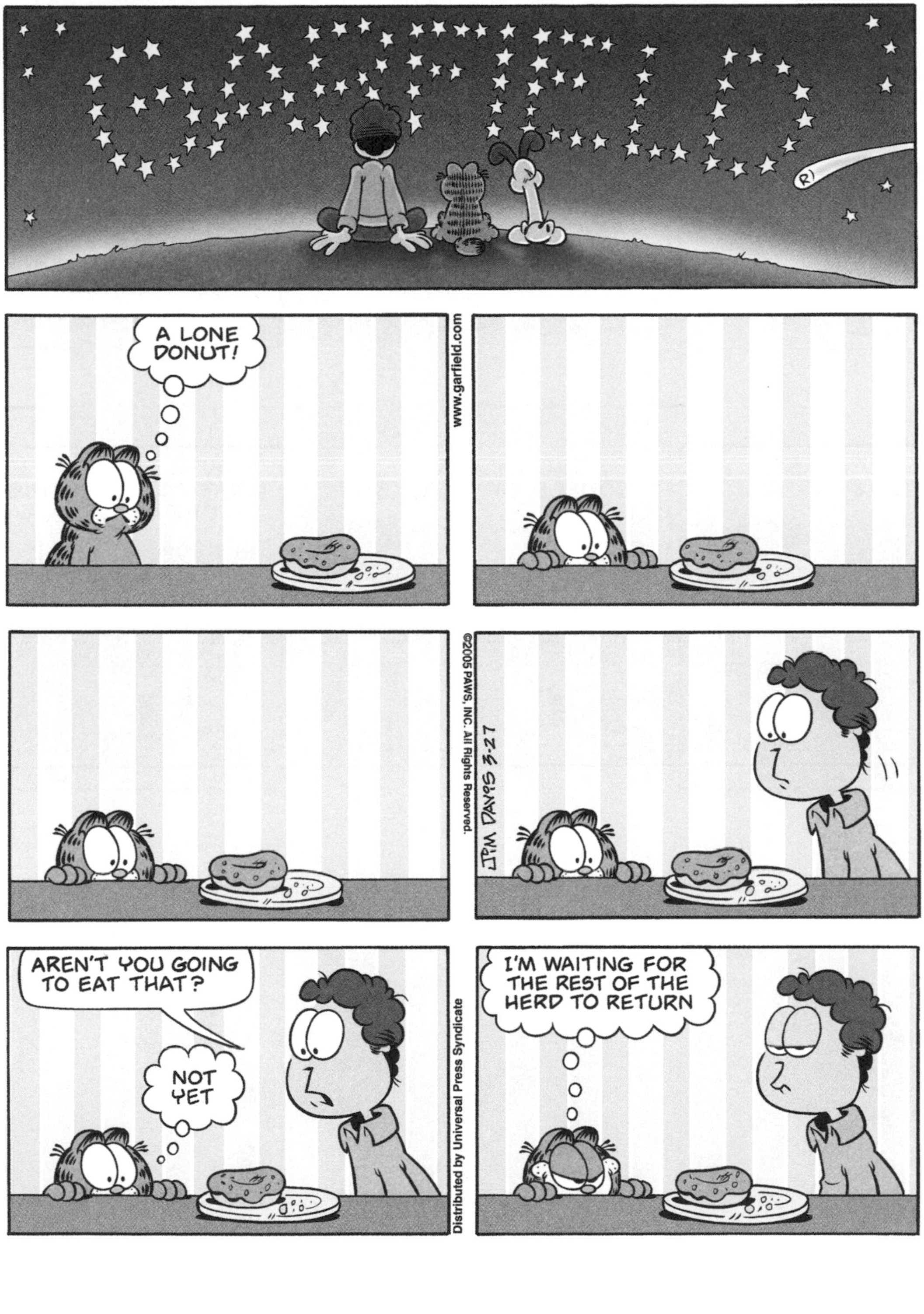
GARFIELD
A LONE DONUT!
www.garfield.com
©2005 PAWS, INC. All Rights Reserved.
JPM DAVIS 3-27
AREN'T YOU GOING TO EAT THAT?
NOT YET
Distributed by Universal Press Syndicate
I'M WAITING FOR THE REST OF THE HERD TO RETURN

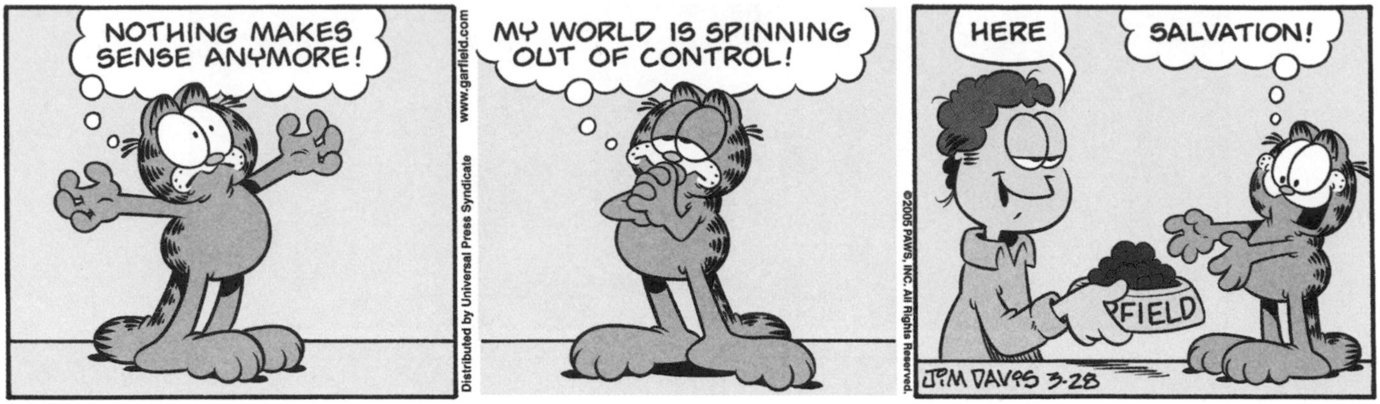
NOTHING MAKES SENSE ANYMORE!
MY WORLD IS SPINNING OUT OF CONTROL!
HERE
SALVATION!
FIELD
JIM DAVIS 3-28
www.garfield.com Distributed by Universal Press Syndicate
©2005 PAWS, INC. All Rights Reserved.

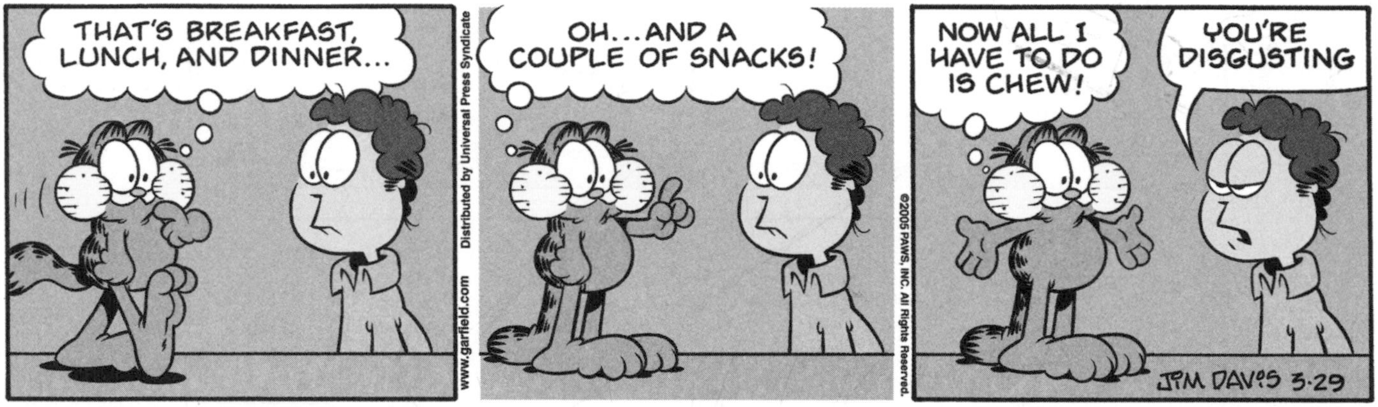
THAT'S BREAKFAST, LUNCH, AND DINNER...
OH...AND A COUPLE OF SNACKS!
NOW ALL I HAVE TO DO IS CHEW!
YOU'RE DISGUSTING
JIM DAVIS 3-29
Distributed by Universal Press Syndicate www.garfield.com
©2005 PAWS, INC. All Rights Reserved.

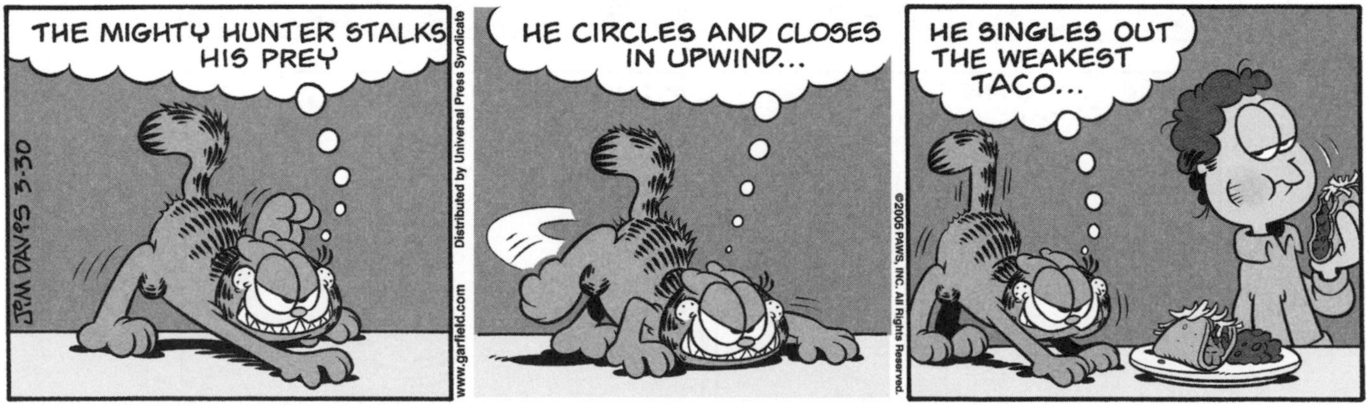
THE MIGHTY HUNTER STALKS HIS PREY
JIM DAVIS 3-30
HE CIRCLES AND CLOSES IN UPWIND...
HE SINGLES OUT THE WEAKEST TACO...
Distributed by Universal Press Syndicate www.garfield.com
©2005 PAWS, INC. All Rights Reserved.

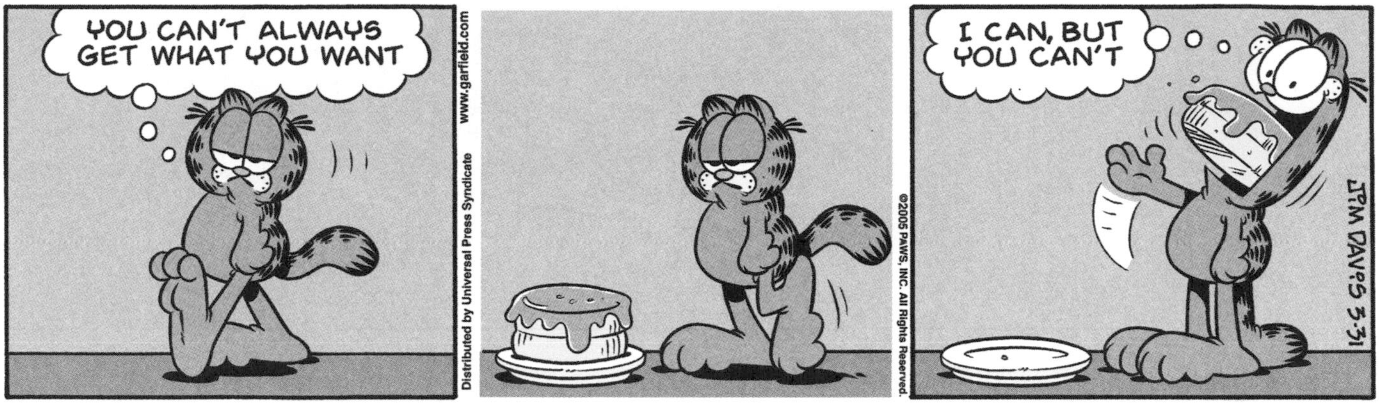
YOU CAN'T ALWAYS GET WHAT YOU WANT
I CAN, BUT YOU CAN'T
JIM DAVIS 3-31
www.garfield.com
Distributed by Universal Press Syndicate
©2005 PAWS, INC. All Rights Reserved.

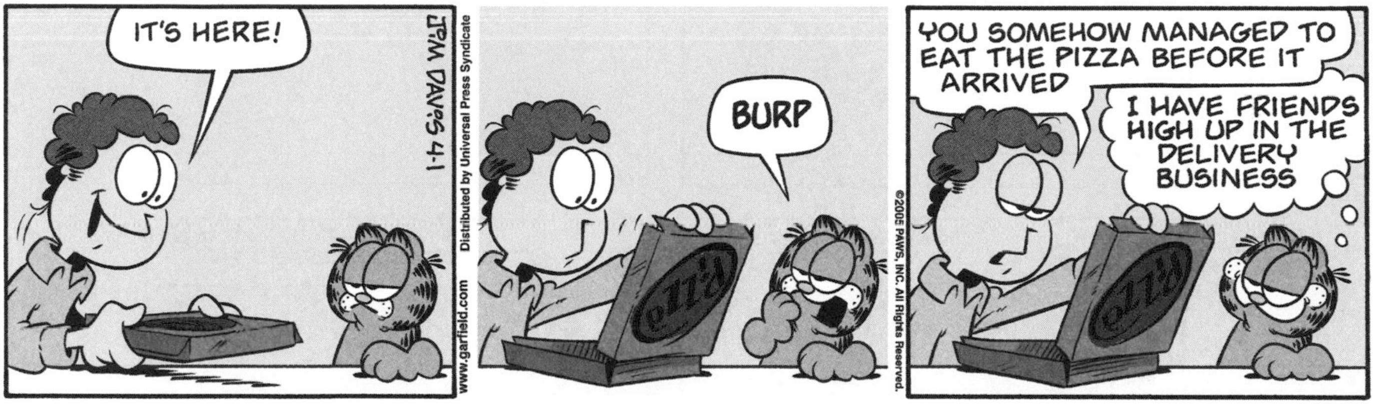
IT'S HERE!
JIM DAVIS 4-1
BURP
PIZZA
YOU SOMEHOW MANAGED TO EAT THE PIZZA BEFORE IT ARRIVED
I HAVE FRIENDS HIGH UP IN THE DELIVERY BUSINESS
www.garfield.com
Distributed by Universal Press Syndicate
©2005 PAWS, INC. All Rights Reserved.

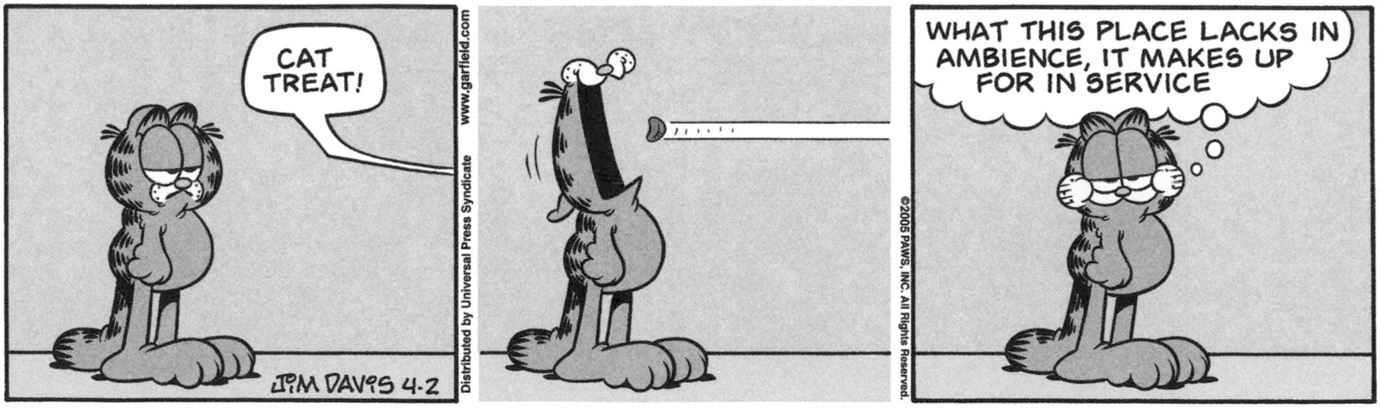
CAT TREAT!
JIM DAVIS 4-2
WHAT THIS PLACE LACKS IN AMBIENCE, IT MAKES UP FOR IN SERVICE
www.garfield.com
Distributed by Universal Press Syndicate
©2005 PAWS, INC. All Rights Reserved.

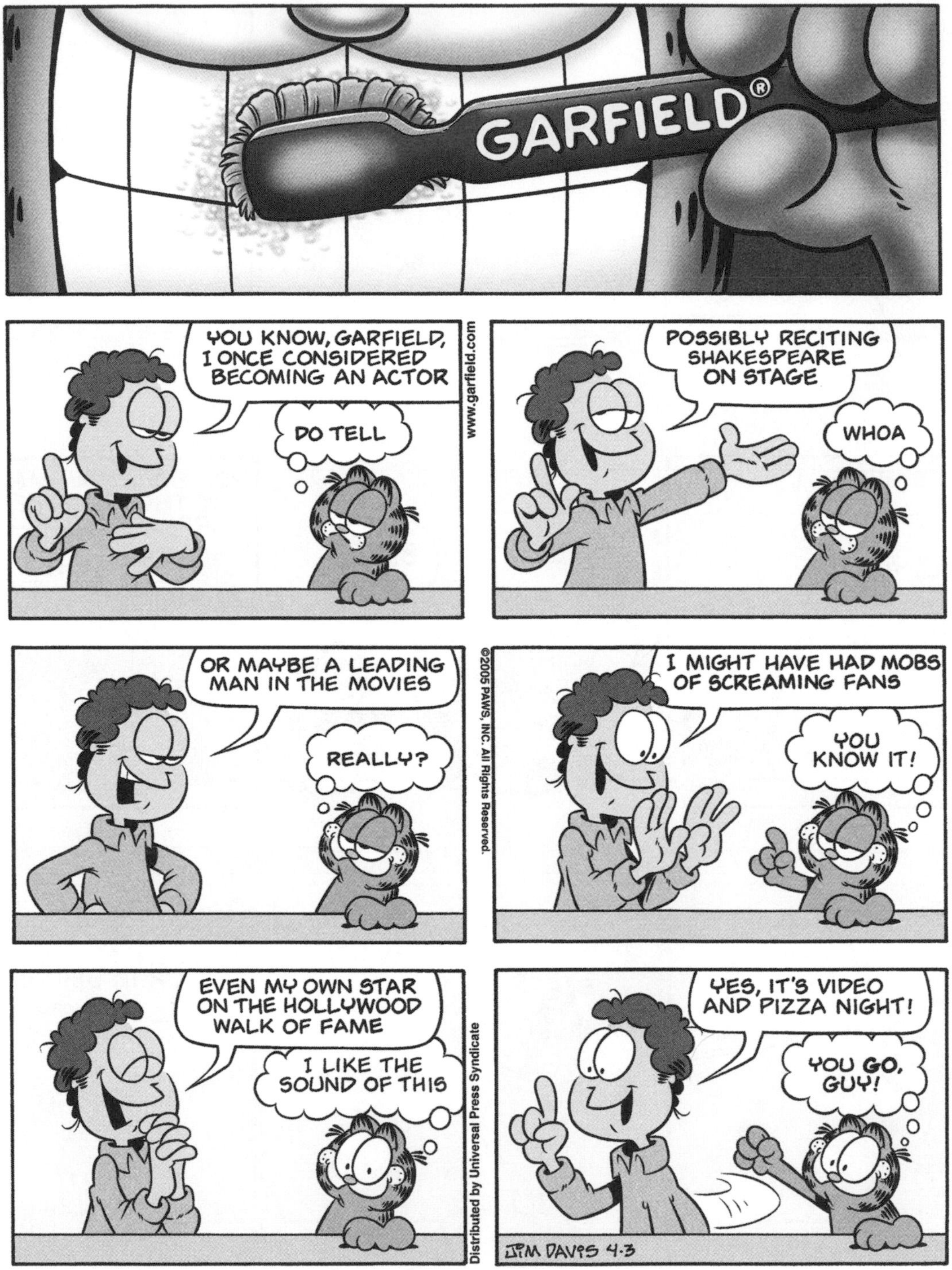
GARFIELD®
YOU KNOW, GARFIELD, I ONCE CONSIDERED BECOMING AN ACTOR
DO TELL
www.garfield.com
POSSIBLY RECITING SHAKESPEARE ON STAGE
WHOA
OR MAYBE A LEADING MAN IN THE MOVIES
REALLY?
©2005 PAWS, INC. All Rights Reserved.
I MIGHT HAVE HAD MOBS OF SCREAMING FANS
YOU KNOW IT!
EVEN MY OWN STAR ON THE HOLLYWOOD WALK OF FAME
I LIKE THE SOUND OF THIS
Distributed by Universal Press Syndicate
YES, IT'S VIDEO AND PIZZA NIGHT!
YOU GO, GUY!
JIM DAVIS 4-3

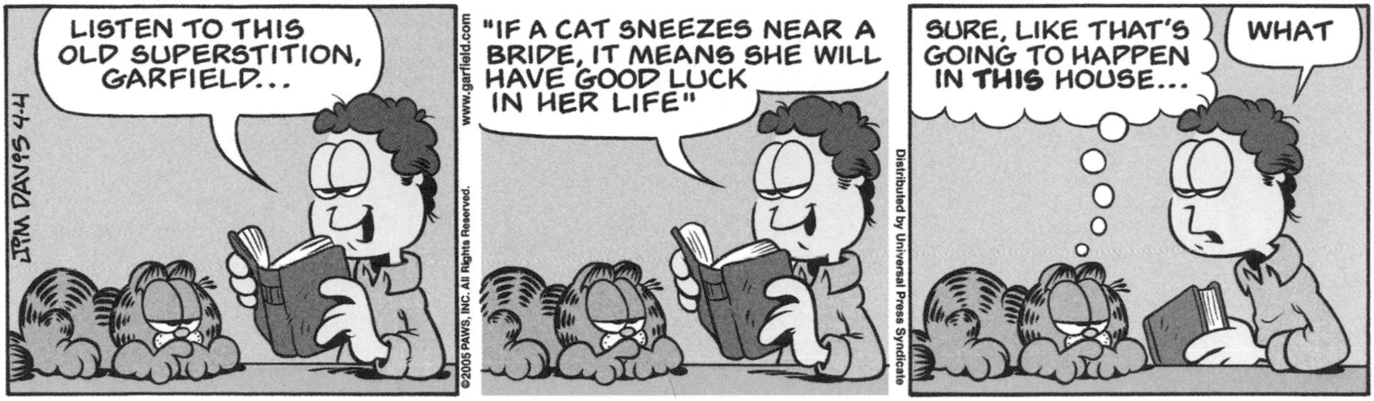
JIM DAVIS 4-4
LISTEN TO THIS OLD SUPERSTITION, GARFIELD...
"IF A CAT SNEEZES NEAR A BRIDE, IT MEANS SHE WILL HAVE GOOD LUCK IN HER LIFE"
SURE, LIKE THAT'S GOING TO HAPPEN IN **THIS** HOUSE...
WHAT
©2005 PAWS, INC. All Rights Reserved. www.garfield.com
Distributed by Universal Press Syndicate

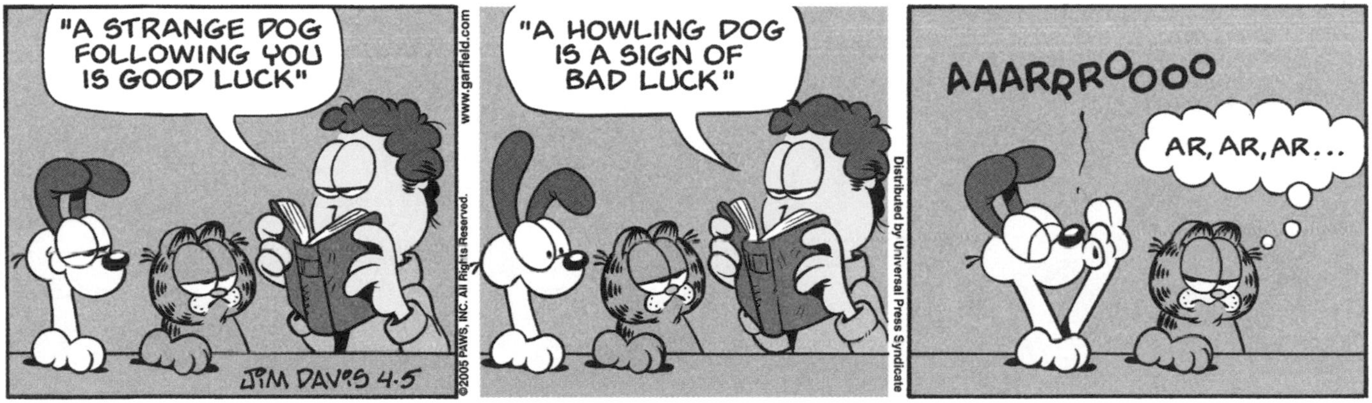
"A STRANGE DOG FOLLOWING YOU IS GOOD LUCK"
JIM DAVIS 4-5
"A HOWLING DOG IS A SIGN OF BAD LUCK"
AAARRROOOO
AR, AR, AR...
©2005 PAWS, INC. All Rights Reserved. www.garfield.com
Distributed by Universal Press Syndicate

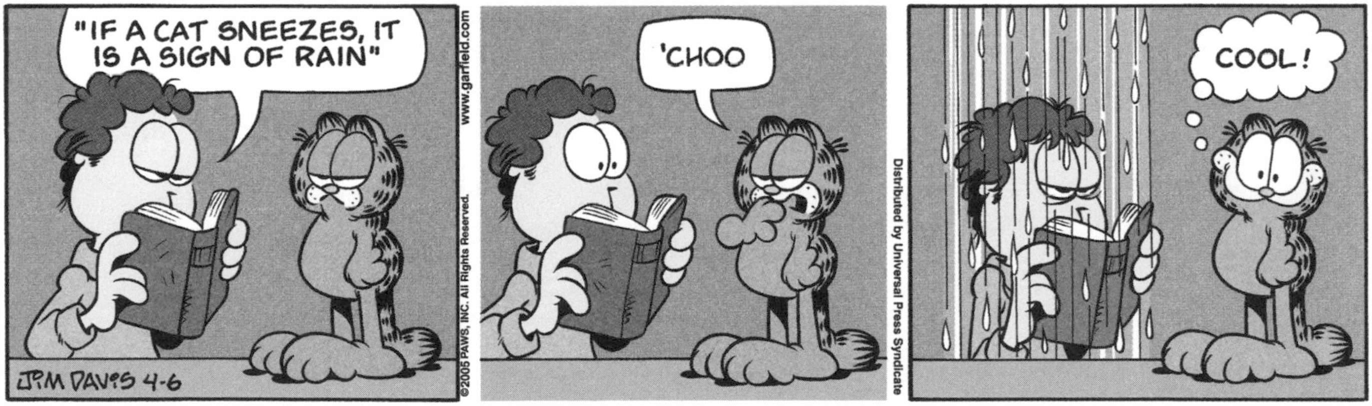
"IF A CAT SNEEZES, IT IS A SIGN OF RAIN"
JIM DAVIS 4-6
'CHOO
COOL!
©2005 PAWS, INC. All Rights Reserved. www.garfield.com
Distributed by Universal Press Syndicate

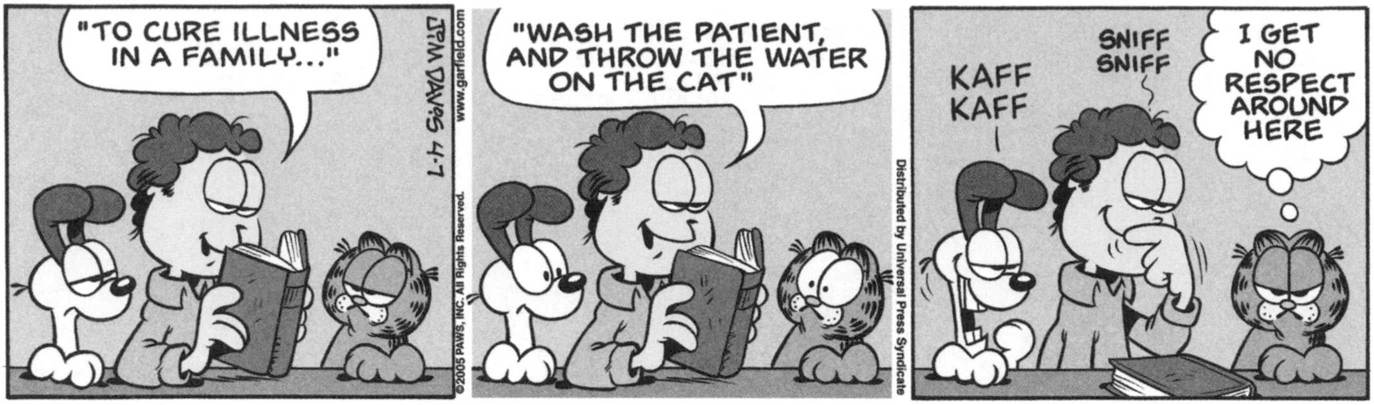
"TO CURE ILLNESS IN A FAMILY..."
JIM DAVIS 4-7
"WASH THE PATIENT, AND THROW THE WATER ON THE CAT"
KAFF KAFF
SNIFF SNIFF
I GET NO RESPECT AROUND HERE
©2005 PAWS, INC. All Rights Reserved. www.garfield.com
Distributed by Universal Press Syndicate

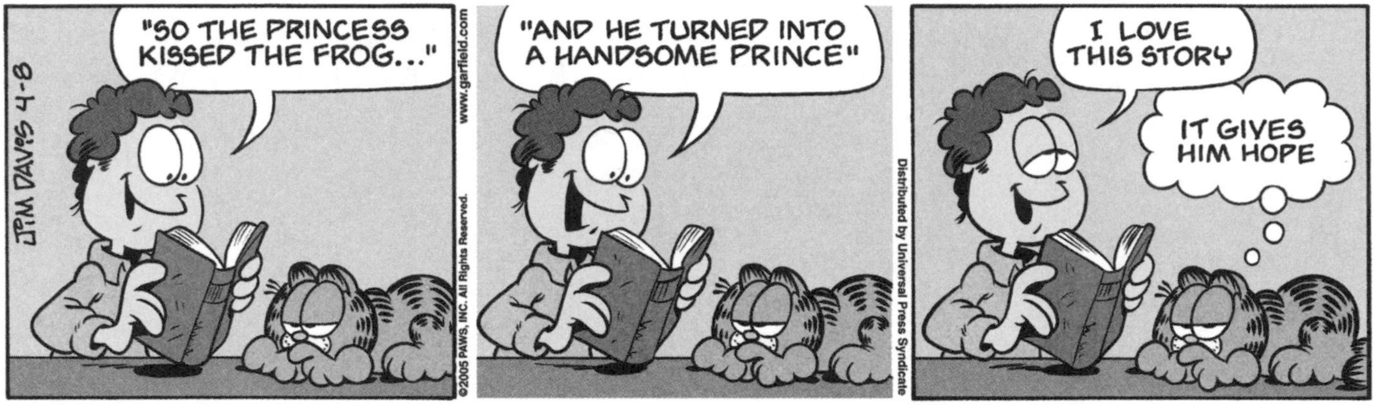
JIM DAVIS 4-8
"SO THE PRINCESS KISSED THE FROG..."
"AND HE TURNED INTO A HANDSOME PRINCE"
I LOVE THIS STORY
IT GIVES HIM HOPE
©2005 PAWS, INC. All Rights Reserved. www.garfield.com
Distributed by Universal Press Syndicate

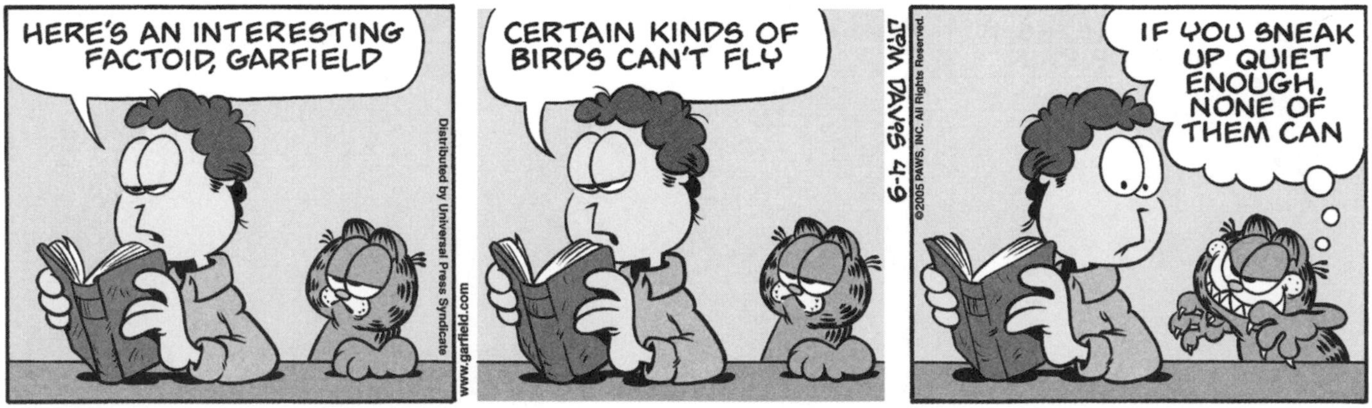
HERE'S AN INTERESTING FACTOID, GARFIELD
CERTAIN KINDS OF BIRDS CAN'T FLY
JIM DAVIS 4-9
IF YOU SNEAK UP QUIET ENOUGH, NONE OF THEM CAN
Distributed by Universal Press Syndicate www.garfield.com
©2005 PAWS, INC. All Rights Reserved.

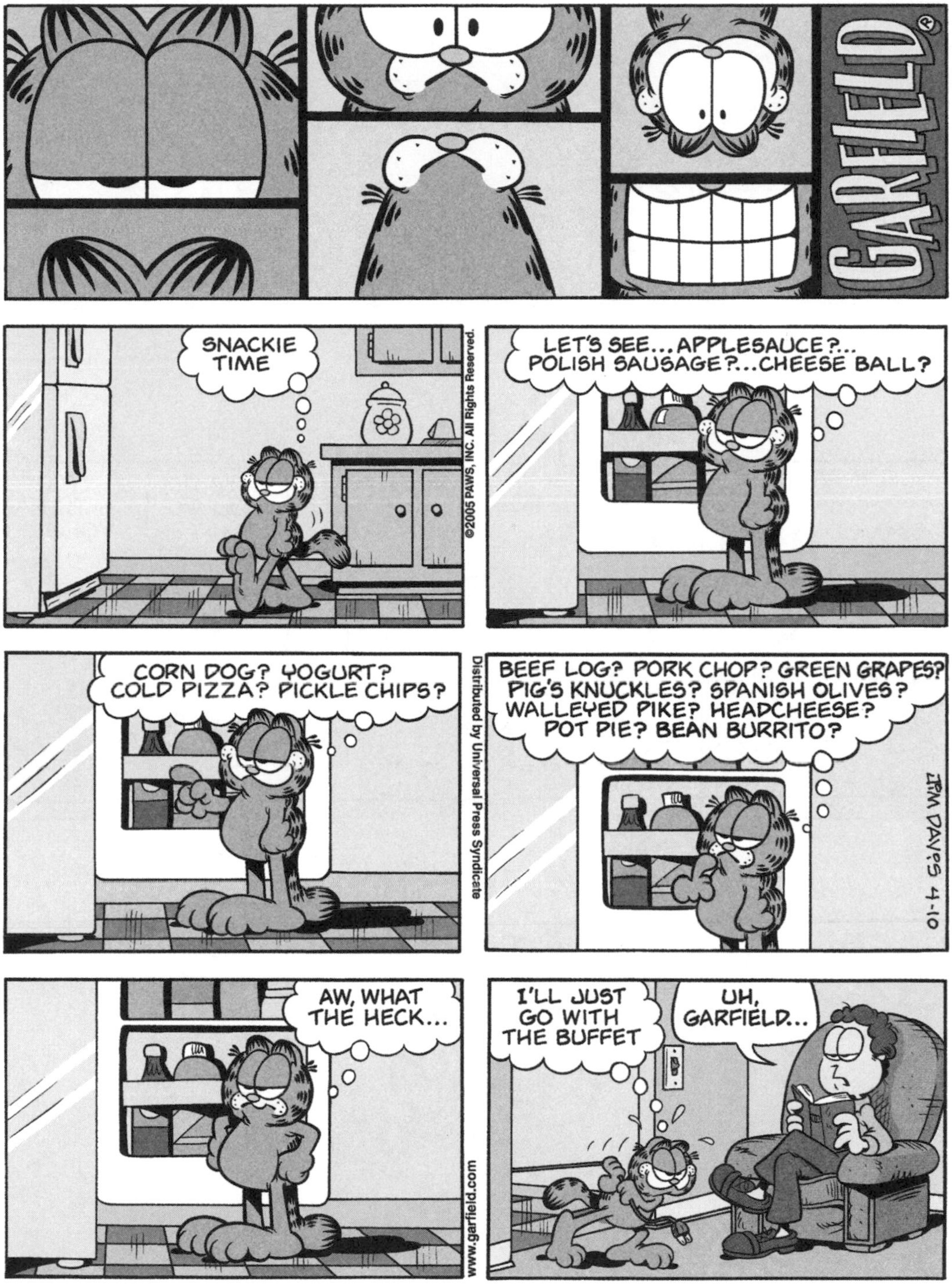
GARFIELD®
SNACKIE TIME
LET'S SEE... APPLESAUCE?... POLISH SAUSAGE?...CHEESE BALL?
CORN DOG? YOGURT? COLD PIZZA? PICKLE CHIPS?
BEEF LOG? PORK CHOP? GREEN GRAPES? PIG'S KNUCKLES? SPANISH OLIVES? WALLEYED PIKE? HEADCHEESE? POT PIE? BEAN BURRITO?
JIM DAVIS 4-10
AW, WHAT THE HECK...
I'LL JUST GO WITH THE BUFFET
UH, GARFIELD...
©2005 PAWS, INC. All Rights Reserved.
Distributed by Universal Press Syndicate
www.garfield.com

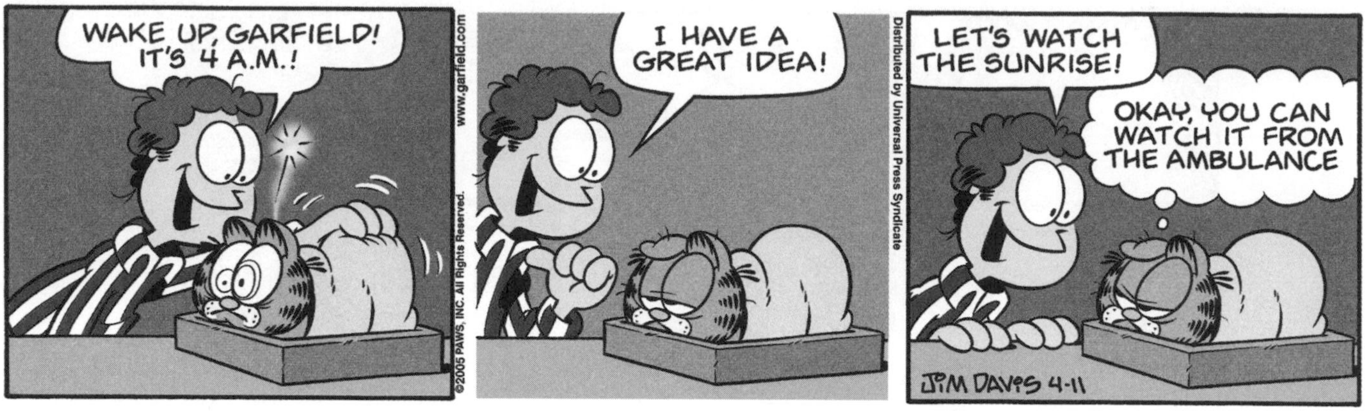
WAKE UP, GARFIELD! IT'S 4 A.M.!
I HAVE A GREAT IDEA!
LET'S WATCH THE SUNRISE!
OKAY, YOU CAN WATCH IT FROM THE AMBULANCE
JIM DAVIS 4-11
©2005 PAWS, INC. All Rights Reserved. www.garfield.com
Distributed by Universal Press Syndicate

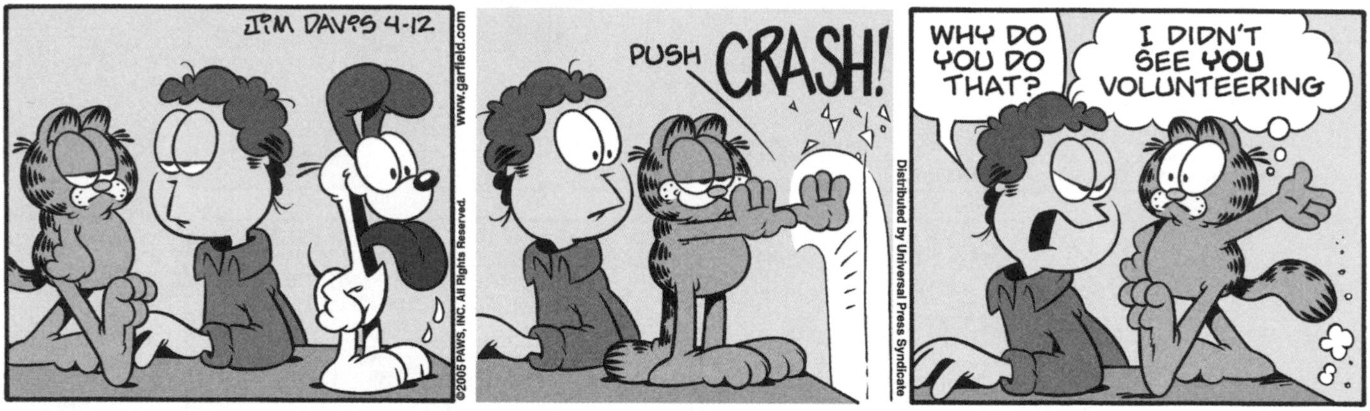
JIM DAVIS 4-12
PUSH
CRASH!
WHY DO YOU DO THAT?
I DIDN'T SEE **YOU** VOLUNTEERING
©2005 PAWS, INC. All Rights Reserved. www.garfield.com
Distributed by Universal Press Syndicate

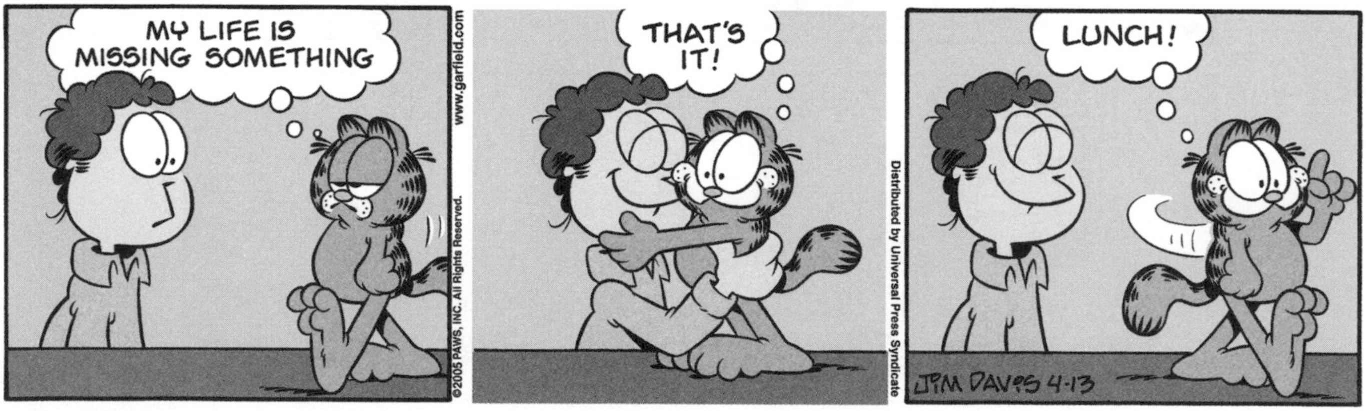
MY LIFE IS MISSING SOMETHING
THAT'S IT!
LUNCH!
JIM DAVIS 4-13
©2005 PAWS, INC. All Rights Reserved. www.garfield.com
Distributed by Universal Press Syndicate

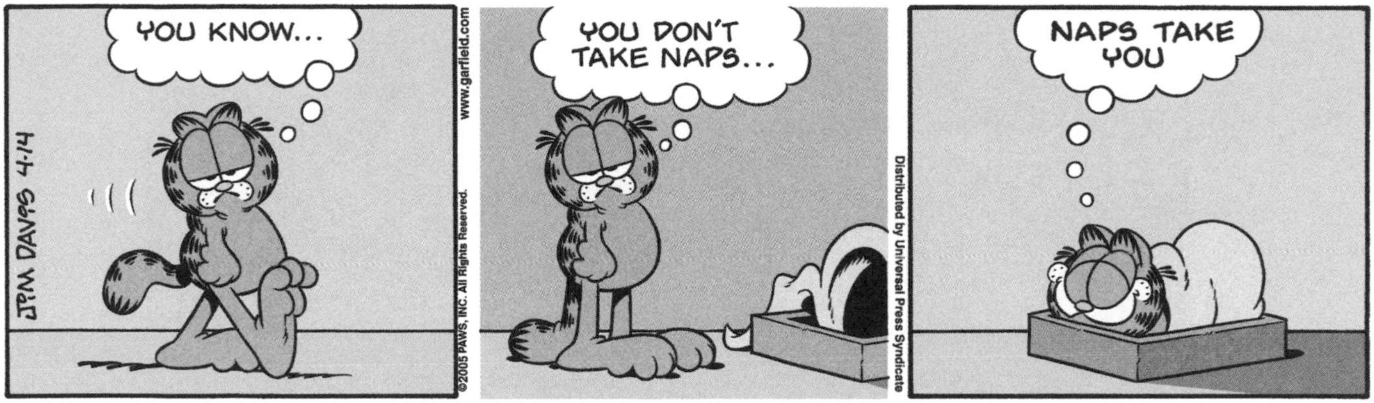
YOU KNOW...
JIM DAVIS 4·14
www.garfield.com
©2005 PAWS, INC. All Rights Reserved.
YOU DON'T TAKE NAPS...
Distributed by Universal Press Syndicate
NAPS TAKE YOU

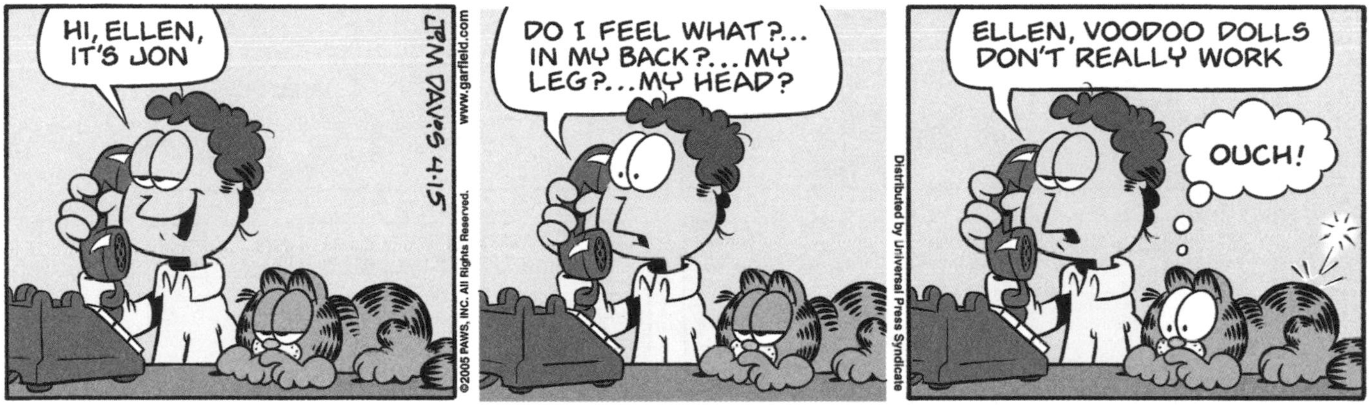
HI, ELLEN, IT'S JON
JIM DAVIS 4·15
www.garfield.com
©2005 PAWS, INC. All Rights Reserved.
DO I FEEL WHAT?... IN MY BACK?... MY LEG?... MY HEAD?
Distributed by Universal Press Syndicate
ELLEN, VOODOO DOLLS DON'T REALLY WORK
OUCH!

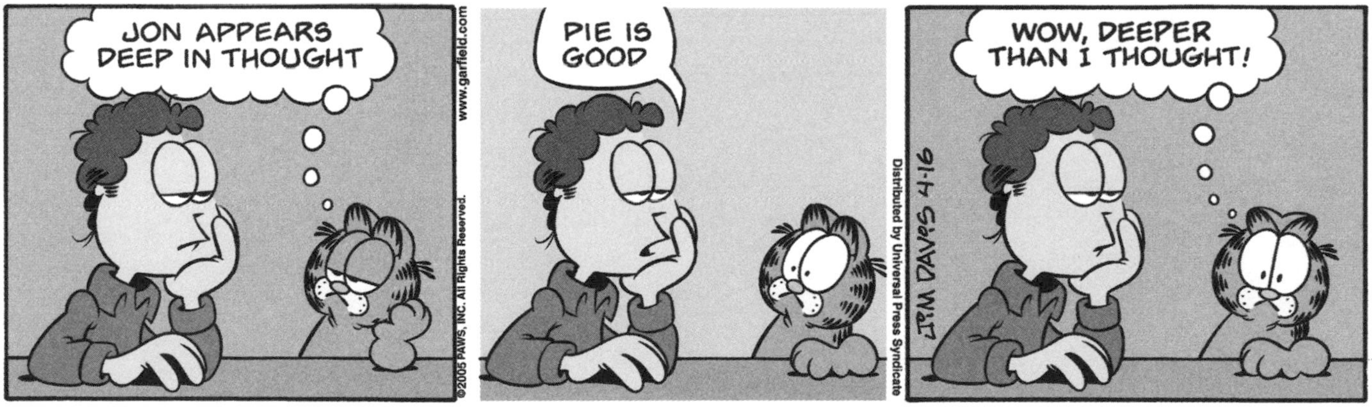
JON APPEARS DEEP IN THOUGHT
www.garfield.com
©2005 PAWS, INC. All Rights Reserved.
PIE IS GOOD
Distributed by Universal Press Syndicate
JIM DAVIS 4·16
WOW, DEEPER THAN I THOUGHT!

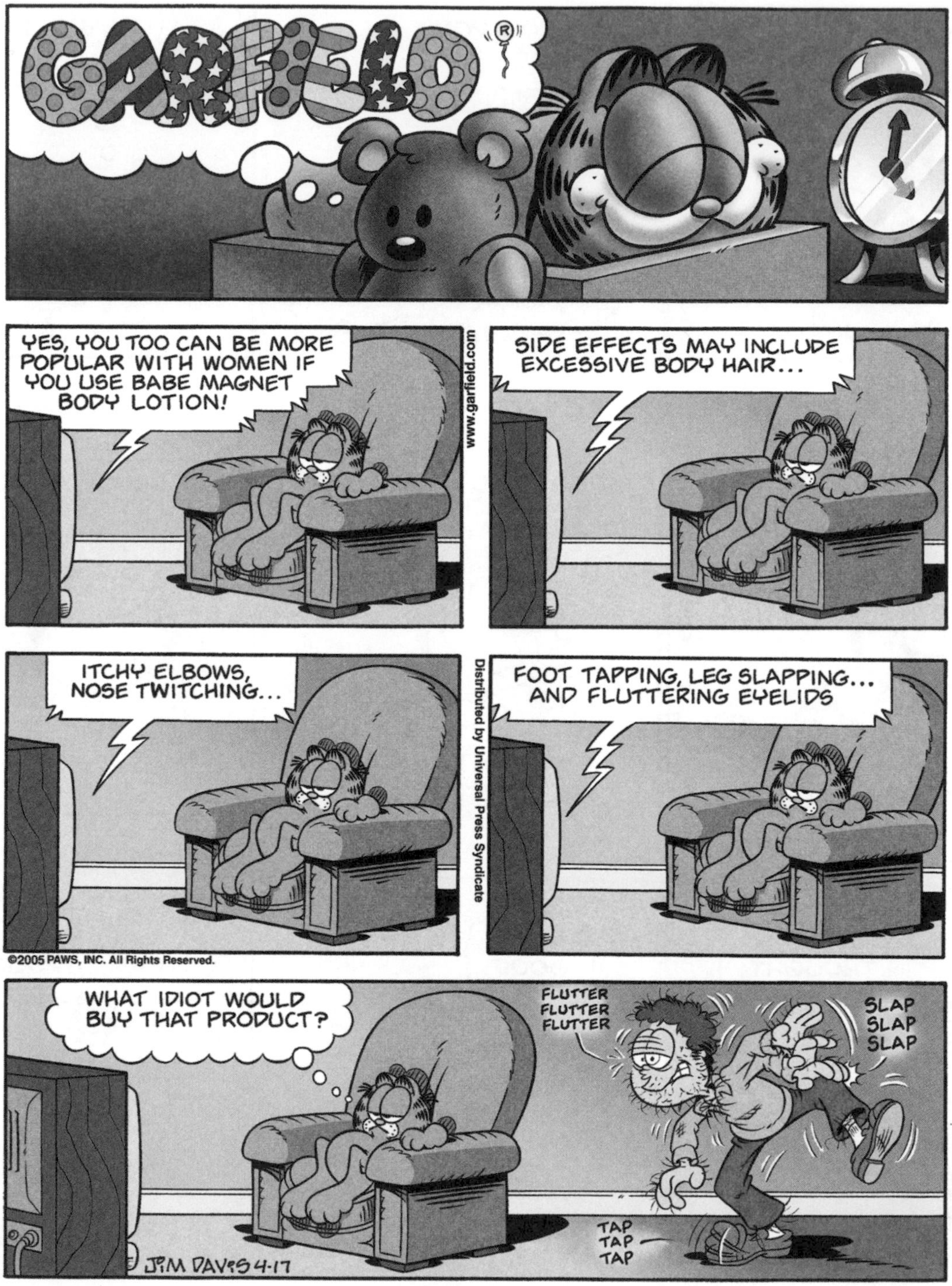
GARFIELD®
YES, YOU TOO CAN BE MORE POPULAR WITH WOMEN IF YOU USE BABE MAGNET BODY LOTION!
www.garfield.com
SIDE EFFECTS MAY INCLUDE EXCESSIVE BODY HAIR...
ITCHY ELBOWS, NOSE TWITCHING...
Distributed by Universal Press Syndicate
FOOT TAPPING, LEG SLAPPING... AND FLUTTERING EYELIDS
©2005 PAWS, INC. All Rights Reserved.
WHAT IDIOT WOULD BUY THAT PRODUCT?
FLUTTER FLUTTER FLUTTER
SLAP SLAP SLAP
TAP TAP TAP
JIM DAVIS 4-17

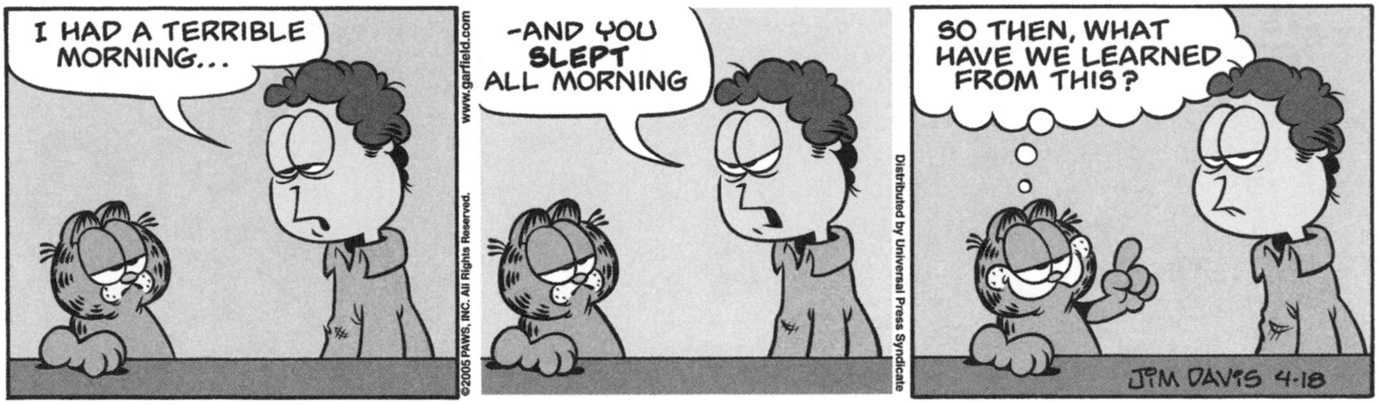
I HAD A TERRIBLE MORNING...
-AND YOU SLEPT ALL MORNING
SO THEN, WHAT HAVE WE LEARNED FROM THIS?
JIM DAVIS 4-18
©2005 PAWS, INC. All Rights Reserved. www.garfield.com
Distributed by Universal Press Syndicate

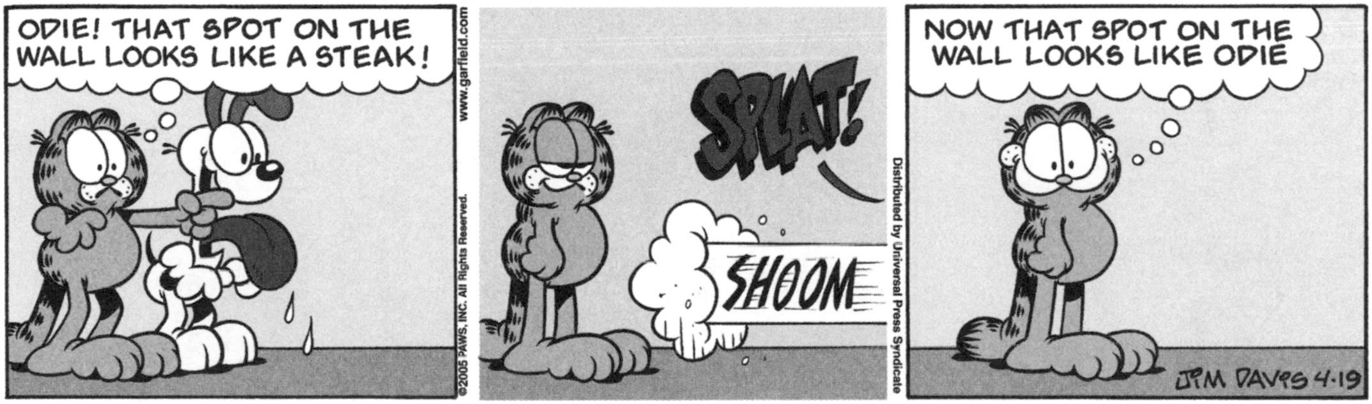
ODIE! THAT SPOT ON THE WALL LOOKS LIKE A STEAK!
SPLAT!
SHOOM
NOW THAT SPOT ON THE WALL LOOKS LIKE ODIE
JIM DAVIS 4-19
©2005 PAWS, INC. All Rights Reserved. www.garfield.com
Distributed by Universal Press Syndicate

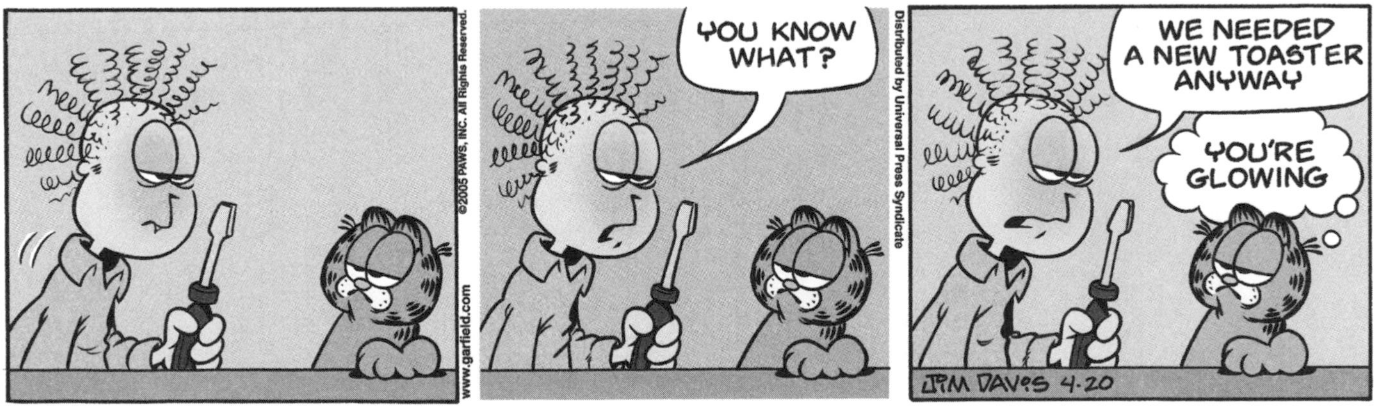
YOU KNOW WHAT?
WE NEEDED A NEW TOASTER ANYWAY
YOU'RE GLOWING
JIM DAVIS 4-20
©2005 PAWS, INC. All Rights Reserved. www.garfield.com
Distributed by Universal Press Syndicate

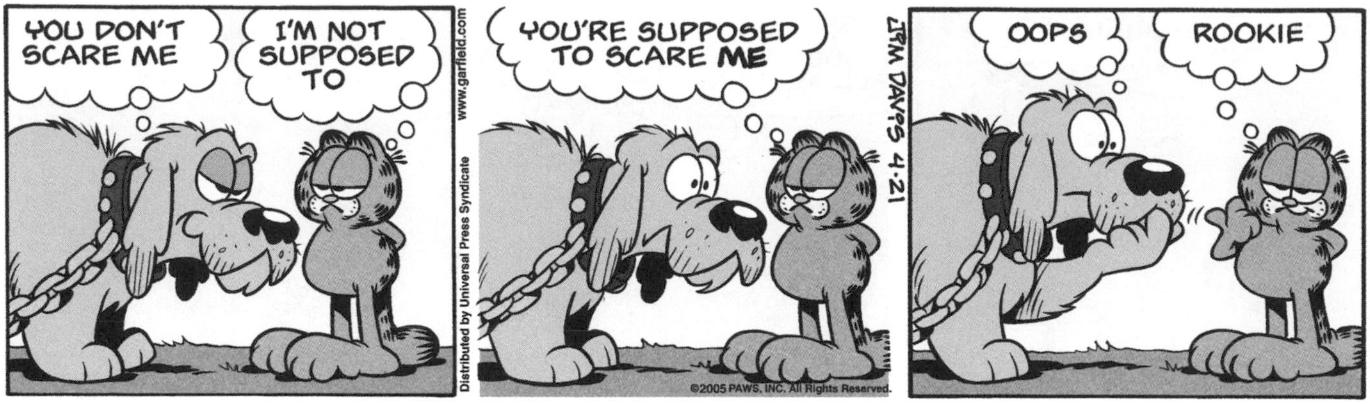
YOU DON'T SCARE ME
I'M NOT SUPPOSED TO
YOU'RE SUPPOSED TO SCARE ME
OOPS
ROOKIE
JIM DAVIS 4·21
www.garfield.com
Distributed by Universal Press Syndicate
©2005 PAWS, INC. All Rights Reserved.

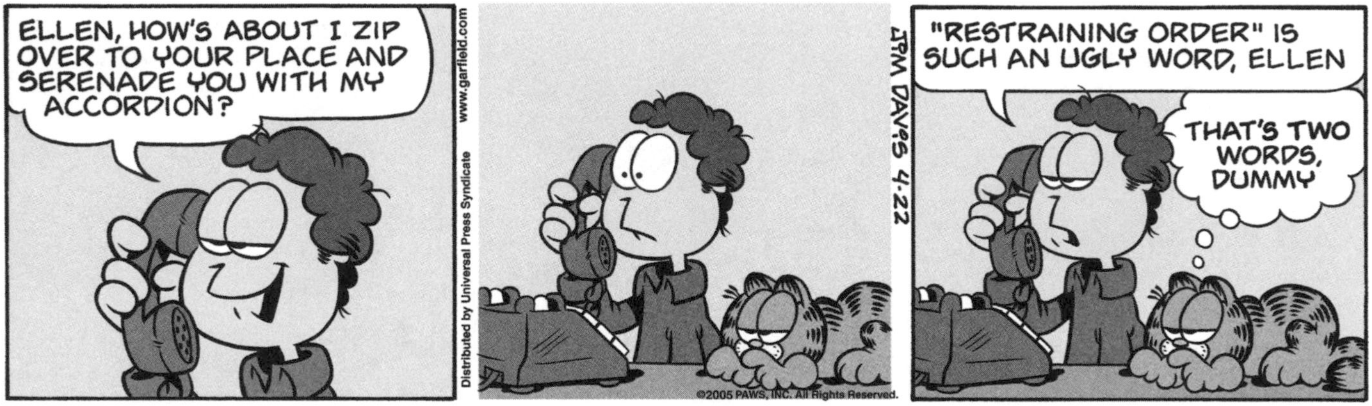
ELLEN, HOW'S ABOUT I ZIP OVER TO YOUR PLACE AND SERENADE YOU WITH MY ACCORDION?
"RESTRAINING ORDER" IS SUCH AN UGLY WORD, ELLEN
THAT'S TWO WORDS, DUMMY
JIM DAVIS 4·22
www.garfield.com
Distributed by Universal Press Syndicate
©2005 PAWS, INC. All Rights Reserved.

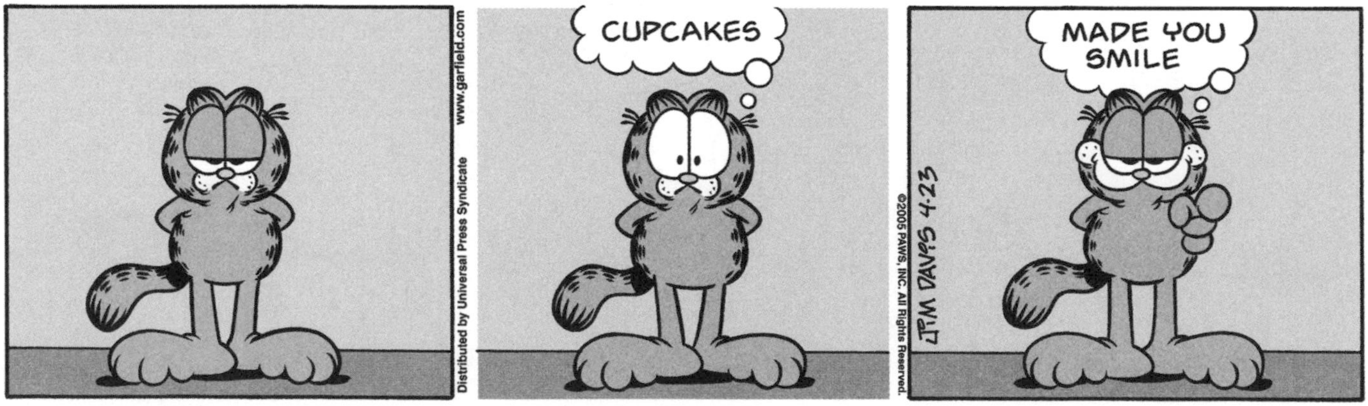
CUPCAKES
MADE YOU SMILE
JIM DAVIS 4·23
www.garfield.com
Distributed by Universal Press Syndicate
©2005 PAWS, INC. All Rights Reserved.

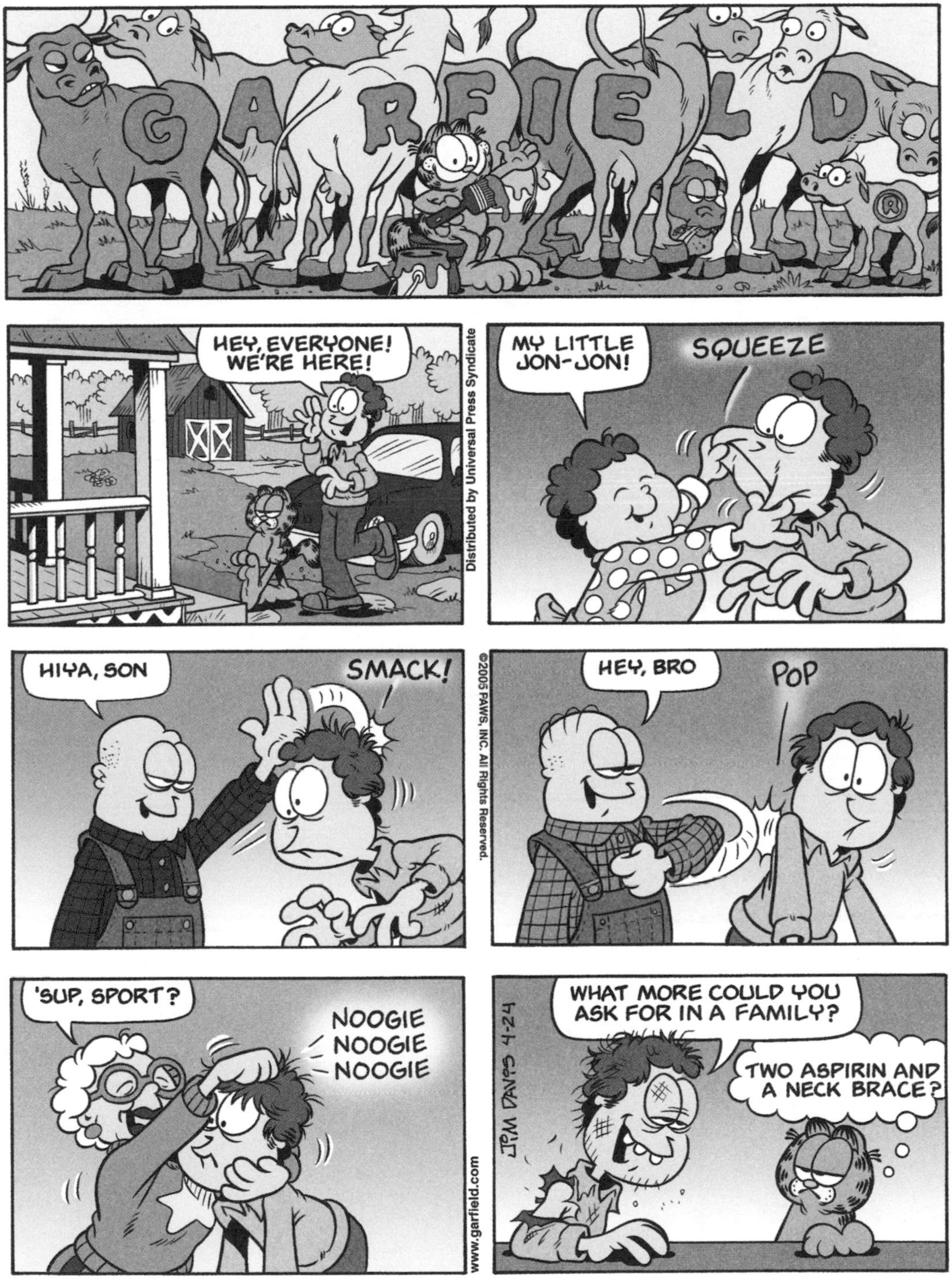
GARFIELD
®
HEY, EVERYONE! WE'RE HERE!
Distributed by Universal Press Syndicate
MY LITTLE JON-JON!
SQUEEZE
HIYA, SON
SMACK!
©2005 PAWS, INC. All Rights Reserved.
HEY, BRO
POP
'SUP, SPORT?
NOOGIE NOOGIE NOOGIE
JIM DAVIS 4-24
www.garfield.com
WHAT MORE COULD YOU ASK FOR IN A FAMILY?
TWO ASPIRIN AND A NECK BRACE?

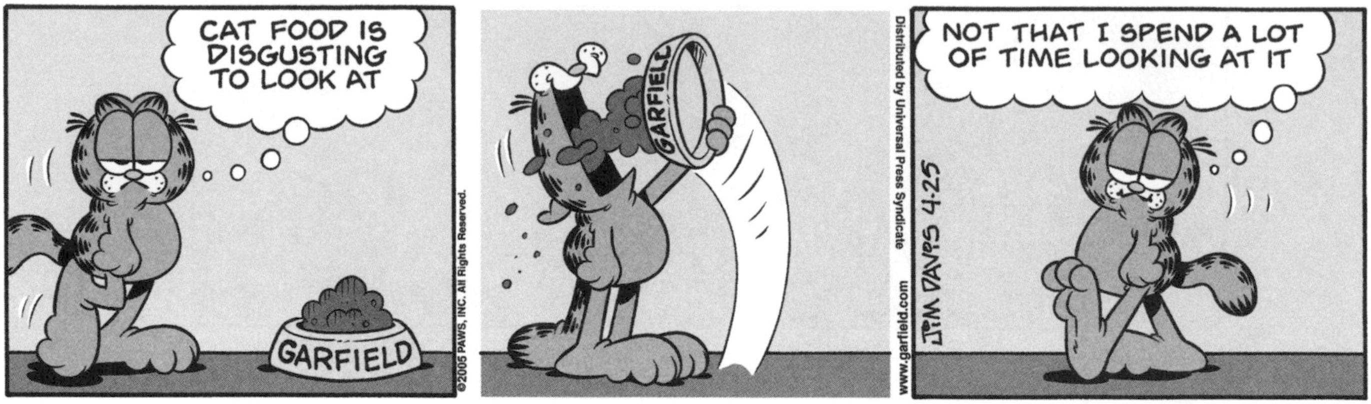
CAT FOOD IS DISGUSTING TO LOOK AT
GARFIELD
NOT THAT I SPEND A LOT OF TIME LOOKING AT IT

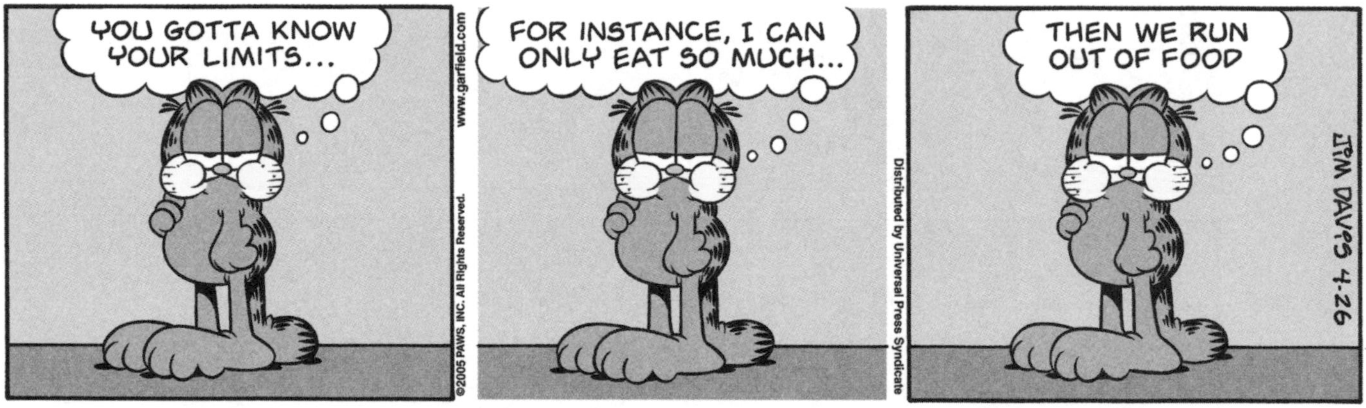
YOU GOTTA KNOW YOUR LIMITS...
FOR INSTANCE, I CAN ONLY EAT SO MUCH...
THEN WE RUN OUT OF FOOD

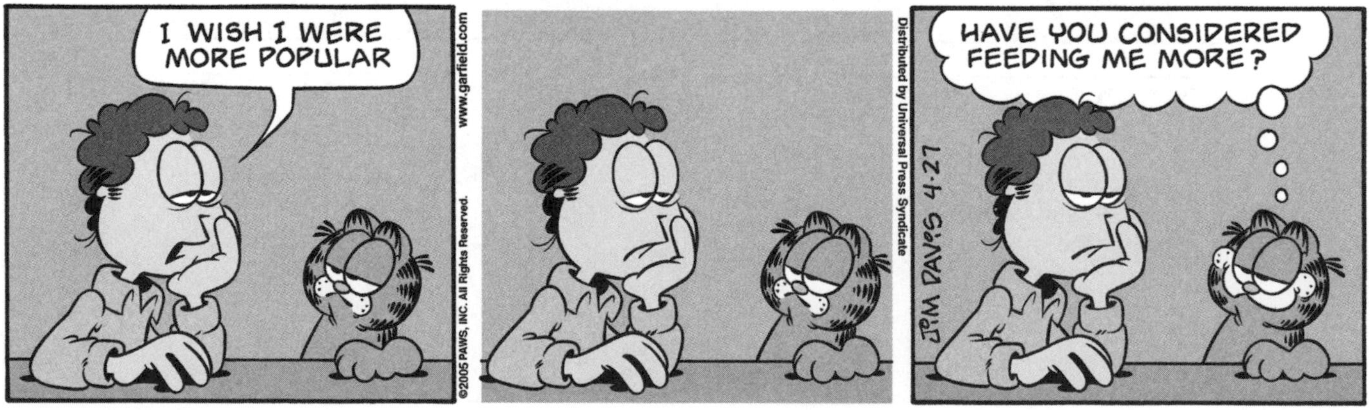
I WISH I WERE MORE POPULAR
HAVE YOU CONSIDERED FEEDING ME MORE?

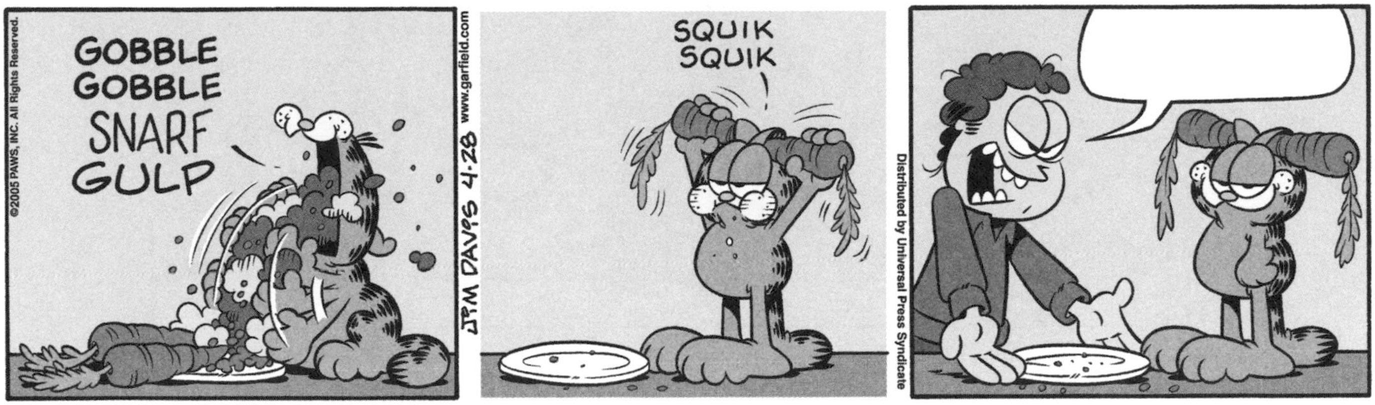
GOBBLE
GOBBLE
SNARF
GULP
©2005 PAWS, INC. All Rights Reserved.
JIM DAVIS 4-28
www.garfield.com
SQUIK
SQUIK
Distributed by Universal Press Syndicate

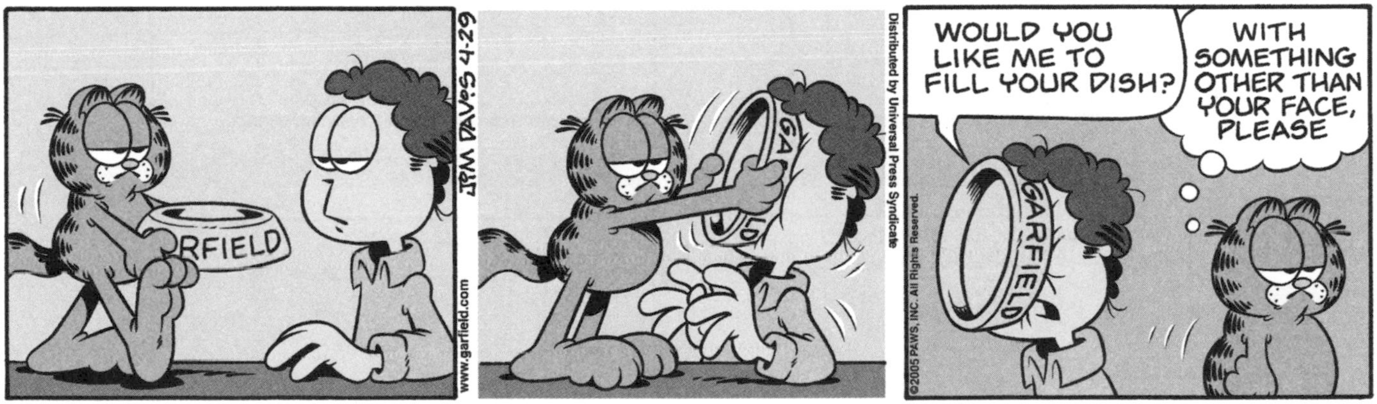
JIM DAVIS 4-29
www.garfield.com
RFIELD
Distributed by Universal Press Syndicate
WOULD YOU LIKE ME TO FILL YOUR DISH?
WITH SOMETHING OTHER THAN YOUR FACE, PLEASE
GARFIELD
©2005 PAWS, INC. All Rights Reserved.

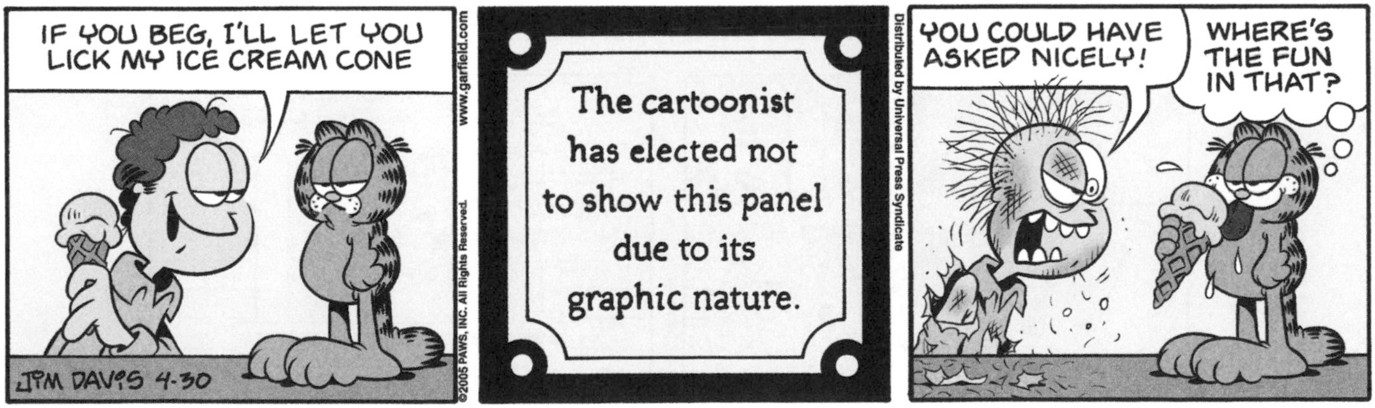
IF YOU BEG, I'LL LET YOU LICK MY ICE CREAM CONE
JIM DAVIS 4-30
www.garfield.com
©2005 PAWS, INC. All Rights Reserved.
The cartoonist has elected not to show this panel due to its graphic nature.
Distributed by Universal Press Syndicate
YOU COULD HAVE ASKED NICELY!
WHERE'S THE FUN IN THAT?

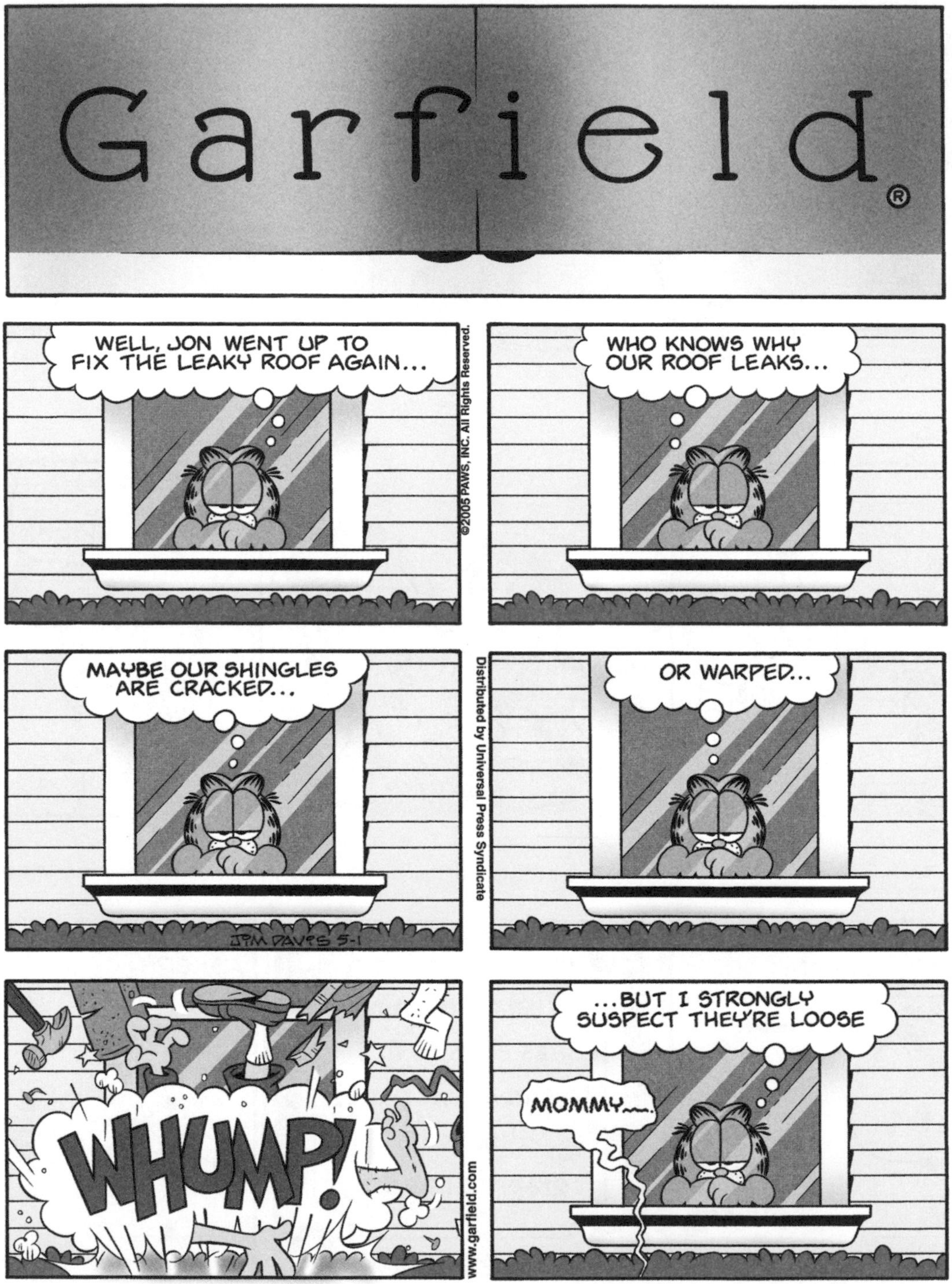
Garfield®
WELL, JON WENT UP TO FIX THE LEAKY ROOF AGAIN...
©2005 PAWS, INC. All Rights Reserved.
WHO KNOWS WHY OUR ROOF LEAKS...
MAYBE OUR SHINGLES ARE CRACKED...
Distributed by Universal Press Syndicate
OR WARPED...
JIM DAVIS 5-1
WHUMP!
www.garfield.com
...BUT I STRONGLY SUSPECT THEY'RE LOOSE
MOMMY....

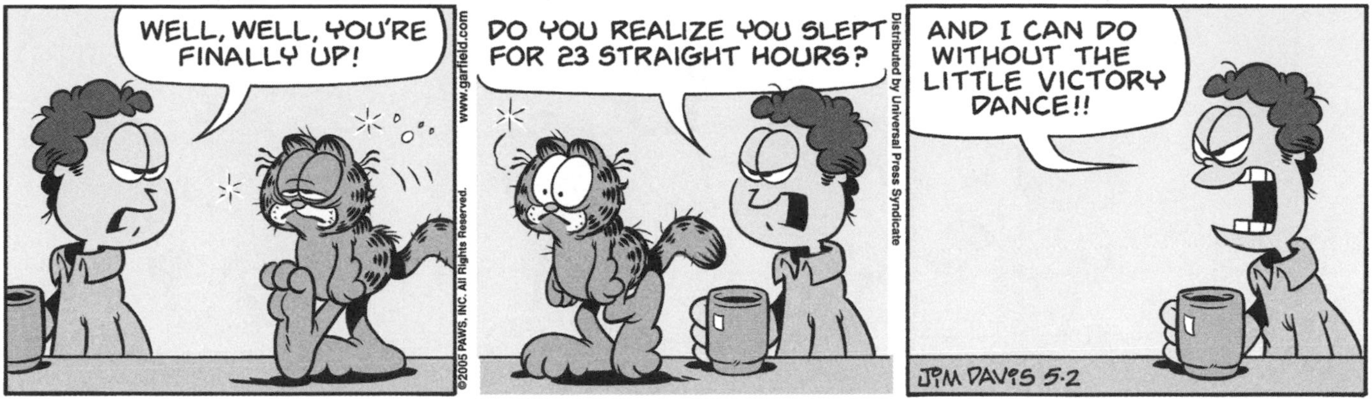
WELL, WELL, YOU'RE FINALLY UP!
www.garfield.com
©2005 PAWS, INC. All Rights Reserved.
DO YOU REALIZE YOU SLEPT FOR 23 STRAIGHT HOURS?
Distributed by Universal Press Syndicate
AND I CAN DO WITHOUT THE LITTLE VICTORY DANCE!!
JIM DAVIS 5-2

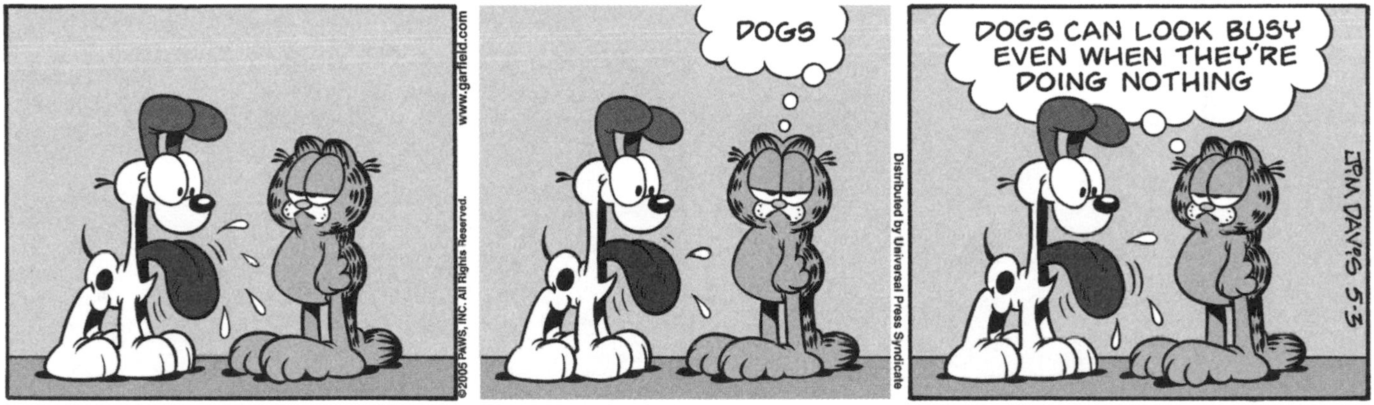
www.garfield.com
©2005 PAWS, INC. All Rights Reserved.
DOGS
Distributed by Universal Press Syndicate
DOGS CAN LOOK BUSY EVEN WHEN THEY'RE DOING NOTHING
JIM DAVIS 5-3

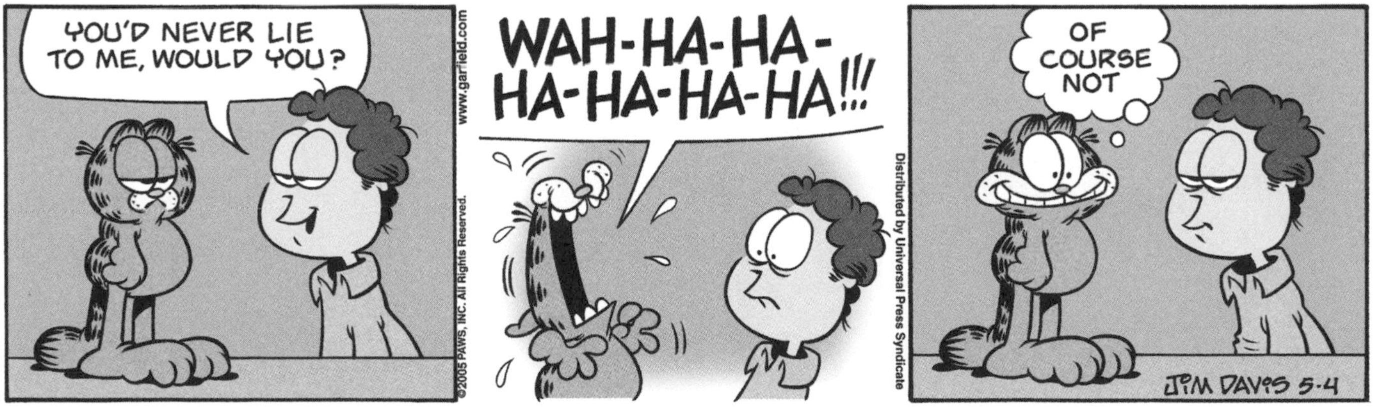
YOU'D NEVER LIE TO ME, WOULD YOU?
www.garfield.com
©2005 PAWS, INC. All Rights Reserved.
WAH-HA-HA-HA-HA-HA-HA!!!
Distributed by Universal Press Syndicate
OF COURSE NOT
JIM DAVIS 5-4

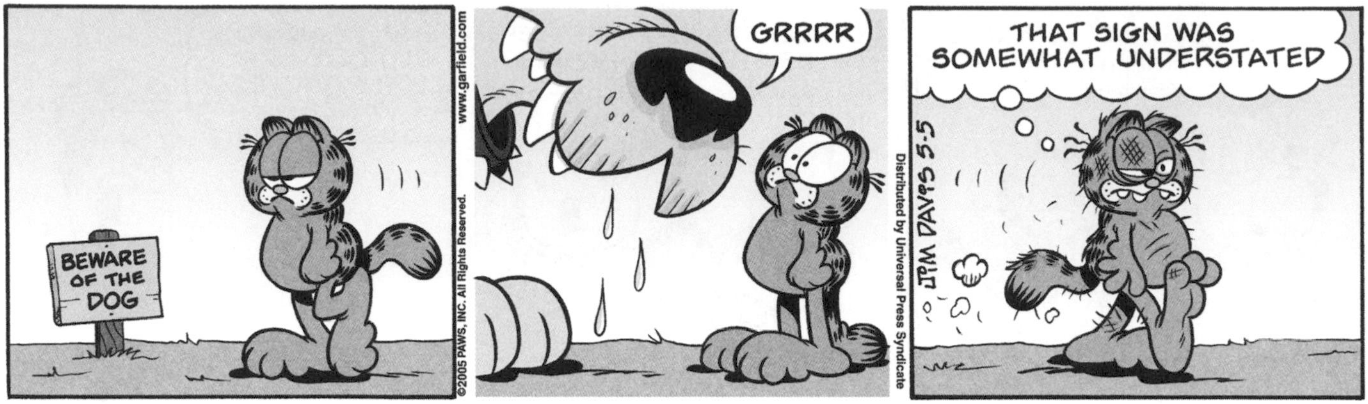
BEWARE OF THE DOG
GRRRR
THAT SIGN WAS SOMEWHAT UNDERSTATED
JIM DAVIS 5-5
©2005 PAWS, INC. All Rights Reserved.
www.garfield.com
Distributed by Universal Press Syndicate

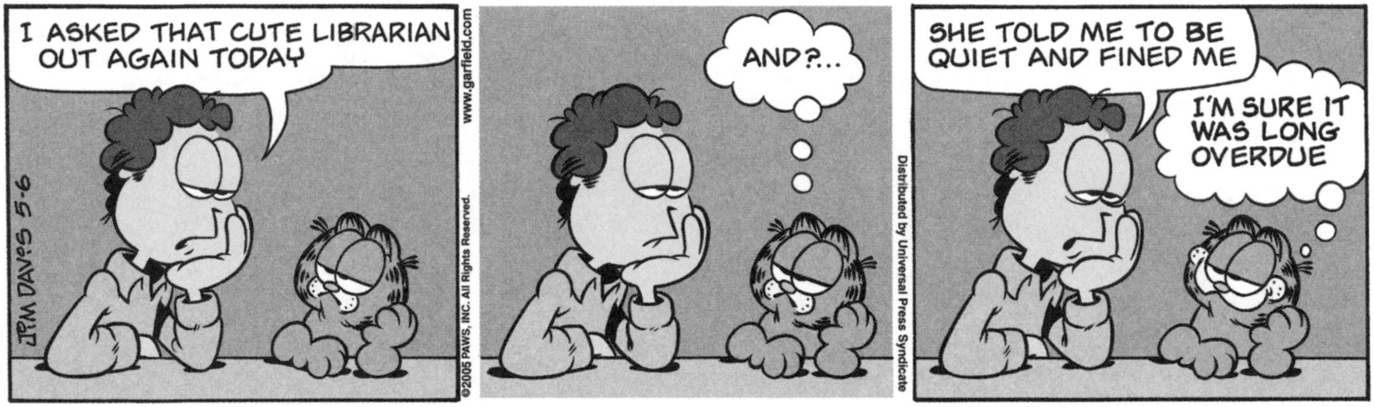
I ASKED THAT CUTE LIBRARIAN OUT AGAIN TODAY
AND?...
SHE TOLD ME TO BE QUIET AND FINED ME
I'M SURE IT WAS LONG OVERDUE
JIM DAVIS 5-6
©2005 PAWS, INC. All Rights Reserved.
www.garfield.com
Distributed by Universal Press Syndicate

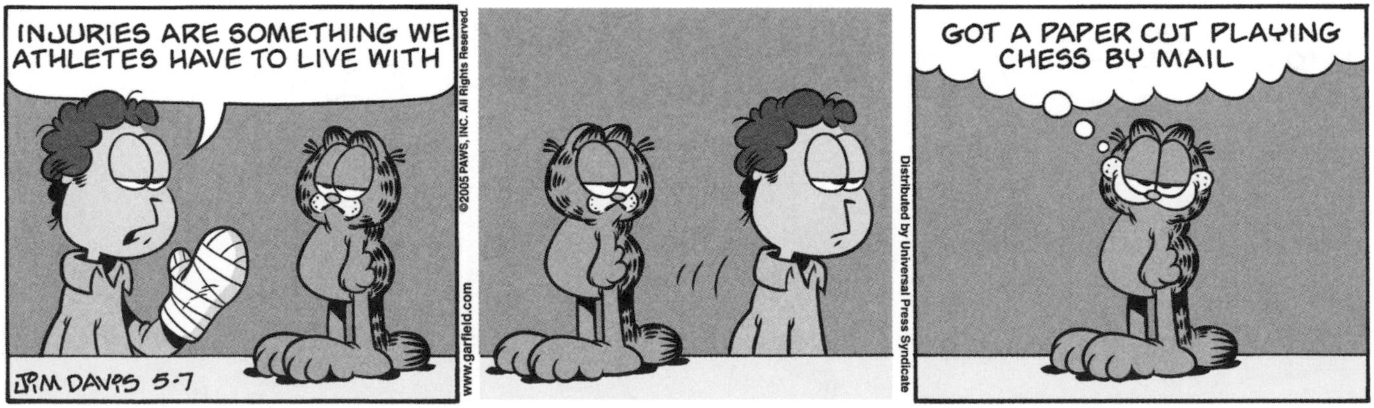
INJURIES ARE SOMETHING WE ATHLETES HAVE TO LIVE WITH
GOT A PAPER CUT PLAYING CHESS BY MAIL
JIM DAVIS 5-7
©2005 PAWS, INC. All Rights Reserved.
www.garfield.com
Distributed by Universal Press Syndicate

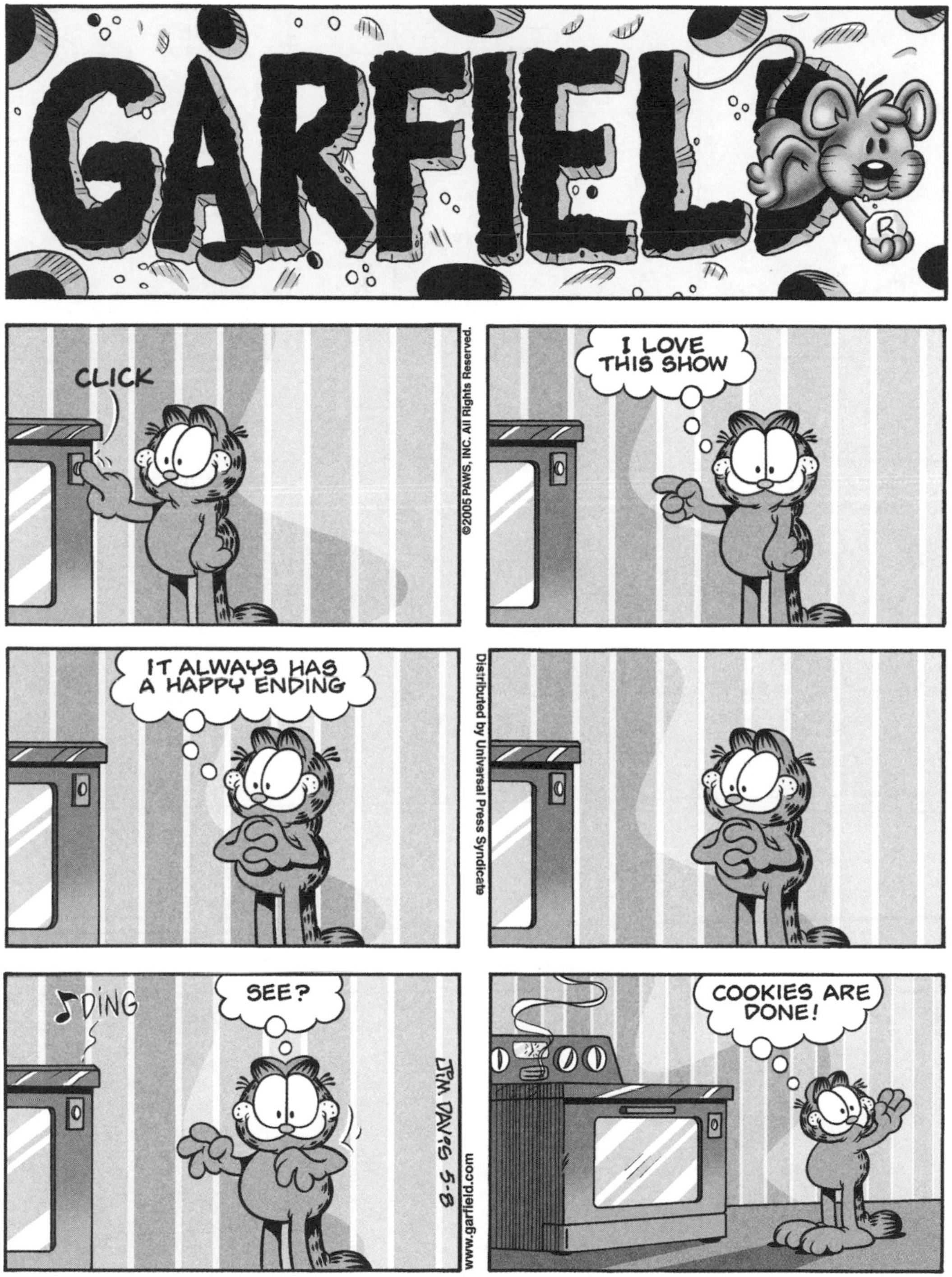
GARFIELD
CLICK
I LOVE THIS SHOW
IT ALWAYS HAS A HAPPY ENDING
DING
SEE?
COOKIES ARE DONE!
JPM DAVIS 5-8
©2005 PAWS, INC. All Rights Reserved.
Distributed by Universal Press Syndicate
www.garfield.com

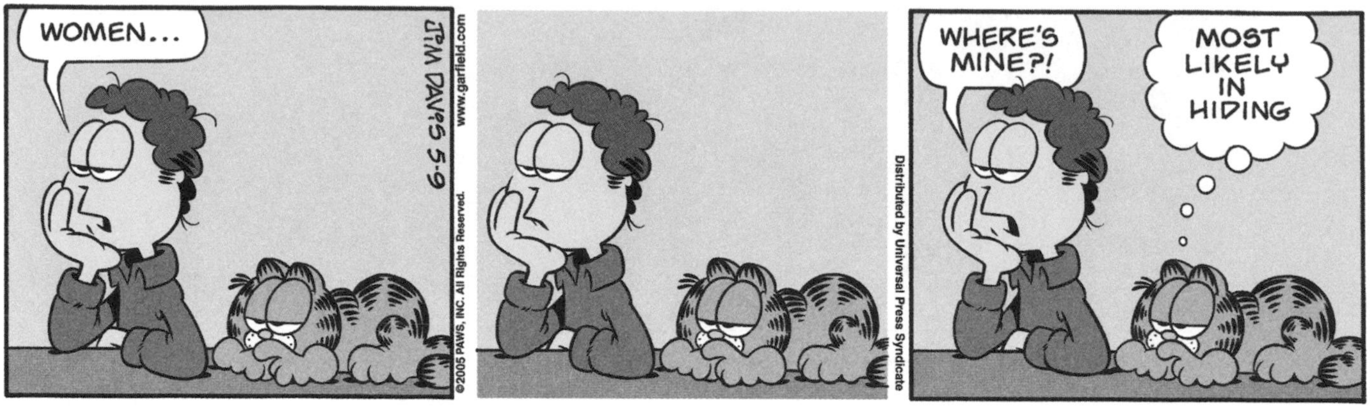
WOMEN...
JIM DAVIS 5-9
www.garfield.com
©2005 PAWS, INC. All Rights Reserved.
Distributed by Universal Press Syndicate
WHERE'S MINE?!
MOST LIKELY IN HIDING

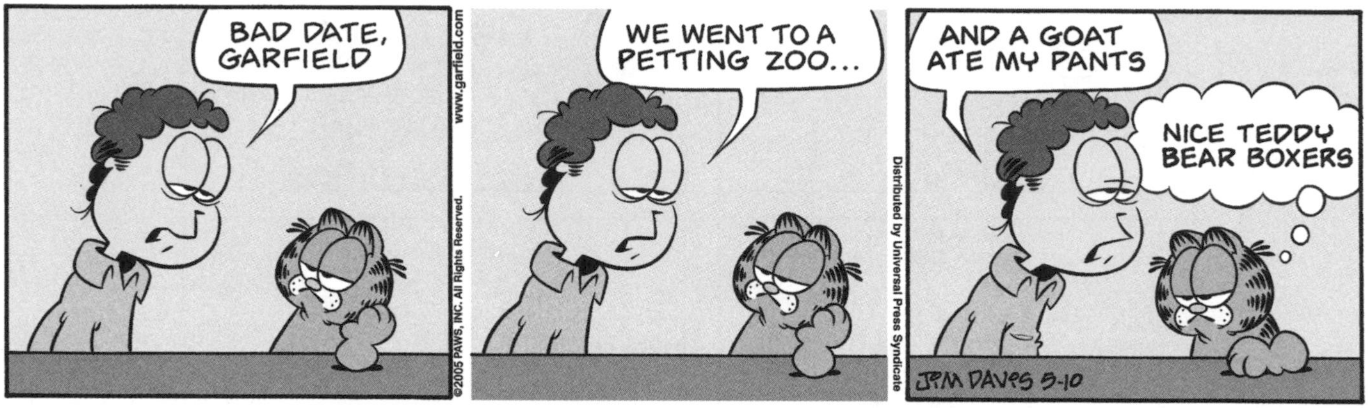
BAD DATE, GARFIELD
www.garfield.com
©2005 PAWS, INC. All Rights Reserved.
WE WENT TO A PETTING ZOO...
Distributed by Universal Press Syndicate
AND A GOAT ATE MY PANTS
NICE TEDDY BEAR BOXERS
JIM DAVIS 5-10

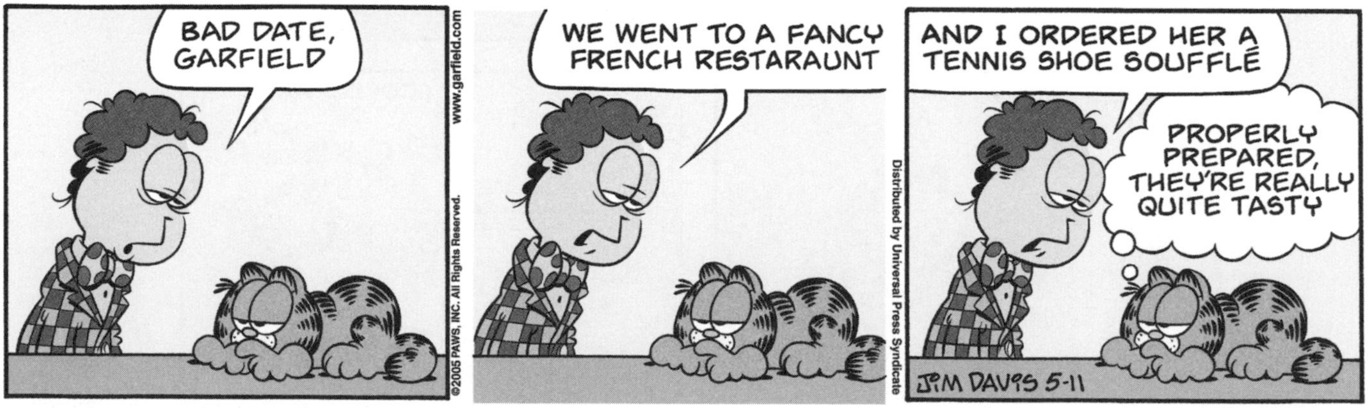
BAD DATE, GARFIELD
www.garfield.com
©2005 PAWS, INC. All Rights Reserved.
WE WENT TO A FANCY FRENCH RESTARAUNT
Distributed by Universal Press Syndicate
AND I ORDERED HER A TENNIS SHOE SOUFFLÉ
PROPERLY PREPARED, THEY'RE REALLY QUITE TASTY
JIM DAVIS 5-11

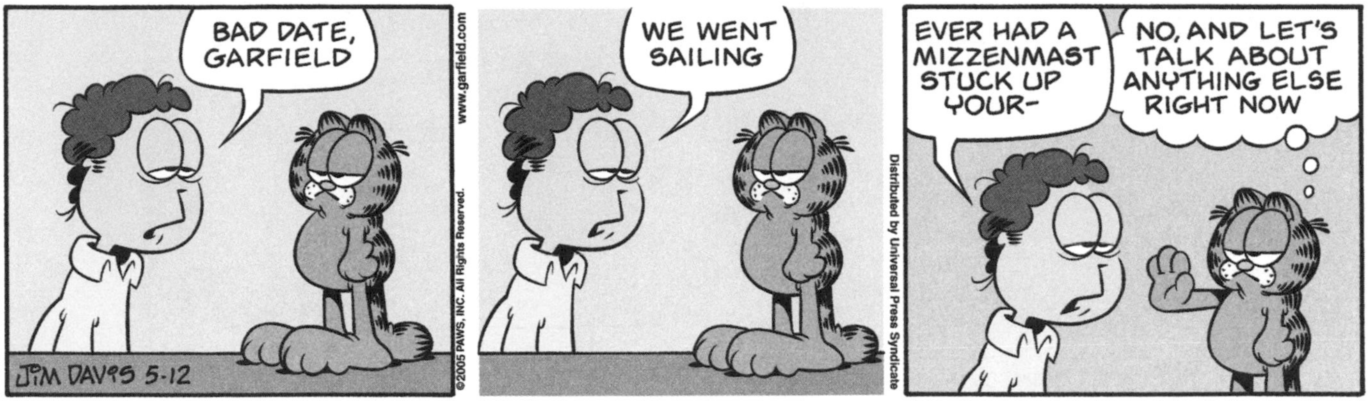
BAD DATE, GARFIELD
JIM DAVIS 5-12
©2005 PAWS, INC. All Rights Reserved. www.garfield.com
WE WENT SAILING
Distributed by Universal Press Syndicate
EVER HAD A MIZZENMAST STUCK UP YOUR-
NO, AND LET'S TALK ABOUT ANYTHING ELSE RIGHT NOW

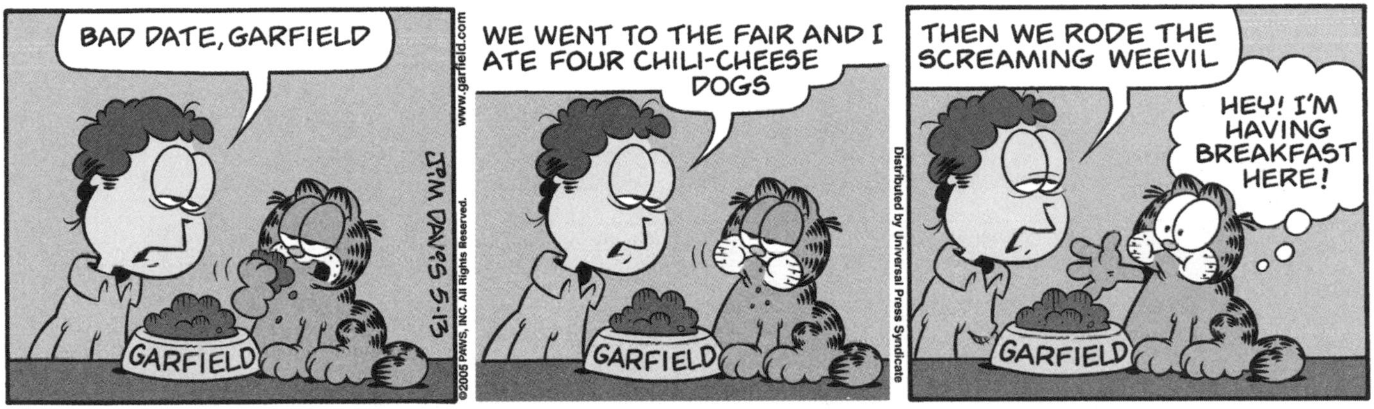
BAD DATE, GARFIELD
GARFIELD
JIM DAVIS 5-13
©2005 PAWS, INC. All Rights Reserved. www.garfield.com
WE WENT TO THE FAIR AND I ATE FOUR CHILI-CHEESE DOGS
GARFIELD
Distributed by Universal Press Syndicate
THEN WE RODE THE SCREAMING WEEVIL
HEY! I'M HAVING BREAKFAST HERE!
GARFIELD

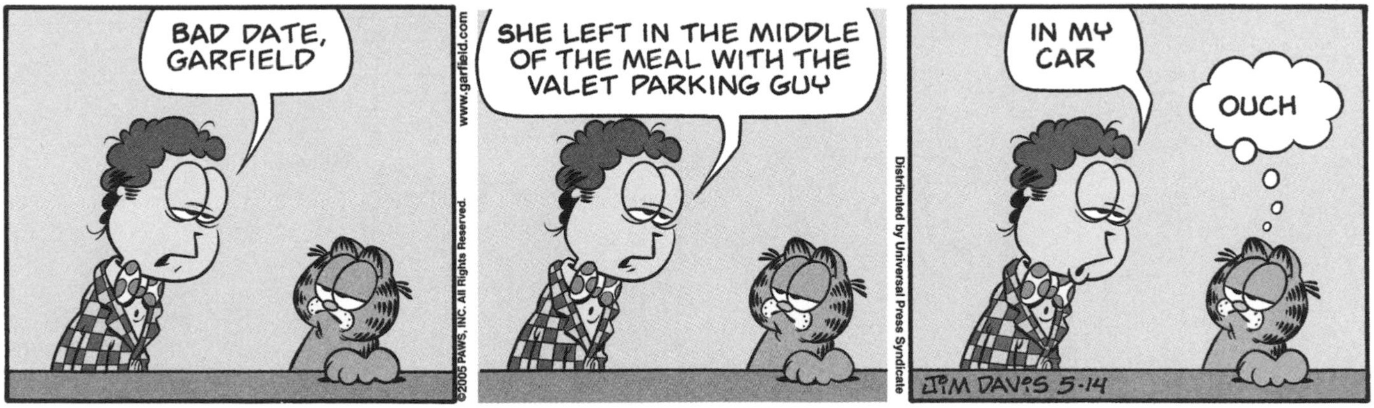
BAD DATE, GARFIELD
©2005 PAWS, INC. All Rights Reserved. www.garfield.com
SHE LEFT IN THE MIDDLE OF THE MEAL WITH THE VALET PARKING GUY
Distributed by Universal Press Syndicate
IN MY CAR
OUCH
JIM DAVIS 5-14

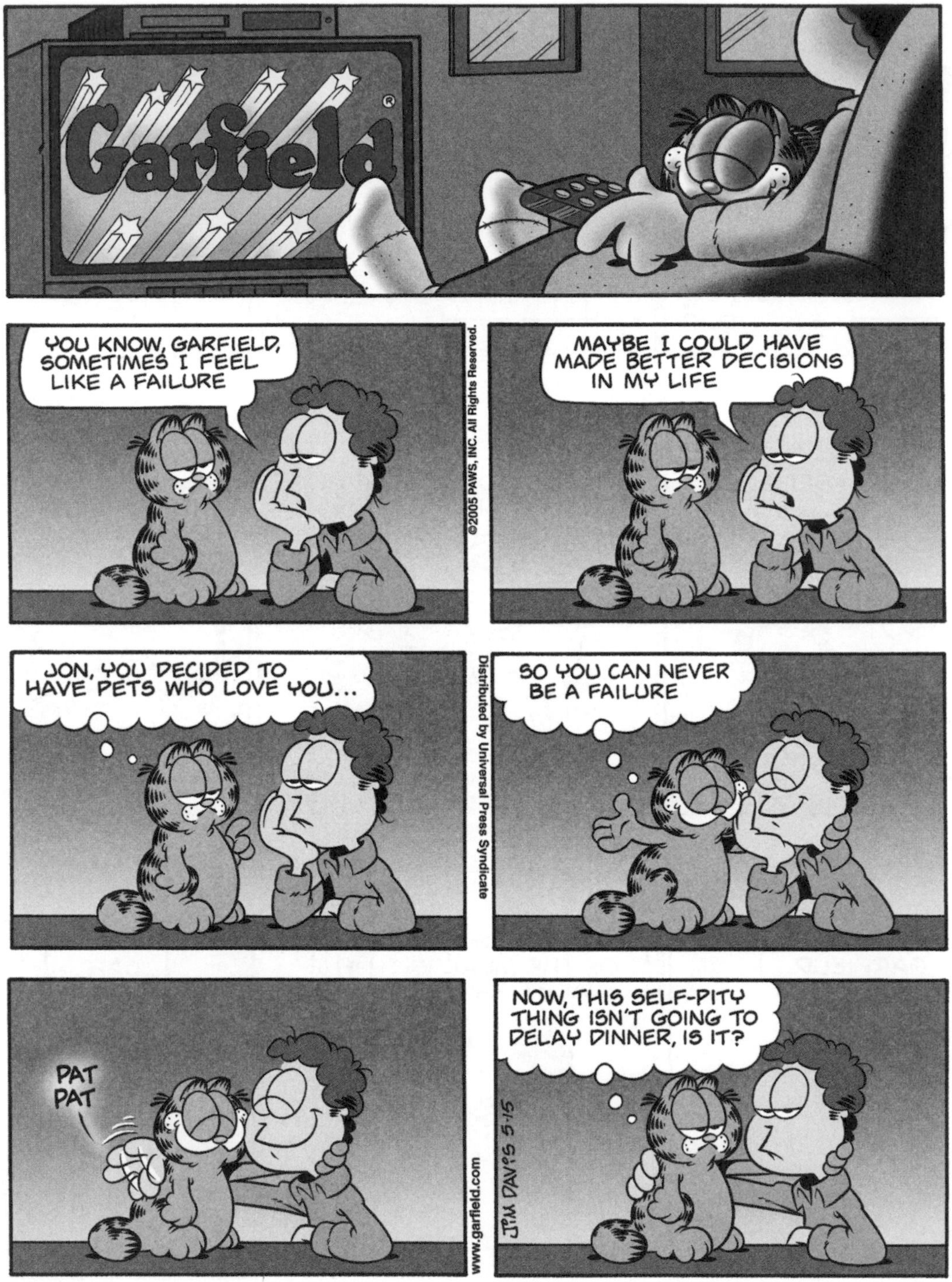
Garfield®
YOU KNOW, GARFIELD, SOMETIMES I FEEL LIKE A FAILURE
MAYBE I COULD HAVE MADE BETTER DECISIONS IN MY LIFE
JON, YOU DECIDED TO HAVE PETS WHO LOVE YOU...
SO YOU CAN NEVER BE A FAILURE
PAT PAT
NOW, THIS SELF-PITY THING ISN'T GOING TO DELAY DINNER, IS IT?
©2005 PAWS, INC. All Rights Reserved.
Distributed by Universal Press Syndicate
www.garfield.com
JPM DAVIS 5-15

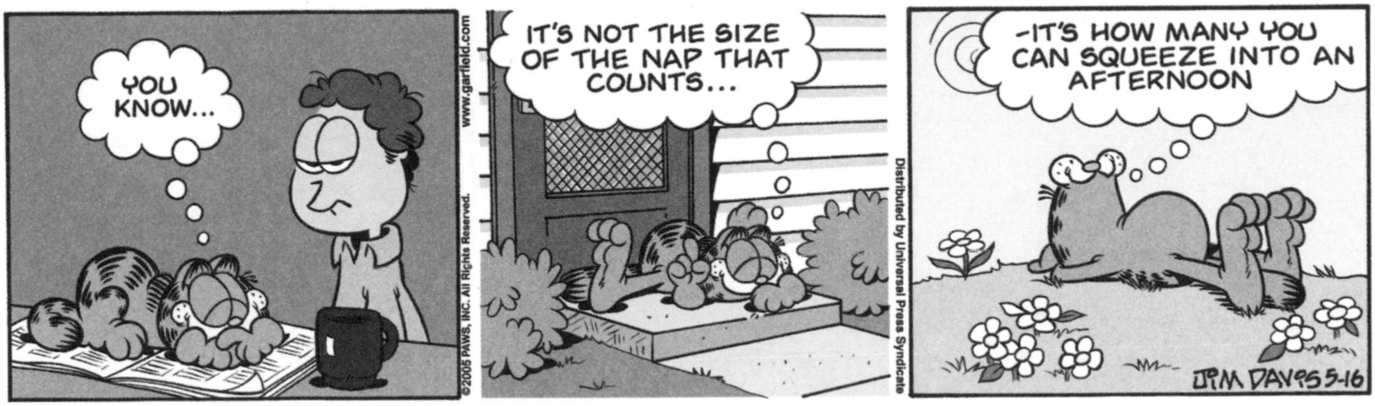
YOU KNOW...
IT'S NOT THE SIZE OF THE NAP THAT COUNTS...
-IT'S HOW MANY YOU CAN SQUEEZE INTO AN AFTERNOON
JIM DAVIS 5-16
©2005 PAWS, INC. All Rights Reserved. www.garfield.com
Distributed by Universal Press Syndicate

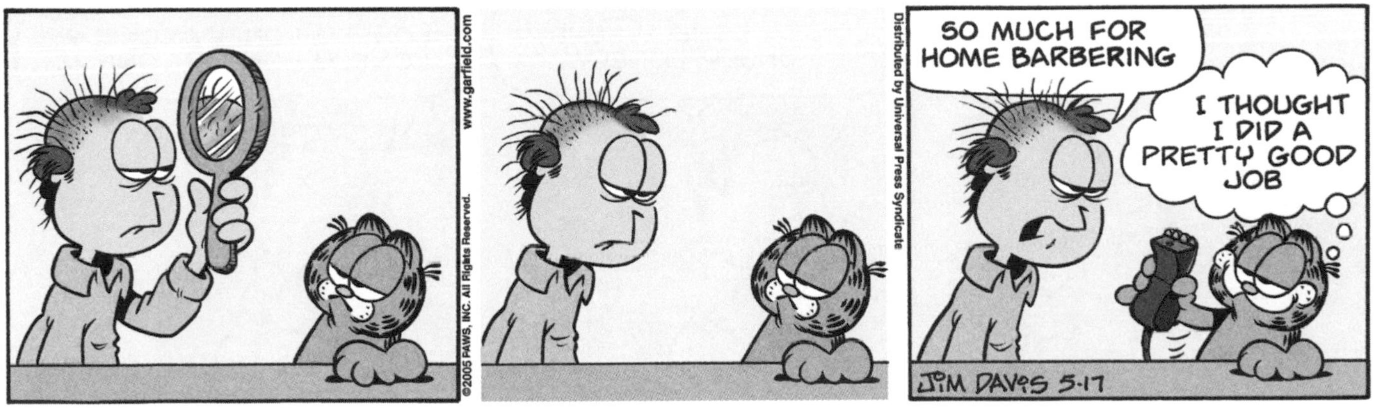
SO MUCH FOR HOME BARBERING
I THOUGHT I DID A PRETTY GOOD JOB
JIM DAVIS 5-17
©2005 PAWS, INC. All Rights Reserved. www.garfield.com
Distributed by Universal Press Syndicate

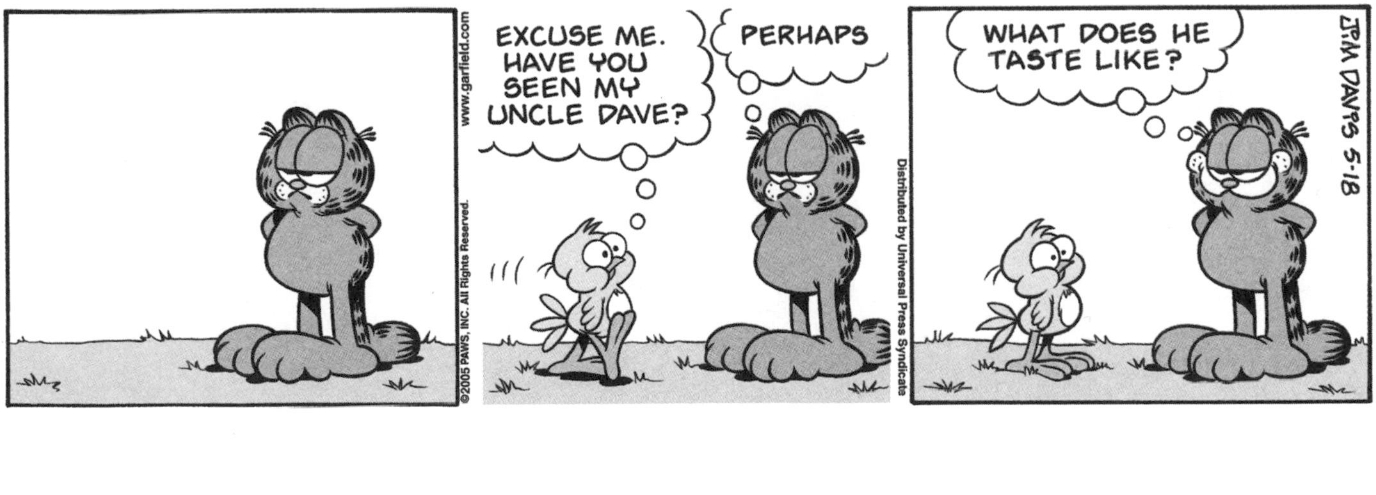
EXCUSE ME. HAVE YOU SEEN MY UNCLE DAVE?
PERHAPS
WHAT DOES HE TASTE LIKE?
JIM DAVIS 5-18
©2005 PAWS, INC. All Rights Reserved. www.garfield.com
Distributed by Universal Press Syndicate

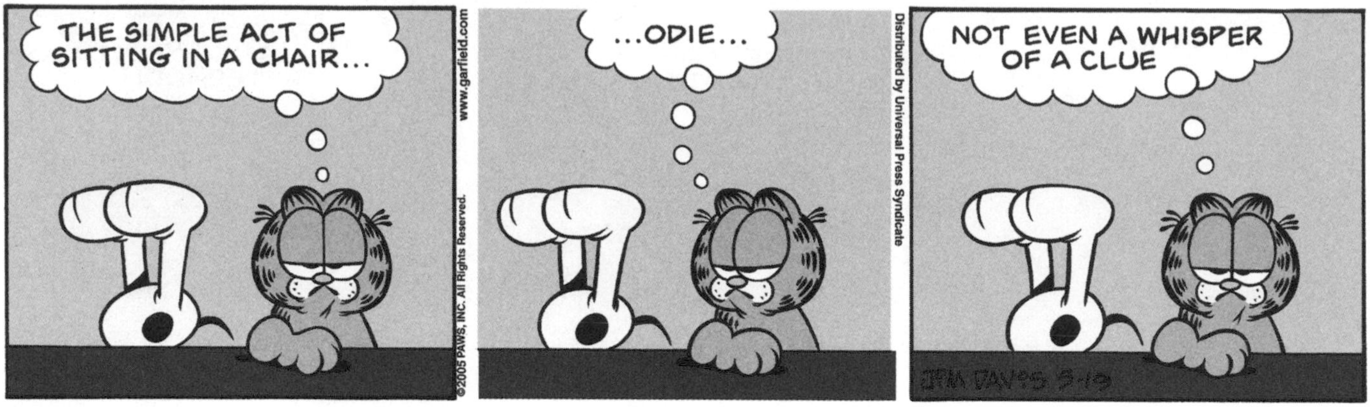
THE SIMPLE ACT OF SITTING IN A CHAIR...
...ODIE...
NOT EVEN A WHISPER OF A CLUE
JIM DAVIS 5-19
©2005 PAWS, INC. All Rights Reserved. www.garfield.com
Distributed by Universal Press Syndicate

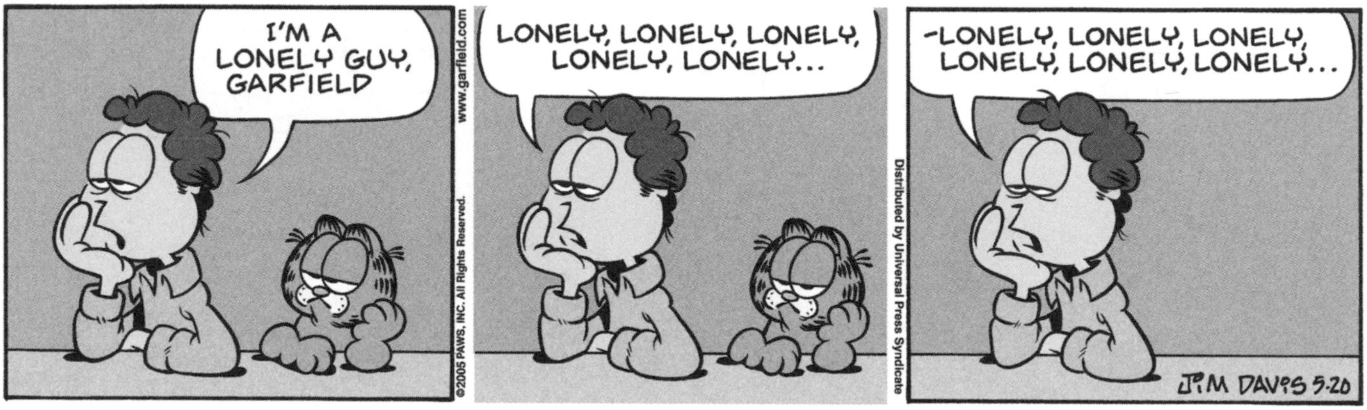
I'M A LONELY GUY, GARFIELD
LONELY, LONELY, LONELY, LONELY, LONELY...
-LONELY, LONELY, LONELY, LONELY, LONELY, LONELY...
JIM DAVIS 5-20
©2005 PAWS, INC. All Rights Reserved. www.garfield.com
Distributed by Universal Press Syndicate

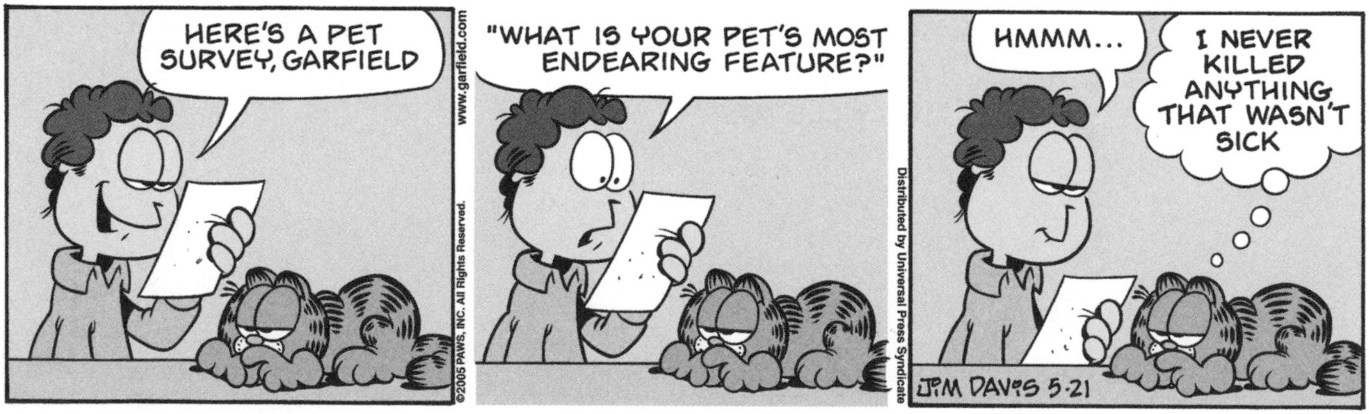
HERE'S A PET SURVEY, GARFIELD
"WHAT IS YOUR PET'S MOST ENDEARING FEATURE?"
HMMM...
I NEVER KILLED ANYTHING THAT WASN'T SICK
JIM DAVIS 5-21
©2005 PAWS, INC. All Rights Reserved. www.garfield.com
Distributed by Universal Press Syndicate

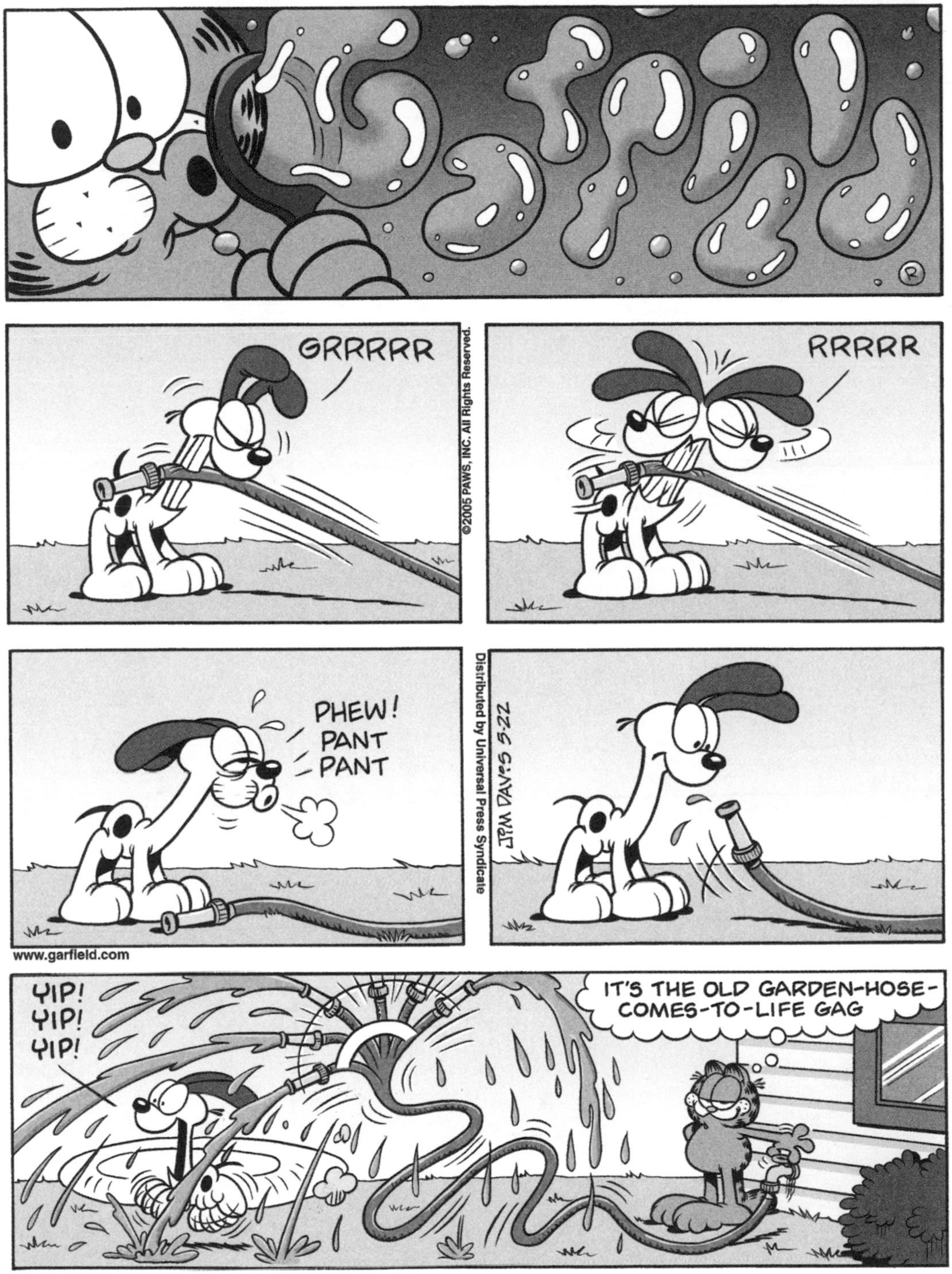
GRRRRR
©2005 PAWS, INC. All Rights Reserved.
RRRRR
PHEW!
PANT
PANT
Distributed by Universal Press Syndicate
JPM DAVIS 5-22
www.garfield.com
YIP!
YIP!
YIP!
IT'S THE OLD GARDEN-HOSE-
COMES-TO-LIFE GAG

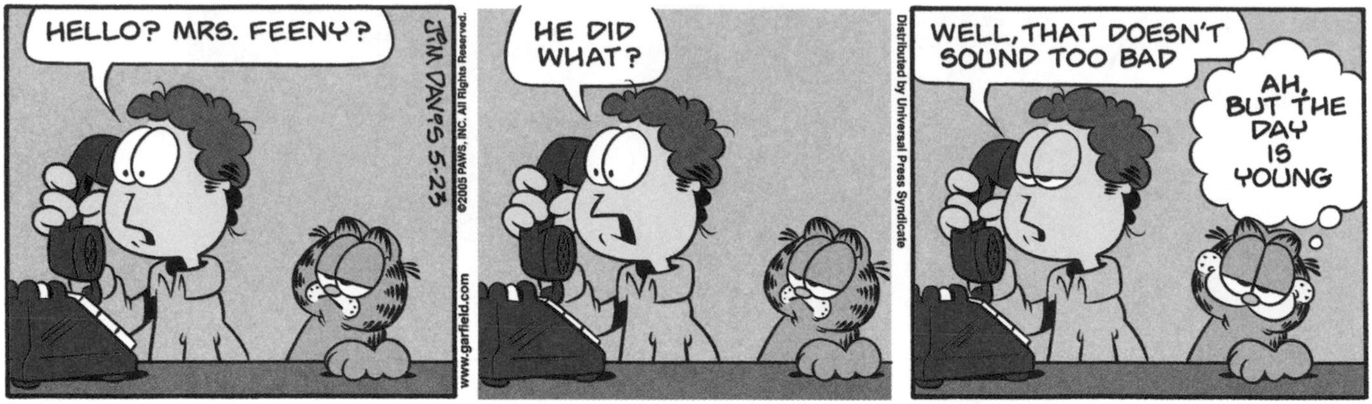
HELLO? MRS. FEENY?
JIM DAVIS 5-23
©2005 PAWS, INC. All Rights Reserved.
www.garfield.com
HE DID WHAT?
Distributed by Universal Press Syndicate
WELL, THAT DOESN'T SOUND TOO BAD
AH, BUT THE DAY IS YOUNG

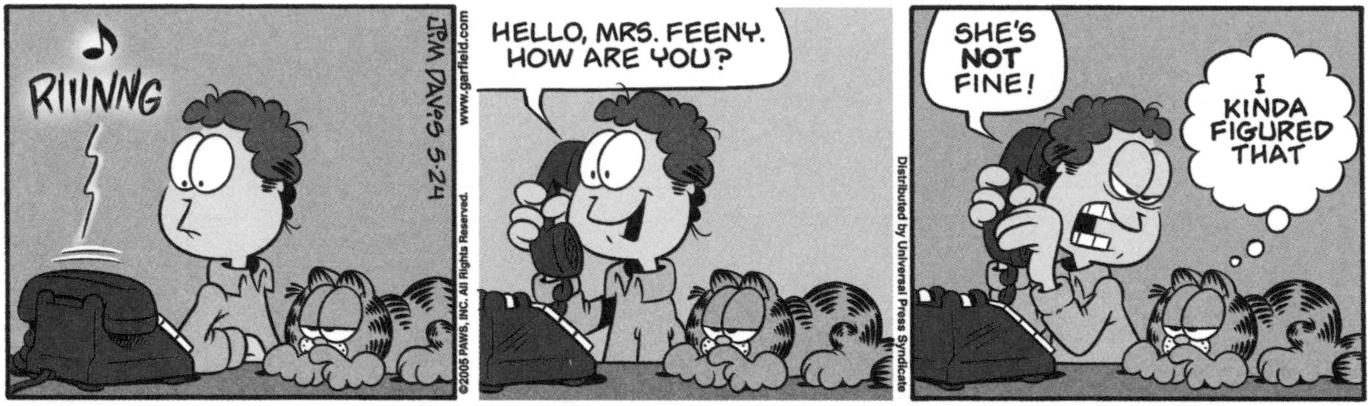
RIIINNG
JIM DAVIS 5-24
www.garfield.com
©2005 PAWS, INC. All Rights Reserved.
HELLO, MRS. FEENY. HOW ARE YOU?
Distributed by Universal Press Syndicate
SHE'S **NOT** FINE!
I KINDA FIGURED THAT

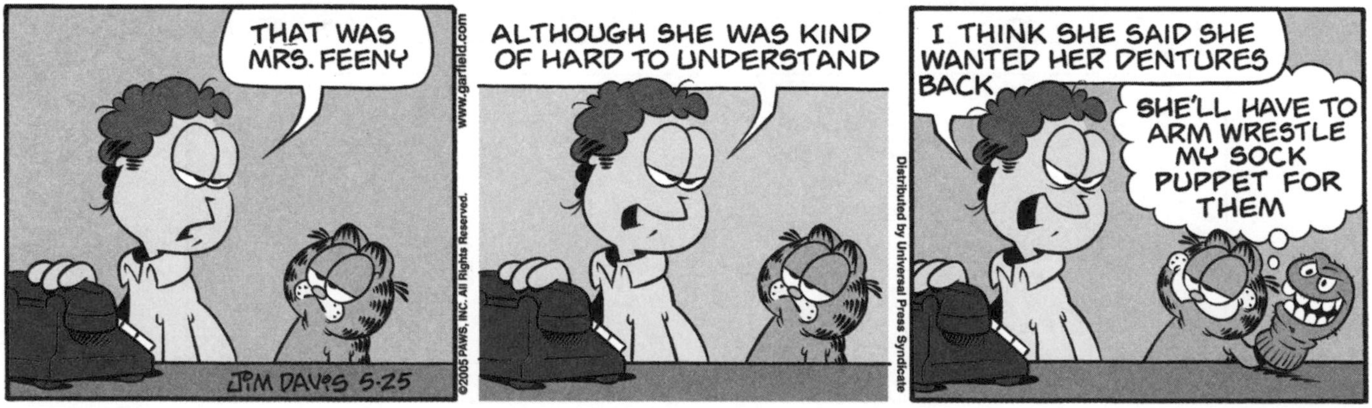
THAT WAS MRS. FEENY
JIM DAVIS 5-25
www.garfield.com
©2005 PAWS, INC. All Rights Reserved.
ALTHOUGH SHE WAS KIND OF HARD TO UNDERSTAND
Distributed by Universal Press Syndicate
I THINK SHE SAID SHE WANTED HER DENTURES BACK
SHE'LL HAVE TO ARM WRESTLE MY SOCK PUPPET FOR THEM

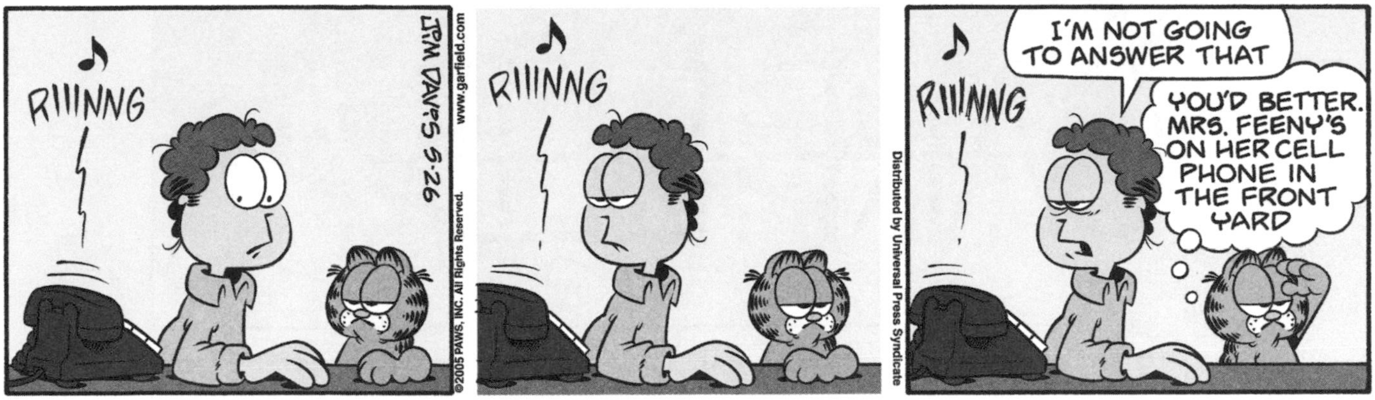
RIIINNG
JIM DAVIS 5-26
©2005 PAWS, INC. All Rights Reserved. www.garfield.com
RIIINNG
Distributed by Universal Press Syndicate
RIIINNG
I'M NOT GOING TO ANSWER THAT
YOU'D BETTER. MRS. FEENY'S ON HER CELL PHONE IN THE FRONT YARD

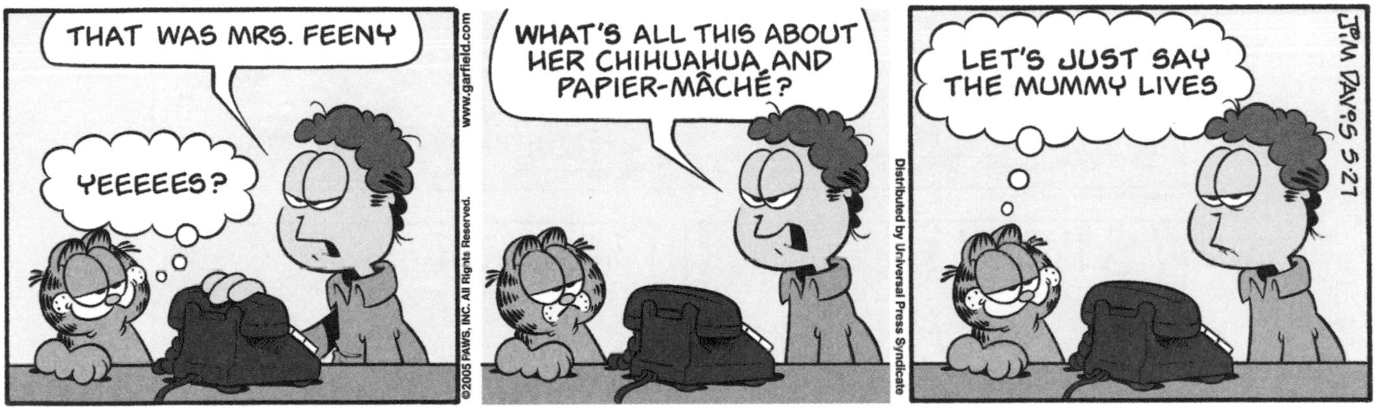
THAT WAS MRS. FEENY
YEEEEES?
©2005 PAWS, INC. All Rights Reserved. www.garfield.com
WHAT'S ALL THIS ABOUT HER CHIHUAHUA AND PAPIER-MÂCHÉ?
Distributed by Universal Press Syndicate
LET'S JUST SAY THE MUMMY LIVES
JIM DAVIS 5-27

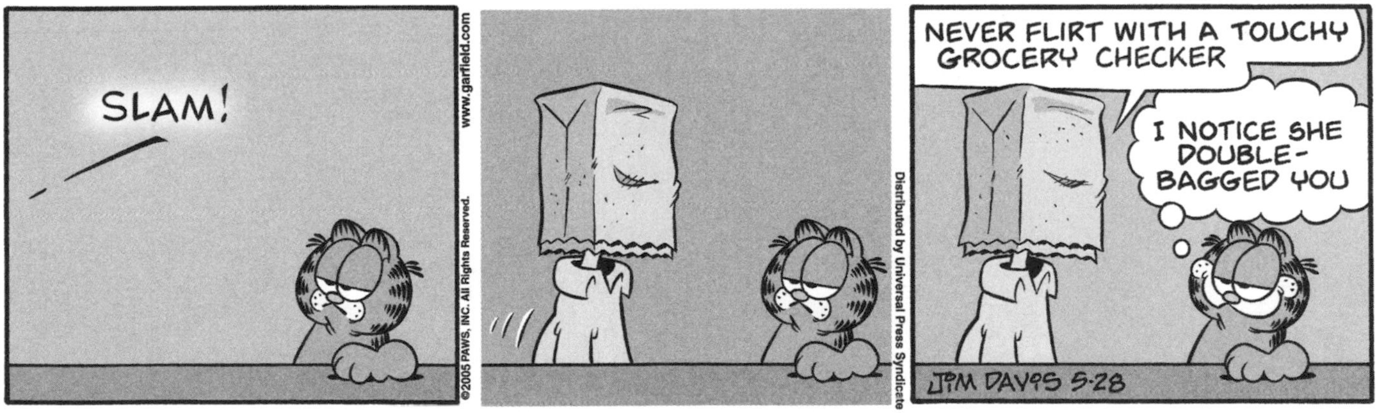
SLAM!
©2005 PAWS, INC. All Rights Reserved. www.garfield.com
Distributed by Universal Press Syndicate
NEVER FLIRT WITH A TOUCHY GROCERY CHECKER
I NOTICE SHE DOUBLE-BAGGED YOU
JIM DAVIS 5-28

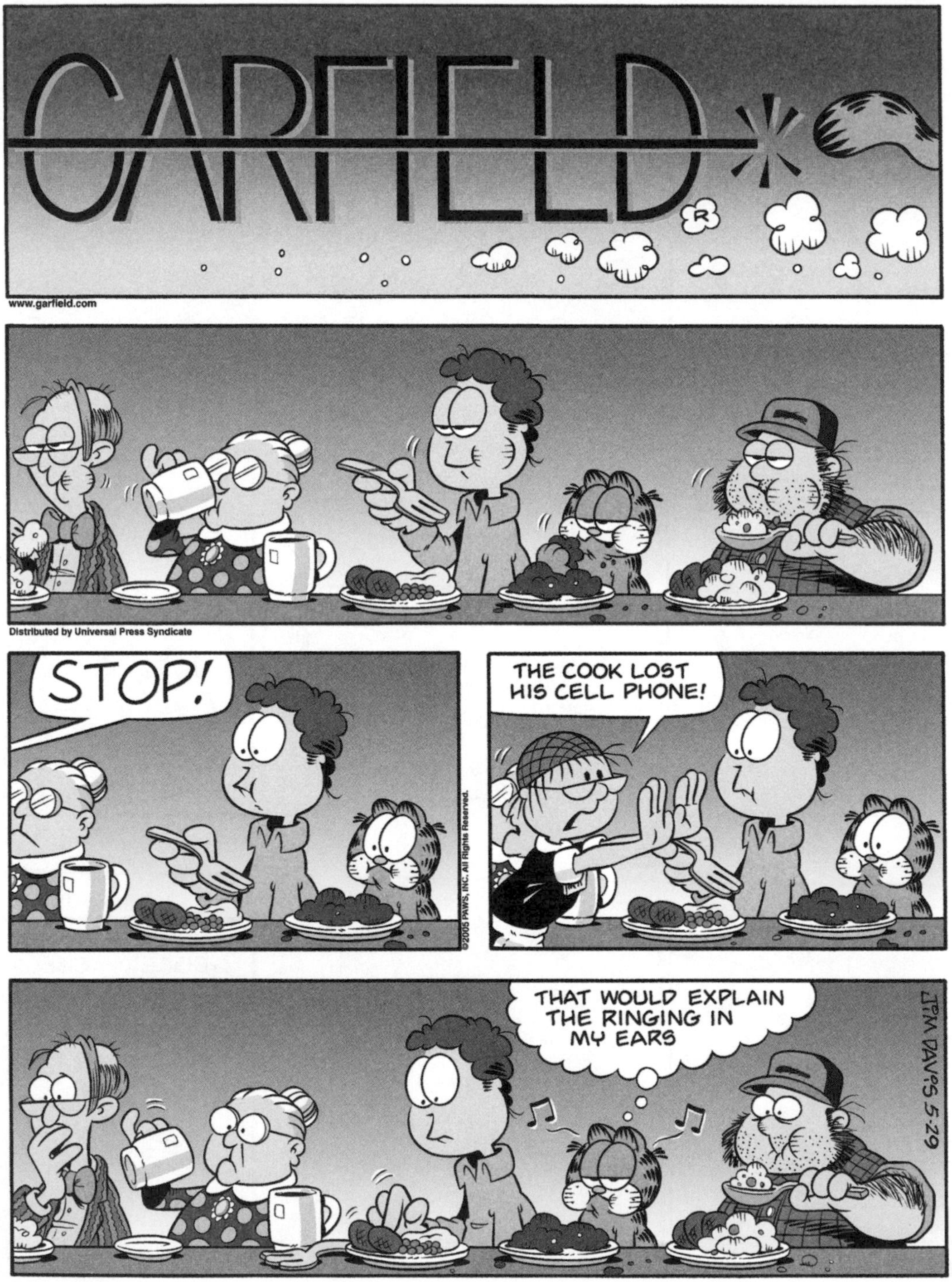
GARFIELD
www.garfield.com
Distributed by Universal Press Syndicate
STOP!
©2005 PAWS, INC. All Rights Reserved.
THE COOK LOST HIS CELL PHONE!
THAT WOULD EXPLAIN THE RINGING IN MY EARS
JIM DAVIS 5-29

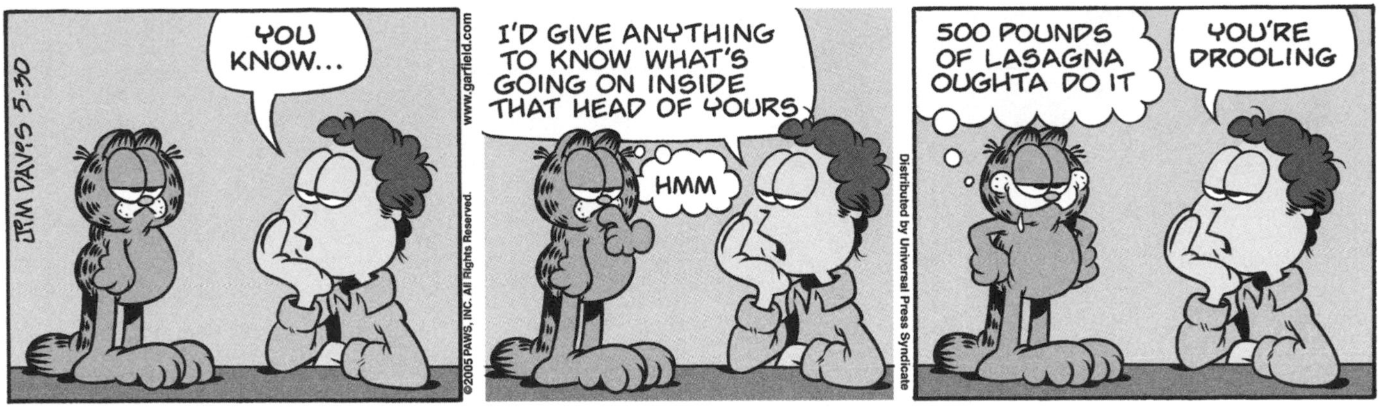
JIM DAVIS 5-30
YOU KNOW...
©2005 PAWS, INC. All Rights Reserved. www.garfield.com
I'D GIVE ANYTHING TO KNOW WHAT'S GOING ON INSIDE THAT HEAD OF YOURS
HMM
Distributed by Universal Press Syndicate
500 POUNDS OF LASAGNA OUGHTA DO IT
YOU'RE DROOLING

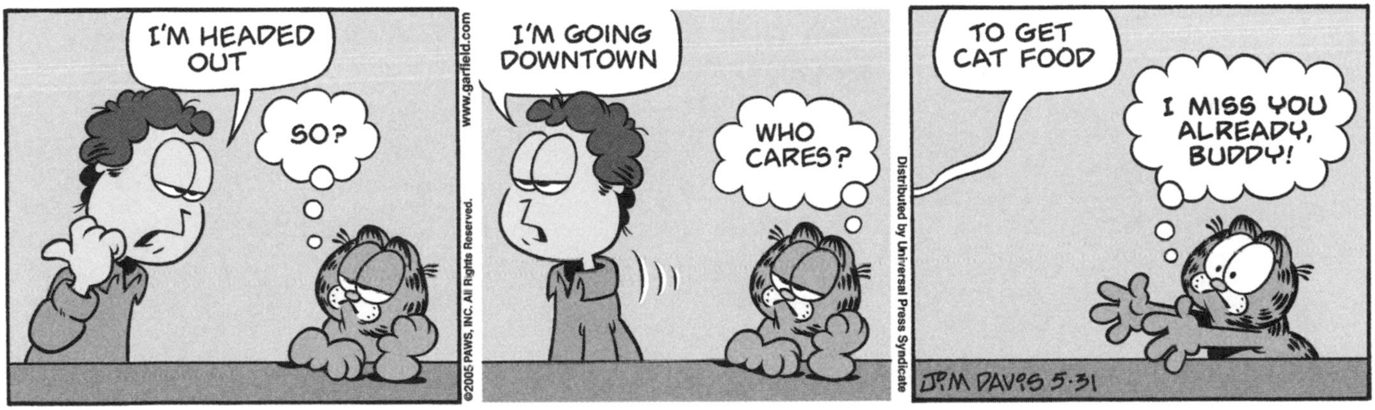
I'M HEADED OUT
SO?
©2005 PAWS, INC. All Rights Reserved. www.garfield.com
I'M GOING DOWNTOWN
WHO CARES?
Distributed by Universal Press Syndicate
TO GET CAT FOOD
I MISS YOU ALREADY, BUDDY!
JIM DAVIS 5-31

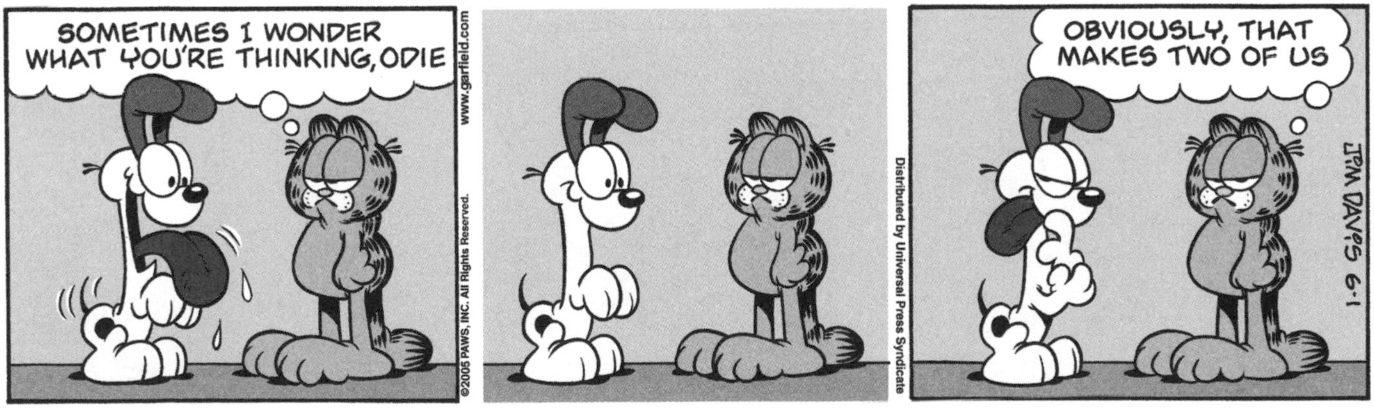
SOMETIMES I WONDER WHAT YOU'RE THINKING, ODIE
©2005 PAWS, INC. All Rights Reserved. www.garfield.com
Distributed by Universal Press Syndicate
OBVIOUSLY, THAT MAKES TWO OF US
JIM DAVIS 6-1

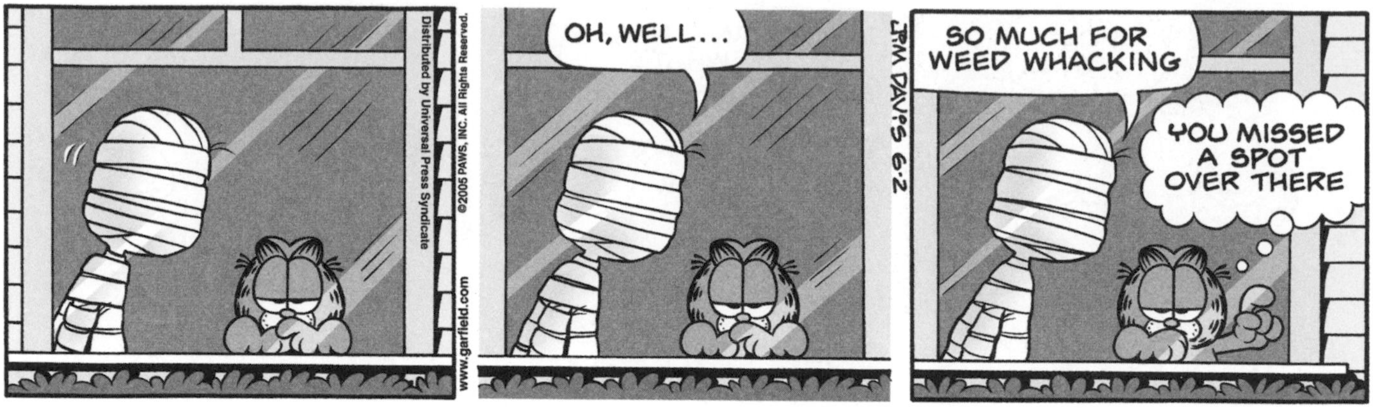
©2005 PAWS, INC. All Rights Reserved.
Distributed by Universal Press Syndicate
www.garfield.com
OH, WELL...
JIM DAVIS 6-2
SO MUCH FOR WEED WHACKING
YOU MISSED A SPOT OVER THERE

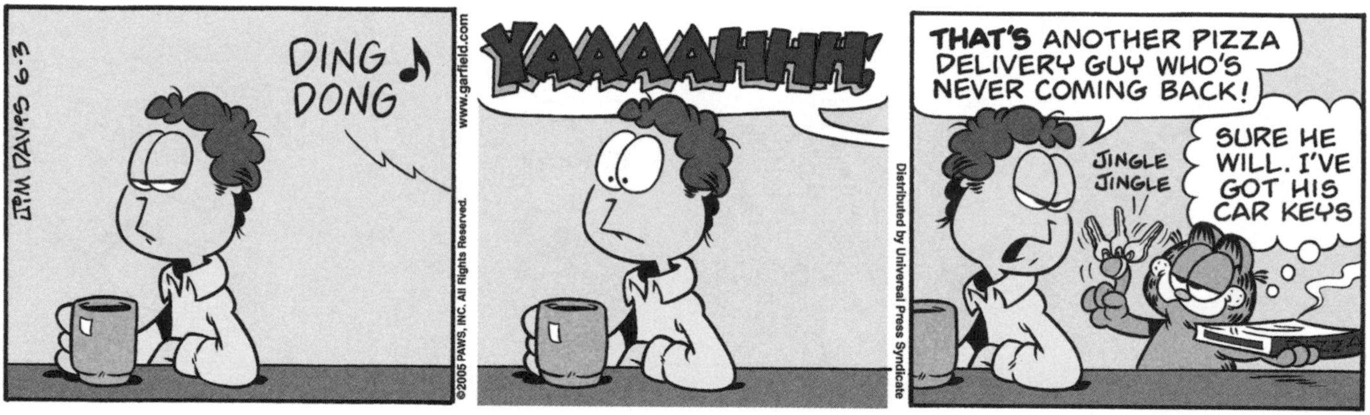
JIM DAVIS 6-3
DING DONG
www.garfield.com
©2005 PAWS, INC. All Rights Reserved.
YAAAAHHH!
Distributed by Universal Press Syndicate
THAT'S ANOTHER PIZZA DELIVERY GUY WHO'S NEVER COMING BACK!
JINGLE JINGLE
SURE HE WILL. I'VE GOT HIS CAR KEYS

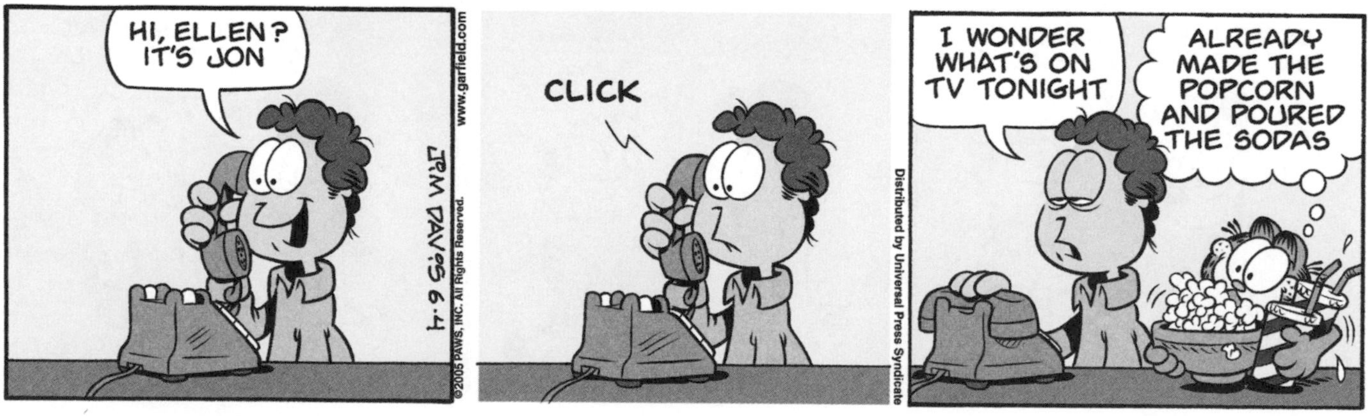
HI, ELLEN? IT'S JON
www.garfield.com
JIM DAVIS 6-4
©2005 PAWS, INC. All Rights Reserved.
CLICK
I WONDER WHAT'S ON TV TONIGHT
ALREADY MADE THE POPCORN AND POURED THE SODAS
Distributed by Universal Press Syndicate

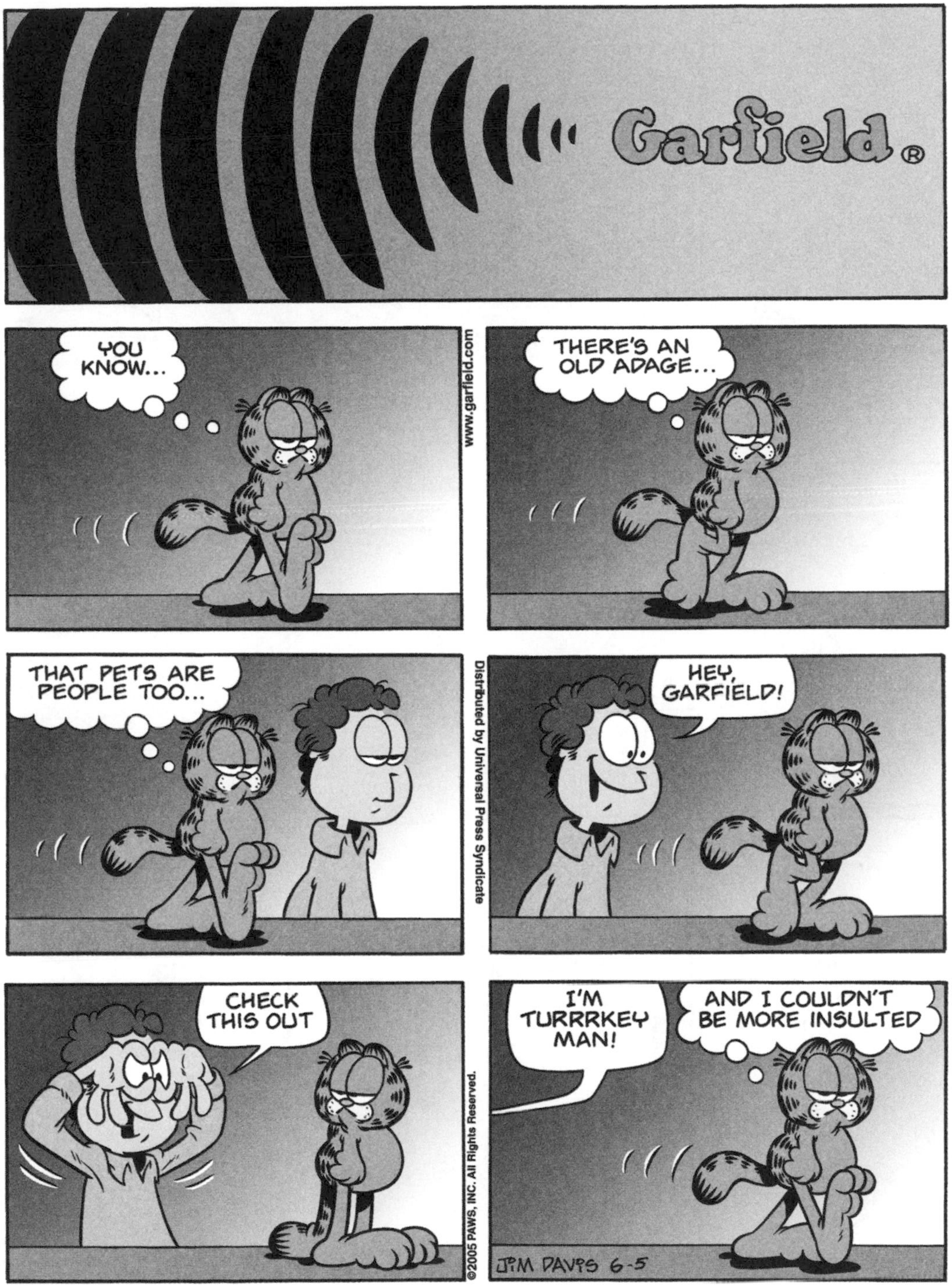
Garfield®
YOU KNOW...
THERE'S AN OLD ADAGE...
THAT PETS ARE PEOPLE TOO...
HEY, GARFIELD!
CHECK THIS OUT
I'M TURRRKEY MAN!
AND I COULDN'T BE MORE INSULTED
JIM DAVIS 6-5
www.garfield.com
Distributed by Universal Press Syndicate
©2005 PAWS, INC. All Rights Reserved.

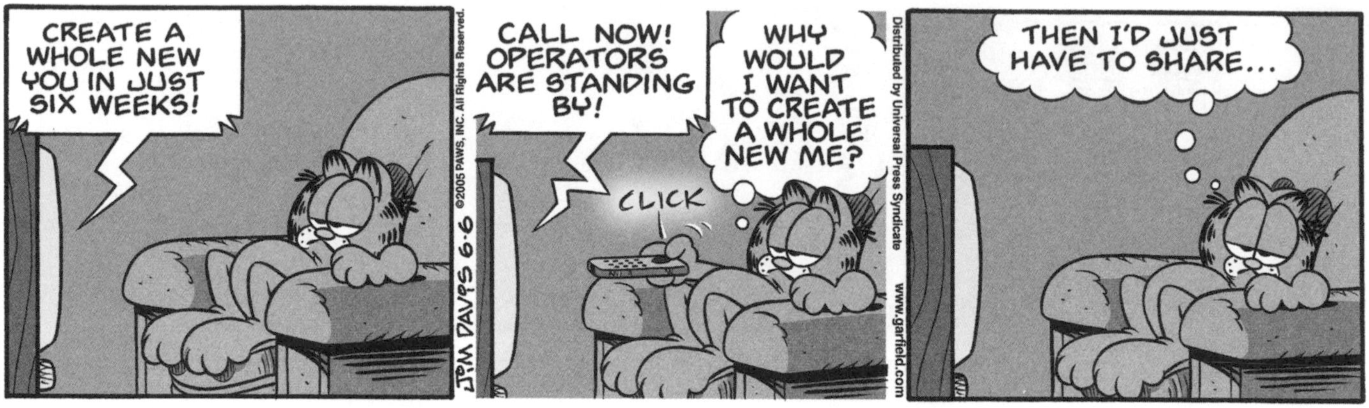
CREATE A WHOLE NEW YOU IN JUST SIX WEEKS!
©2005 PAWS, INC. All Rights Reserved.
JPM DAVPS 6-6
CALL NOW! OPERATORS ARE STANDING BY!
CLICK
WHY WOULD I WANT TO CREATE A WHOLE NEW ME?
Distributed by Universal Press Syndicate www.garfield.com
THEN I'D JUST HAVE TO SHARE...

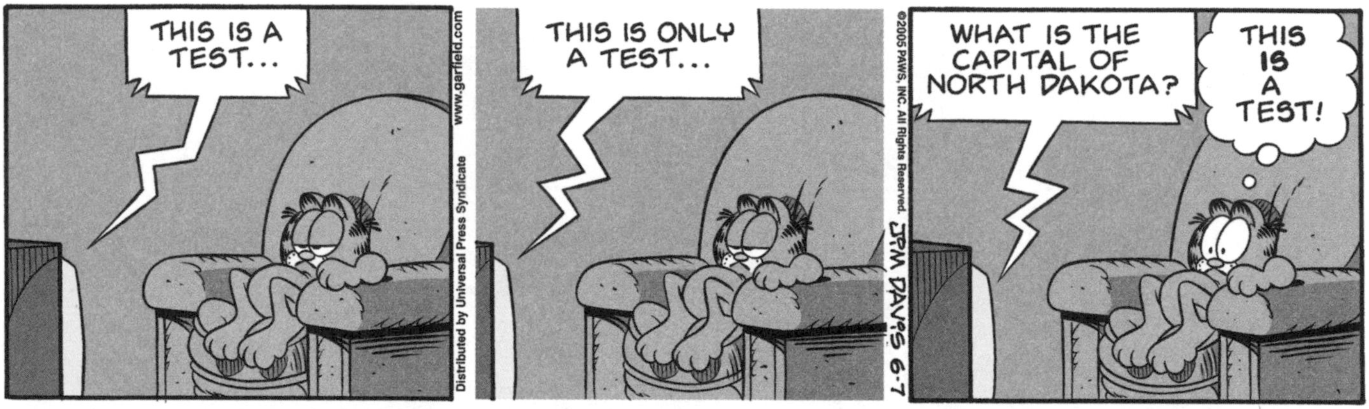
THIS IS A TEST...
Distributed by Universal Press Syndicate www.garfield.com
THIS IS ONLY A TEST...
JPM DAVPS 6-7
©2005 PAWS, INC. All Rights Reserved.
WHAT IS THE CAPITAL OF NORTH DAKOTA?
THIS IS A TEST!

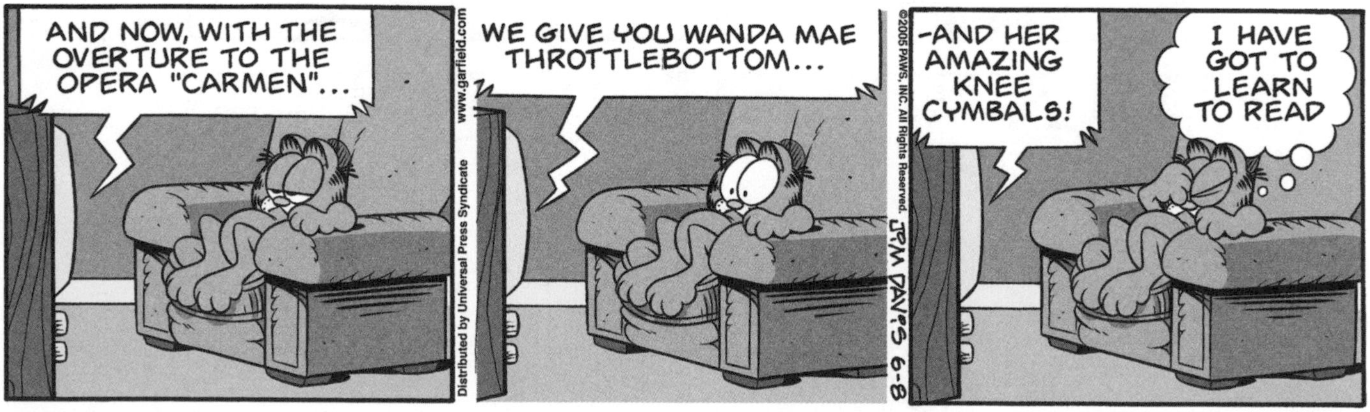
AND NOW, WITH THE OVERTURE TO THE OPERA "CARMEN"...
Distributed by Universal Press Syndicate www.garfield.com
WE GIVE YOU WANDA MAE THROTTLEBOTTOM...
JPM DAVPS 6-8
©2005 PAWS, INC. All Rights Reserved.
-AND HER AMAZING KNEE CYMBALS!
I HAVE GOT TO LEARN TO READ

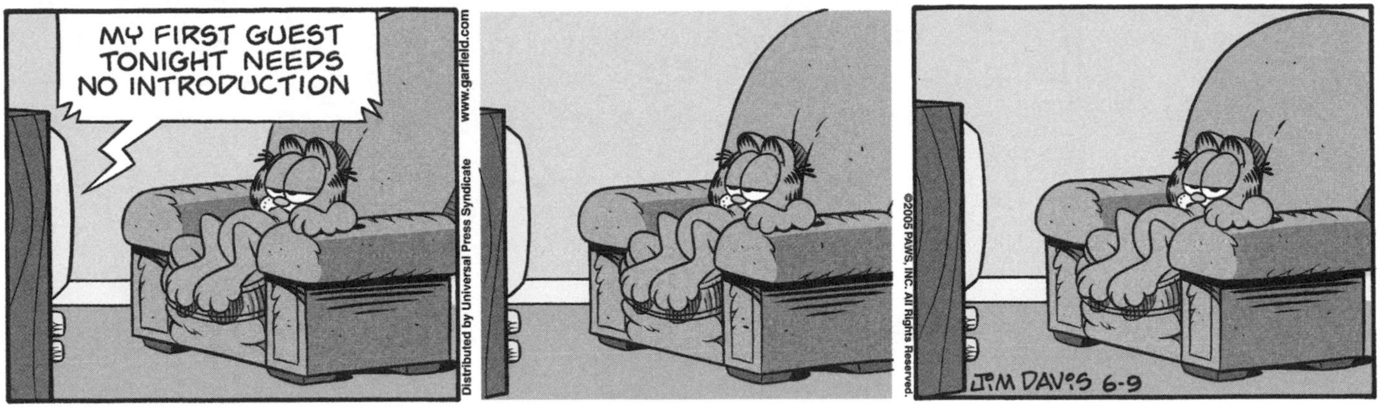
MY FIRST GUEST TONIGHT NEEDS NO INTRODUCTION
www.garfield.com
Distributed by Universal Press Syndicate
©2005 PAWS, INC. All Rights Reserved.
JIM DAVIS 6-9

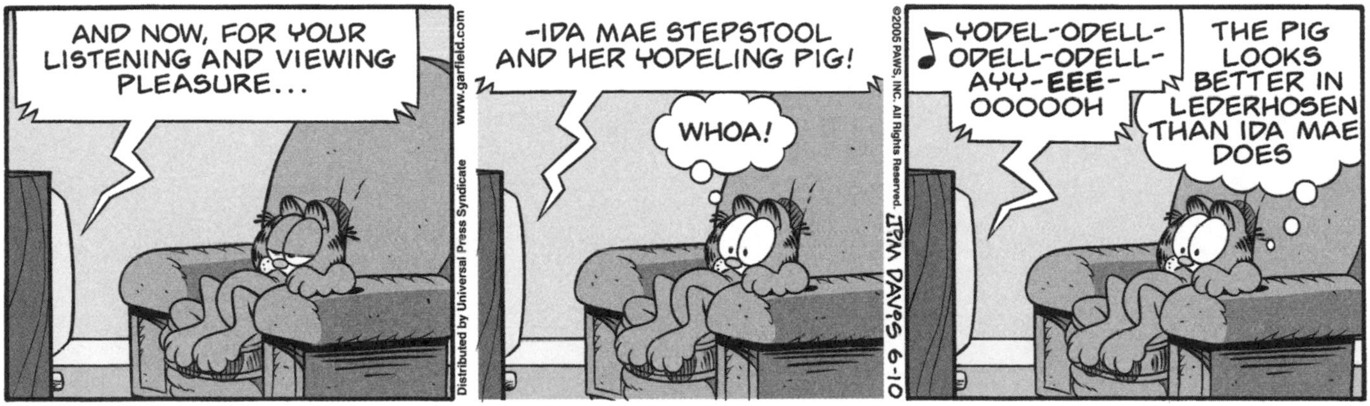
AND NOW, FOR YOUR LISTENING AND VIEWING PLEASURE...
www.garfield.com
Distributed by Universal Press Syndicate
-IDA MAE STEPSTOOL AND HER YODELING PIG!
WHOA!
©2005 PAWS, INC. All Rights Reserved.
JIM DAVIS 6-10
YODEL-ODELL-ODELL-ODELL-AYY-EEE-OOOOOH
THE PIG LOOKS BETTER IN LEDERHOSEN THAN IDA MAE DOES

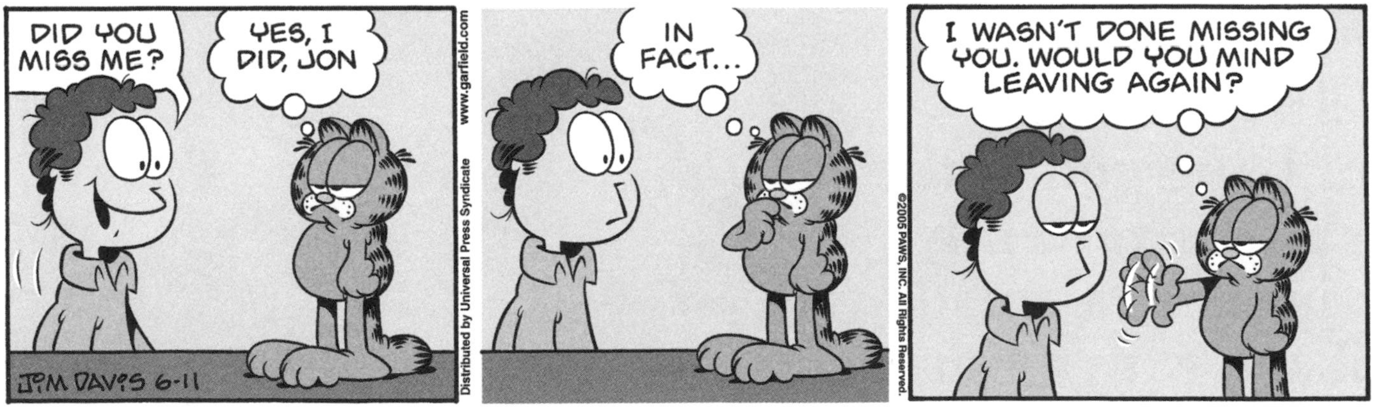
DID YOU MISS ME?
YES, I DID, JON
JIM DAVIS 6-11
www.garfield.com
Distributed by Universal Press Syndicate
IN FACT...
©2005 PAWS, INC. All Rights Reserved.
I WASN'T DONE MISSING YOU. WOULD YOU MIND LEAVING AGAIN?

MYTH MADNESS

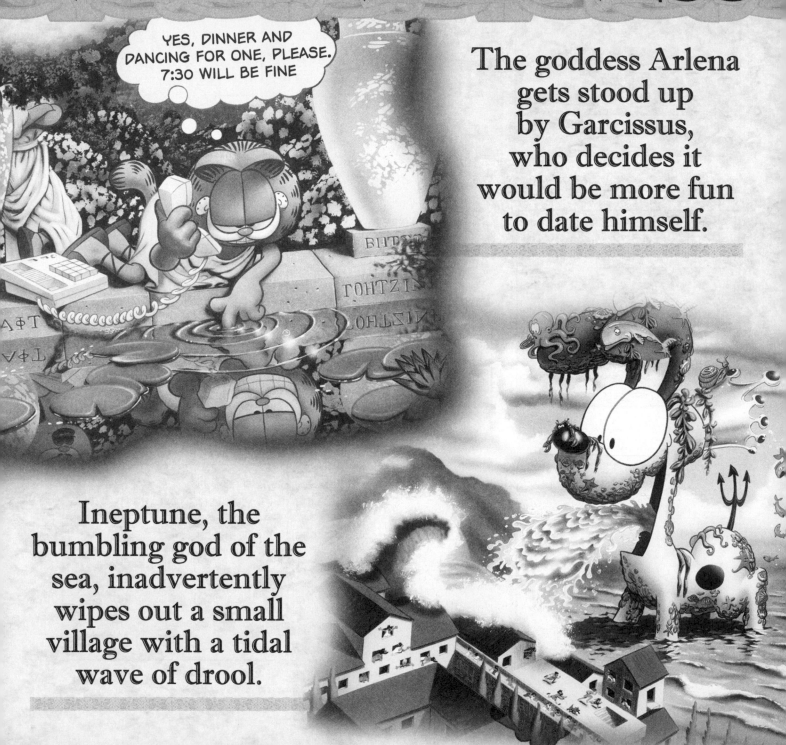

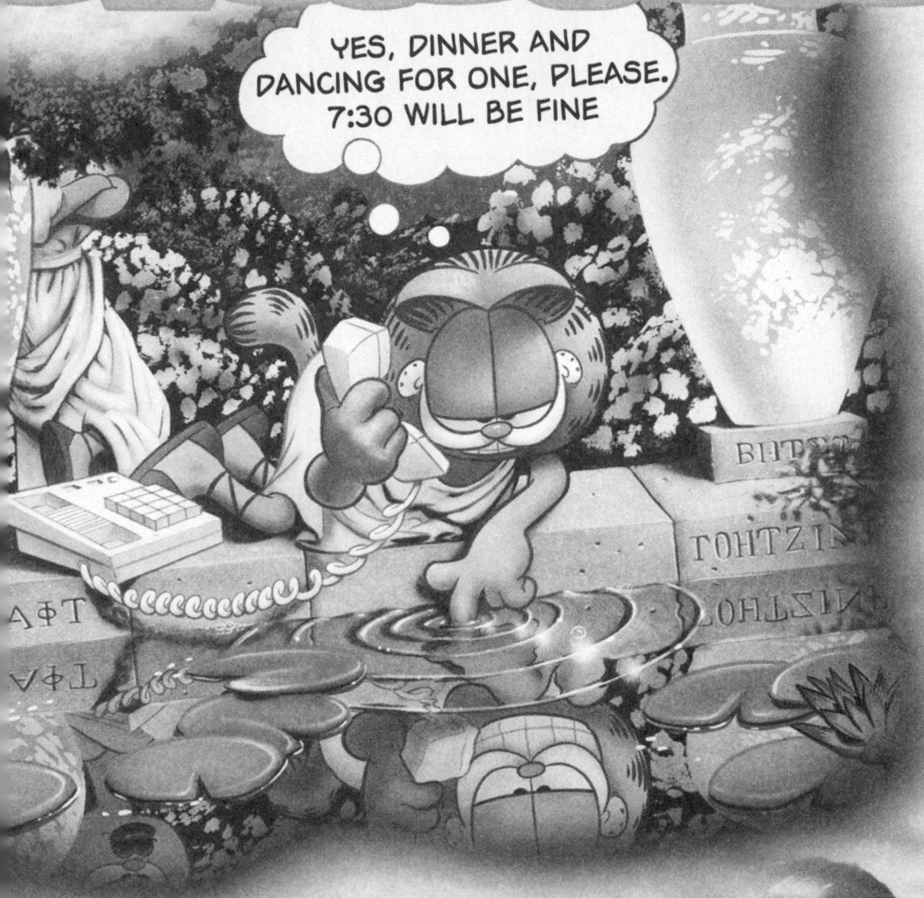
YES, DINNER AND DANCING FOR ONE, PLEASE. 7:30 WILL BE FINE

The goddess Arlena gets stood up by Garcissus, who decides it would be more fun to date himself.

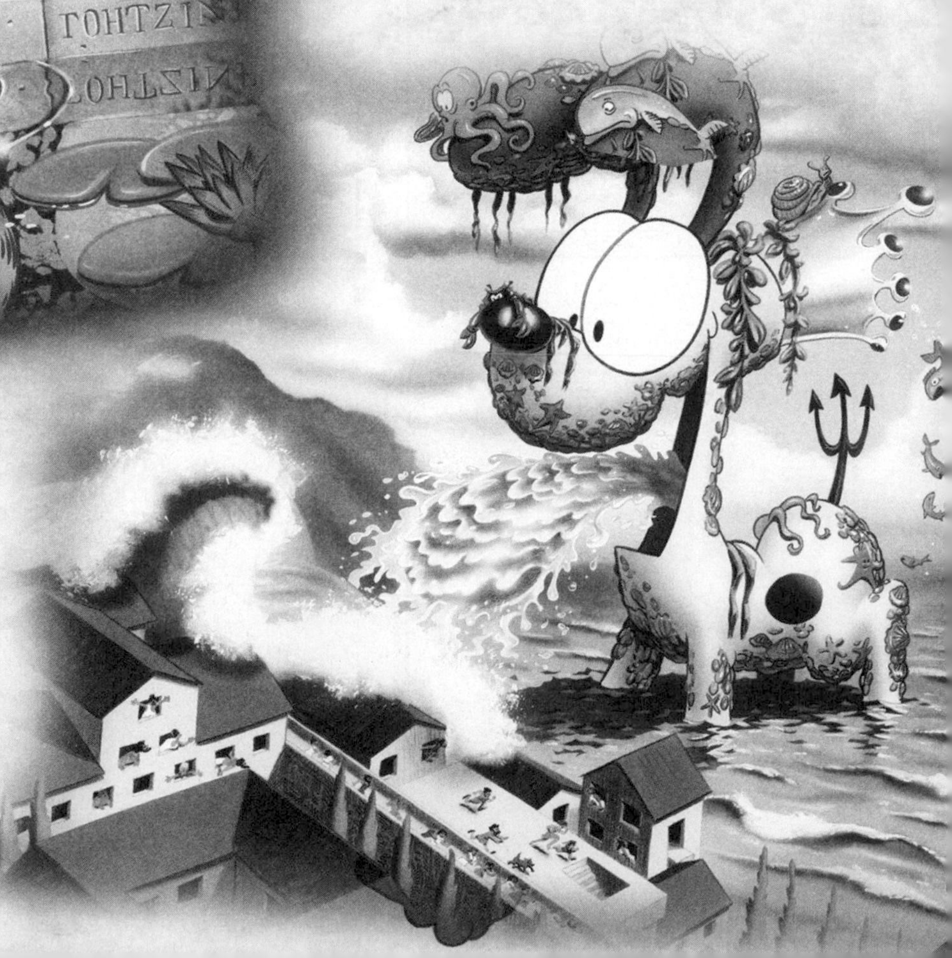

Ineptune, the bumbling god of the sea, inadvertently wipes out a small village with a tidal wave of drool.

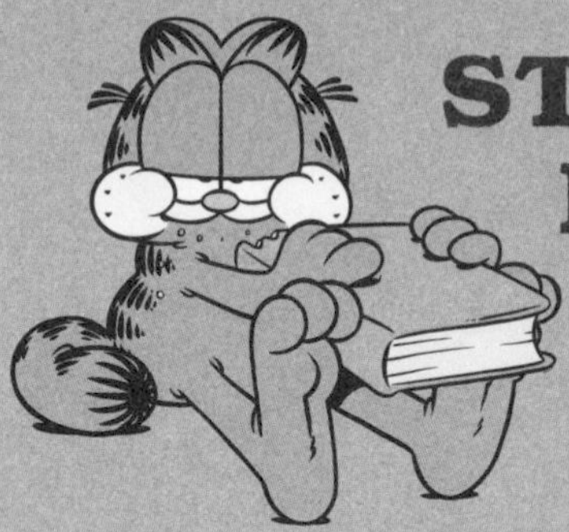

STRIPS, SPECIALS, OR BESTSELLING BOOKS . . . GARFIELD'S ON EVERYONE'S MENU.

Don't miss even one episode in the Tubby Tabby's hilarious series!

- GARFIELD AT LARGE ....(#1) 978-0-345-44382-3
- GARFIELD GAINS WEIGHT ....(#2) 978-0-345-44975-7
- GARFIELD BIGGER THAN LIFE ....(#3) 978-0-345-45027-2
- GARFIELD WEIGHS IN ....(#4) 978-0-345-45205-4
- GARFIELD TAKES THE CAKE ....(#5) 978-0-345-44978-8
- GARFIELD EATS HIS HEART OUT........(#6) 978-0-345-46459-0
- GARFIELD SITS AROUND THE HOUSE..(#7) 978-0-345-46463-7
- GARFIELD TIPS THE SCALES ....(#8) 978-0-345-46909-0
- GARFIELD LOSES HIS FEET.................(#9) 978-0-345-46467-5
- GARFIELD MAKES IT BIG ....(#10) 978-0-345-46468-2
- GARFIELD ROLLS ON ....(#11) 978-0-345-47561-9
- GARFIELD OUT TO LUNCH.................(#12) 978-0-345-47562-6
- GARFIELD FOOD FOR THOUGHT......(#13) 978-0-345-47563-3
- GARFIELD SWALLOWS HIS PRIDE....(#14) 978-0-345-91386-9
- GARFIELD WORLDWIDE ....(#15) 978-0-345-91754-6
- GARFIELD ROUNDS OUT....................(#16) 978-0-345-49169-5
- GARFIELD CHEWS THE FAT...............(#17) 978-0-345-49170-1
- GARFIELD GOES TO WAIST ....(#18) 978-0-345-36430-2
- GARFIELD HANGS OUT.......................(#19) 978-0-345-36835-5
- GARFIELD TAKES UP SPACE ....(#20) 978-0-345-37029-7
- GARFIELD SAYS A MOUTHFUL ....(#21) 978-0-345-37368-7
- GARFIELD BY THE POUND.................(#22) 978-0-345-37579-7
- GARFIELD KEEPS HIS CHINS UP ......(#23) 978-0-345-37959-7
- GARFIELD TAKES HIS LICKS..............(#24) 978-0-345-38170-5
- GARFIELD HITS THE BIG TIME ....(#25) 978-0-345-38332-7
- GARFIELD PULLS HIS WEIGHT..........(#26) 978-0-345-38666-3
- GARFIELD DISHES IT OUT..................(#27) 978-0-345-39287-9
- GARFIELD LIFE IN THE FAT LANE .....(#28) 978-0-345-39776-8
- GARFIELD TONS OF FUN....................(#29) 978-0-345-40386-5
- GARFIELD BIGGER AND BETTER......(#30) 978-0-345-40770-2
- GARFIELD HAMS IT UP ....(#31) 978-0-345-41241-6
- GARFIELD THINKS BIG.......................(#32) 978-0-345-41671-1
- GARFIELD THROWS HIS WEIGHT AROUND ....(#33) 978-0-345-42749-6
- GARFIELD LIFE TO THE FULLEST.....(#34) 978-0-345-43239-1
- GARFIELD FEEDS THE KITTY ....(#35) 978-0-345-43673-3
- GARFIELD HOGS THE SPOTLIGHT ...(#36) 978-0-345-43922-2
- GARFIELD BEEFS UP ....(#37) 978-0-345-44109-6
- GARFIELD GETS COOKIN' ....(#38) 978-0-345-44582-7
- GARFIELD EATS CROW ....(#39) 978-0-345-45201-6
- GARFIELD SURVIVAL OF THE FATTEST ....(#40) 978-0-345-46458-3
- GARFIELD OLDER AND WIDER..........(#41) 978-0-345-46462-0
- GARFIELD PIGS OUT ....(#42) 978-0-345-46466-8
- GARFIELD BLOTS OUT THE SUN ......(#43) 978-0-345-46615-0
- GARFIELD GOES BANANAS ....(#44) 978-0-345-91346-3
- GARFIELD LARGE & IN CHARGE.......(#45) 978-0-345-49172-5

DVD TIE-INS

- GARFIELD AS HIMSELF................................978-0-345-47805-4
- GARFIELD HOLIDAY CELEBRATIONS.........978-0-345-47930-3
- GARFIELD TRAVEL ADVENTURES 978-0-345-48087-3

AND DON'T MISS...

- GARFIELD AT 25: IN DOG YEARS I'D BE DEAD 978-0-345-45204-7
- GARFIELD'S JOKE ZONE/INSULTS..............978-0-345-46263-3
- GARFIELD FAT CAT 3-PACK/ VOL. 1 978-0-345-46455-2
- GARFIELD FAT CAT 3-PACK/ VOL. 2 978-0-345-46465-1
- GARFIELD FAT CAT 3-PACK/ VOL. 3 978-0-345-48088-0
- GARFIELD FAT CAT 3-PACK/ VOL. 13 978-0-345-46460-6
- SEASON'S EATINGS: A VERY MERRY GARFIELD CHRISTMAS 978-0-345-47560-2
- GARFIELD'S GUIDE TO EVERYTHING 978-0-345-46461-3
- ODIE UNLEASHED! 978-0-345-46464-4
- GARFIELD'S BOOK OF CAT NAMES............978-0-345-48516-8
- THE GARFIELD JOURNAL............................978-0-345-46469-9
- LIGHTS, CAMERA, HAIRBALLS!: GARFIELD AT THE MOVIES 978-0-345-49134-3

New larger, full-color format! (books #1–#17)